Applying Project Management in the Workplace

Fourth Edition

Jeff Crow

Blackbird Publishing
Portland, Oregon

Applying Project Management in the Workplace
Fourth Edition

© 2003 Jeff D. Crow
All Rights Reserved

ISBN: 0-9660469-3-5

Printed in the United States of America

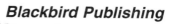

Blackbird Publishing

PO Box 80746
Portland,OR 97280-1746
1-888-674-0010
E-Mail: info@blackbirdpub.com

*With heartfelt thanks to all the students
and workshop participants who, over the
years, have contributed so much to the
content, organization, and presentation of
this book and to my own understanding of
project management inside organizations.*

Table of Contents

Introduction

Welcome

This book is the result of many years of experience as a project leader and many hours (days, weeks, months) of research into the available information on project management. Over the years, I have experimented with the various concepts, tools, and techniques I've found, thought up, and heard about. The basic text was created as a training handout for a specific client with a specific problem in about 1985. Since then, it has undergone countless revisions and updates.

This is the current version of the results of an on-going search for project-management-type tools and techniques that work in the in-house business environment. Over all the years that I have been a project leader and have taught project management, both in the university and community college arenas and in numerous public and private sector organizations, one thing has become glaringly obvious:

> *Employees working on projects inside organizations need simple, portable, flexible tools, to plan and manage their projects in order to succeed. In addition, these tools need to be scalable to meet the needs of a wide array of projects.*

The concepts, tools, and techniques in this book are aimed at addressing the particular needs of employees working on projects developed by them or assigned to them as part of their work. I have included multiple versions of a tool when options are available. There should be more tools here than any one project leader would ordinarily need. The intention is that you, the reader, try several options and choose and adapt those that work best in your individual circumstances.

Online Resources

As an adjunct to this book, there are two web sites that contain related information:

www.crowdevelopment.com is the web site of my consulting and training company. On this site you will find news and information about the company, its clients, and our services. There is a password-protected section of the site called the "Client's Area" where customers have access to specific information unavailable through other sources.

www.ProjectManagementTools.com is a password-access-only resources site exclusively for readers of this book and participants in our project-management and process-improvement training programs. All of the tools, forms, and checklists in this book are available for download from this site. Information on how to obtain your password to both of these sites is provided on page 4.

This is the fourth edition of this book. The first edition was published in 1997. So, obviously, this is a work in progress. I am constantly seeking to improve and expand the information in this book and on these web sites. Many of the revisions in this edition are a result of discussions with students in my workshops and experimentation with clients. Some are from other professionals in the project management field. I encourage you to contact me with your comments and suggestions. I can be reached at:

Crow Development Corporation
PO Box 80746
Portland, OR 97280-1746
E-mail: jcrow@crowdevelopment.com

A Working Definition of Project Management

If they buy the premise, they'll buy the joke.
Johnny Carson
Former Tonight Show Host

Just to be sure that we're all starting from the same point, this is the definition of project management used in this book:

Project Management is the process by which actions are planned, resources organized, and activities initiated and managed to achieve a specific goal or purpose, or to produce a specified deliverable.

This book presents an approach to project management that is somewhat different from those commonly used. The difference centers around a basic assumption about how projects are handled by employees within organizations:

The project leader within an organization is rarely a manager in a traditional sense. He or she rarely has the managerial authority necessary to "make things happen."

Frequently, individuals are given responsibility for a project based on their expertise in the area that the project impacts. For example, a technically-oriented individual may be given responsibility for a development project based solely on his or her perceived expertise in that technology — not on their management ability, position in the organization, or project planning and management experience. Project leaders in organizations are almost always expected to be active participants in the work of their projects — they are not expected (or even allowed) to be "managers" in the traditional sense. A more appropriate title would be "project leader."

This characteristic of projects undertaken by employees within organizations uncovers some problems with the more traditional approaches to project management. Since project leaders within organizations are frequently not in management positions, they generally do not have the organizational hierarchy behind them. They usually do not have "hire-and-fire" authority. They don't have responsibility for employee performance reviews. They don't have the power to grant raises or promotions, take disciplinary action, etc. Even in the cases of those project leaders who are managers in the traditional sense, their projects frequently require that they work them using at least some personnel who are not in their reporting chain. The problems this situation can create are not usually addressed by project management methodologies which assume true managerial authority and responsibility as a prerequisite for undertaking a project.

This text addresses the lack of managerial authority in several ways:

* There is information on negotiation, which is a tool a project leader can use to staff and develop a team. It is also useful when trying to secure the technical and support resources necessary to successfully complete a project without relying on non-existent authority.

* There is a section dealing specifically with leadership with an emphasis on leading project teams.

* There is a section on the origins and use of power and authority within organizations that provides insights into how truly effective project leaders achieve goals and gather support without relying on "position power" (power granted by one's position within the hierarchy of the organization).

* There is information and tools for developing and working with teams made up of individuals who are not dedicated to the project on a full-time basis.

Most of the tools, techniques, and forms described in this text are designed for non-managers.

Remember, the tools in this book are also available online at:

www.ProjectManagementTools.com

Instructions for obtaining a password are in the next section: Using the Tools and Online Access.

The Structure and Features of the Text

For the most part, this book is organized to follow the way most projects unfold. It begins with this introductory chapter which is devoted to some basic concepts about projects and project management. This is followed by chapters covering project pre-work and preliminary planning; project teams and people skills; project planning; project implementation; and the transfer of project output and close-out of the project. A chapter addressing some of the unique issues faced by distributed (geographically disbursed) teams and projects rounds out the main text. Four Appendices finish out the book. Appendix A: *Project Planning and Management Checklists*, contains 21 checklists covering a wide range of project situations. Appendix B: *Project Planning and Management Forms*, has full-size versions of all of the forms presented in the text as well as some additional tools that might be useful. Appendix C: *A Problem-Solving Process*, lays out the steps of a structured problem-solving process that can be used when problems do not have obvious solutions. And Appendix D: *Problem-Solving Tools*, contains all the tools referenced in the process description. You are encouraged to select the ones most appropriate for your projects and leadership style.

Throughout the text, you'll find boxed sections titled "Process Tip." These sections contain specific suggestions for implementing the concepts or tools described in the text around them.

At the end of chapters 1, 2, 4, 5, and 6, information has been included under the heading "Issues by Project Type." This information is based on the idea that most projects fall into one of three broad categories:

- Projects to develop or enhance processes for doing work within the organization

- Projects to develop or enhance the products or services of the organization that are offered to the organization's customers

- Projects to develop software for either internal use or external sale

As mentioned earlier, this book is organized to parallel how most projects unfold. These "Special Concerns by Project Type" sections are intended to call attention to issues of special concern when dealing with each type of project related to the material covered in the chapter.

Chapter 3: *People Skills for Project Leaders*, is the odd-man-out in the follow-the-project structure. The material in this chapter applies and is useful throughout the life of a project. Many of the "Process Tips" reference skills and techniques that are covered in the people-skills material.

Using the Tools and Online Access

Many chapters contain descriptions of specific techniques and examples of tools that can be used to plan or manage the issues being discussed. These tools, in the form of fill-in-the-blank forms and checklists, are available to you in a couple of ways:

- Appendix A: *Project Planning and Management Checklists* and Appendix B: *Project Planning and Management Forms*, contain master copies of each of the tools included in the text as well as some additional tools and descriptions of techniques not discussed in the text. Since the "one-size-fits-all" approach almost never works in practice, tools and techniques in a wide range of "sizes" have been included. When available, more than one version of a form is provided so you can select the one that best suits your needs. Try some of them on and see what "fits."

- Downloadable versions of all of the forms and checklists and many of the problem-solving tools in Appendix B are available on the web site www.projectmanagementtools.com. In addition, new tools, forms, and checklists are added to this online library all the time. Forms and checklists are available in Microsoft® Word or Microsoft® Excel format (depending on the form), and all contain "pop-up" instructions for using the tool.

This online library is available to anyone who has purchased a copy of this book. You will need a user name and password to access the forms. To get your user name and password for access to this online toolkit, do one of the following:

Send an e-mail with "Forms Access Request" in the subject line to:

- **info@crowdevelopment.com**. Include your preference for a user name and password. If possible, we will use the user name and password you request. If your requested user name and password are already in use, we will create a substitute that closely parallels your requested combination. Your user name and password will be returned to you by e-mail.

- Go to **www.ProjectManagementTools.com**. On the Home Page there is form to "Request Access to Forms". Complete the form and click the "Submit" button at the bottom.

Your user name and password combination will be returned to you by email.

Privacy Statement

We will retain your e-mail address within our system for use only to return your user name and password to you and to notify you of significant changes to the contents of the www.ProjectManagementTools.com web site. Under no circumstances will your personal information be sold, traded, or otherwise shared with any other entity.

This book is designed to be a reference and resource manual for project leaders. Not all concepts apply to all projects. Not all tools are appropriate for every project leader or project. Not all techniques will work in every case. Examine the concepts in light of what you know about your own situation and work environment. Try the tools and techniques that appeal to you. Adopt and adapt those that work.

Good luck on your projects!

Jeff Crow
Portland, Oregon
February, 2003

1

Basic Concepts

Why Projects?

Projects have been with us for a very long time. People have been undertaking them since the earliest days of organized human activity. The hunting parties of our prehistoric forebears were projects, for example; they were temporary undertakings directed at the goal of obtaining meat for the community. Large, complex projects have also been with us for a long time. The pyramids, the Great Wall of China, and Hadrian's Wall were projects that, in their time, were roughly the same dimensions of the Manhattan Project or the Apollo Project to send a man to the moon.

J. Davidson Frame
American author
Managing Projects
in Organizations

Organizations undertake projects for a variety of reasons. One of the most common is to allow the organization to do something it has never done before. There was a time in the not-so-distant past when this idea of doing something "new" would have been assigned to some specific part of the organization that specialized in doing "new" things; research and development for example. Well, those days are gone, probably forever. Most organizations are doing "new" things every day. And they're not relying on R&D to get them done. There are very few job descriptions out there anymore that don't include something about "projects as assigned." Most jobs now involve at least some degree of unique one-of-a-kind or first-of-a-kind activity. The degree of uniqueness varies greatly from organization to organization and job to job, but overall, projects are undertaken to do something that can't be done within the normal operating systems of the business.

Most organizations place a high value on predictability. The organizational operating systems are in place for the express purpose of controlling activities and predicting what will happen in both the short-term and the long-term. Accounting systems are set up to track and detail the use of the organization's financial resources. Production control systems are in use to predict, monitor, and control the manufacturing processes of the business. Even marketing forecasting systems are intended to predict demand for the company's products or services.

Innovation (doing something new) is, by its very nature, unpredictable. It does not respond to the same controls as ongoing operations. And, very definitely, projects in most of their guises are forms of innovation.

Projects are undertaken to develop new products, improve or develop a process, write software, enhance methods of accomplishing work, or to accomplish any of a thousand other objectives. Whatever the reason for the project, it's likely that ongoing business operating systems will demand more predictability and require more control than can reasonably be expected when doing something new.

The controls and systems of established businesses are very good at doing things millions of times with great reliability and predictability. They are not good at doing things for the first time. This is where projects come in. The solution that has emerged is the acceptance of the basic concepts, tools, and techniques of project management as the "method of choice" for getting things done. Unfortunately, not all of the traditional elements of project management make the transition to the in-house environment as cleanly as we might like. Foremost among the translation problems is the fact that, as mentioned in the Introduction, project leaders within organizations rarely have the full scope of managerial authority the title implies. Working within these constraints is one of the main themes of this text.

Another major theme is that many of the projects that individuals undertake inside organizations are not on the grand scale of building dams, writing the next "killer app" software, or designing the next consumer-product superstar. The projects most people get involved in are more modest in scale. They tend to be fairly short in duration, utilize only a few resources, and usually don't have "world-changing" impacts on either the organization or the world. Consequently, some of the traditional tools (some of the major software packages in particular), could be characterized as "killing flies with a sledge hammer."

The approach presented here is one of practical application of simple tools to accomplish the goals of a project. This approach is certainly scalable for projects from the simple to the complex, but the focus is on moderate sized projects.

The Characteristics of Projects

Projects come in all shapes, sizes, and levels of complexity. There are, however, some characteristics they all share that help to define a project as something separate from the day-to-day operations of an organization:

- A beginning and an ending
- A uniqueness
- A specific goal to be achieved

- The involvement of several people, usually on an ad-hoc basis
- Limited resources
- A sequencing of activities

A Beginning and an Ending

Every accomplishment starts with the decision to try.

Anonymous

This is probably the most obvious characteristic of projects. Projects usually start and stop within a time-frame that is most often established at the outset of the project. Sometimes this time frame is determined by the actual time that will be required to produce the output of the project — after project planning is complete. But, more often than not, the project's deadline is determined by factors outside the actual project such as: Meeting a specific market introduction date; having a new or changed process on-line by a specific date; or, completing the construction of a new facility in time for a major organizational move.

The time between the beginning and end of the project, multiplied by the time each project-team member can devote to its achievement, is the total number of person-hours (days, weeks, etc.) that can be applied to project work. This time-frame is usually the most demanding constraint on a project. In many cases, schedule trumps output. Organizations will frequently accept a less-than-perfect output if it can be delivered on time.

This seems to be based on that old axiom: "We never seem to have the time to do it right but we always find the time to do it over." In the interest of not setting unrealistic expectations as to what project management tools and techniques can do for you, it is important to recognize that, for most project leaders inside organizations, there is little that you can do, individually, to overcome this rather foolish approach. You will most likely have to work within the deadlines assigned to your projects. You can build a case for increasing the deadline (or the resources available to do the work) but there is no guarantee that you will win.

There is another aspect to this idea of an ending point for a project. Ongoing support or maintenance should not be part of the project. If you want a single project to become a career, don't separate ongoing support and maintenance from design and implementation. Many in-house projects are undertaken to deliver new work processes. These processes need to be designed, implemented, and debugged and then made a part of ongoing operations. It is the transition between project and ongoing operations that is critical. Designing the maintenance process may well be part of the project. Doing the daily maintenance forever should not be.

A Uniqueness

In order to compose, all you have to do is remember a tune that nobody else has thought of

Robert Schumann
1810-1856
German Composer

Uniqueness is the characteristic that separates projects from the ongoing, predictable activities those business systems are designed to deal with. Most organizations are geared to doing things thousands, or millions, of times. All of the systems of the organization act to support ongoing, repetitive activity. Most organizations, as they are normally structured, are not very good at doing things for the first time. There are, of course, exceptions to this. Many high-tech start-up companies (and some of the more mature high-tech firms) are actually designed to continually do new things. However, this is not the norm for most businesses.

Projects are a form of innovation. As such, in order to be successful, they must fall outside the normal operating and controlling systems of the organization. Innovation is a very nebulous thing. It rarely occurs in a truly systematic fashion. To be sure, there are systems which can help create an environment in which innovation can take place. Some of them even work fairly well within established organizations, but trying to control and monitor innovation in the same manner a company would monitor predictable, established operations (like accounting, for instance) rarely works very well. The need for planning, controlling, and monitoring "controlled chaos" (specifically in the construction industry) is what gave birth to the discipline of project management.

The degree of uniqueness varies with every project. Many projects are essentially variations on past projects. The same basic plans can be duplicated, taking into account the changes necessary to accommodate the requirements of the new material (idea, process, product, etc.) being developed.

Other projects push the boundaries of imagination. They involve exploration of potential technologies; development of completely unique products; evolving areas of thought or research; or implementation of un-tested techniques or processes.

Routine | Most in-house projects | **Unique**

Most projects undertaken by today's organizations fall closer to the left side of this model. They are, to a greater or lesser degree, variations on work that has been done in the past. This is not to say that they are easier or any more predictable than "raw research" projects, but they do have the benefit of being able to use somewhat standardized tools and techniques and readily available information and expertise.

The really good news is that you will likely be able to develop "plan templates" for projects that fall on the left side of the model. Since the projects will probably follow the same general sequence of activities, you can develop a plan that includes those elements and simply change the details as required.

A Specific Goal

If you don't know where you're going, any path will get you there.

Sioux Proverb

Of all of the characteristics of projects, the specific goal to be achieved by a project may be the most difficult to define accurately at the beginning of the activity. You need to determine the start and finish; the activities that must be completed; the deliverables that are expected; the budget for development; the performance or quality expectations; etc. In order to determine all of these, a specific goal must be developed which states exactly what is expected.

The establishment of the project's goal is the first step in actually planning the project. Without a clear, concise goal statement, most projects flounder. The goal sets the expectations of the project team, the project's sponsors, and the project's customers. There are a number of considerations in developing a goal for a project. Many of these and a process for developing the project goal are discussed in the next chapter.

Several People

Fortunately, it appears that most people are more cooperative than the standard economic model suggests
Richard Thaler
Cornell University

For most projects undertaken within organizations, the project teams are made up of individuals who are not assigned to the project full time. For that matter, most leaders are not assigned to a "full time" either. In most organizations, projects are conducted in parallel with ongoing operations. They operate within the confines of the business, use the resources of the business, and are in constant contact with the business. But, they are not managed in the same fashion as the rest of the business. This characteristic places some unique demands on the project leader. Unless the business is a true "matrix organization" the chances are quite good that most of the members of the project team will report (organizationally) to someone other than the project leader. The specific issues this raises are discussed in some detail later in this book.

At this point, we should say that virtually all of the people assigned to a project should be thought of as "borrowed resources." This means they report to someone other than the project leader and the chances are quite good that the person they report to already has plans for their time. Bottom line, this means that they can be called away from the project whenever there is a need for them elsewhere.

Limited Resources

You never know what you can do without until you try.
Franklin Pierce Adams
1881-1960
American journalist

When you are first assigned a project, have you ever had anyone tell you, "We don't care how much it costs or how long it takes, we just want to get it done?" Didn't think so. In even the most research-and-development-driven organizations — those that survive on the development of new products and services — there are limits on resources. For the types of projects that will be discussed here, these limits are very tight. They include all resources — time, people, money, materials, space, all of it. Sometimes the resource limits are flexible enough, or broad enough, to allow project activity to go on without much concern for reaching limits. However, in most cases, the limits placed on resources are a major determining factor in what can be done on the project.

Money is not the currency of most in-house projects. In-house project leaders usually have little, if any, input to or control of project budgets. In fact, in training programs for eighteen to twenty people, when we ask the question, "How many of you have control over your project's budget?" we typically only see two or three hands raised. When we ask the follow-up question, "How many of you even know if your project has a budget?" we may see a couple more hands go up. The fact is, most in-house projects are not budgeted in the traditional sense.

Of all of the resources that will impact a typical in-house project, the time available from the people who must participate in the work is usually the most limited. In fact, the "currency" that is spent to get most projects accomplished is not money, it's time — your time as the project leader and the time of the people who work on the project. And, of all the resources that might be associated with a project, time is the one that is in the most limited supply. There are only so many hours in a person's day. And, thanks to planetary rotation and those pesky laws of physics, there's no known way to get any more.

There are certainly other considerations in the definition of resources associated with a project, but the driving factor in most in-house projects - the thing that really determines when the final output will be delivered - is the time available from the participants.

A Sequencing of Activities

In every affair consider what precedes and what follows, and then undertake it.

Epictetus
circa 60 A.D
Greek Philosopher

The logical sequence of activity is one of the things that makes project planning possible, and project planning is a major part of project management. Some things must be completed before other things can begin. Some things can be done simultaneously. Some things can be done completely separately. But, in all cases, there is a sequence to activities which places some constraints on project activity.

Determining this sequence of activities is one of the main functions of developing a project plan. The sequence of activity forms the basic structure of the project on which all other planning activity is based. Project planning cannot be done with any degree of effectiveness without a sense of the organization of the work to be done, who's going to do it, when it should be done, anticipating problems that might arise, etc. All of the planning and management tools in this book are based on the assumption that a project can be structured in a logical sequence of activities.

The "Triple Constraint"

Quality. Speed. Price. Pick two.

Advertising-Agency Lobby Sign

All projects, regardless of size or complexity, are bounded by a "Triple Constraint" of time, resources, and output.

The triple constraint is usually visualized as a triangle with each constraint placed at a corner of the triangle. The area of the triangle is the "space" within which the project is done. This is sometimes called project scope.

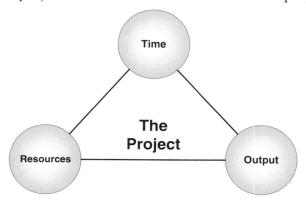

Time

The Time constraint encompasses all of the time limitations on the project: When it must be delivered, the time demands on the people who must be involved, the time demands on the equipment that must be used, the time constraints placed on the project by management, etc.

Schedule is the most common driving constraint on most projects. You may be able to deliver a less-than-optimum output if you deliver it on time. While this may seem to be an extension of the "We never have time to do it right but we always find the time to do it over" mentality, there may be other factors involved. For example, the deadline for a project is not usually just "pulled out of the air." If you ask some questions about it, you will likely find that the deadline is related to some other business need. For example, a process project may need to be implemented by a certain date in order to link up with the delivery of material to be put through the process. A new-product development project may need to be completed to allow the product to be introduced at a national trade show. (It's funny, but those trade show people are really sticky about their dates and they won't delay the show because your product isn't ready.)

Of all of the constraints placed on projects, the deadline for delivery is usually the least flexible. This does not, however, mean that the way in which the time from the initiation of the project to the deadline is used is also inflexible. On most projects, the amount of time that can be devoted to the work is flexible, based on the importance the organization places on completion of the project.

Resources

The Resource constraint encompasses all the limitations placed on the project that involve either money or the things money can buy: Material, outside expertise, machinery and equipment, space, and most of all, the time and expertise of the members of the project team.

If you think of resources as the "currency" you can spend to accomplish your project, then the most common denomination of that currency will be other people's time. Most project leaders in businesses today do not control the budgets for their projects. In many cases, they don't even know what the financial constraints are. Likewise, they do not usually have control over the things that money buys such as outside experts, equipment, raw materials, and space. This doesn't mean project leaders can't influence these expenditures. However, they usually don't have direct authority over them.

Output

The Output constraint encompasses all the requirements placed on the final output of the project. This includes all of the performance and quality characteristics: What must the output be able to do or provide when it is delivered.

Of all the constraints placed on projects, this is generally the most difficult to define clearly at the outset. This is not to say that it is impossible, but it will require work and negotiation to insure that the deliverable at the end meets the expectations set at the beginning. Chapter 2: *Project Pre-work*, has several tools to help clarify and define project output.

PROCESS TIP
One of the constraints is usually the "driver"

In virtually every project, one of the constraints (time, resources, output) drives the project — one is more important than the others. If you can identify which constraint is the driver, you can focus efforts on ensuring that is it met. This can also help with decisions about how to react when the constraints begin to shift (and come into conflict with each other) as the project unfolds.

In many cases, when you ask the question, "Which of these is more important than the others?" the answer will be something like, "They're all equally important." This, of course, is no help whatsoever. Most of the time, history will be the main clue as to which is most important. For example, if other projects seem to be driven by schedule, it's probably a safe bet that your project will also be driven by schedule. What this means is, it problems begin to surface that look like they're going to delay the final output, the focus should probably shift to making sure that the schedule is met, even at the expense of some of the features or an increase in resources. (By the way, in private sector businesses, Schedule is the most common driver, followed by Output/Quality characteristics. In public sector organizations such as government and non-profit agencies, the most common driver by far is Resources/Cost.)

The Impact of Changing a Constraint

> Certainty generally is illusion, and repose is not the destiny of man.
> **Oliver Wendell Holmes, Jr.**
> 1841-1935
> U.S. Supreme Court Justice

As long as the constraints remain stable, all is well. However, stability is not the normal state of most projects. As projects unfold, one or more of the original constraints are likely to change. As the following illustrations show, moving one of the corners of the triangle changes the size and shape of the project's "space." In order to complete the project, changes may be required in the other two constraints.

Unfortunately, constraints rarely get changed in a positive direction. Phrases you are unlikely to hear include:

- "We've decided that the original deadline was just too aggressive so you now have an additional three months to complete the project."

- "We've just discovered several people with nothing to do. Could you use them on your project?"

- "We've thought about it and decided that there were just too many features in the original design. Let's drop a few."

It is rare to get more time, more resources, or reduced output requirements. The opposite is generally the case. Most projects are planned and scheduled to deliver the originally specified output within a fairly tight schedule and with limited flexibility in resources. So, if one or more of the constraints gets tightened, the others must "pick up the slack."

The trap in this situation lies in not acknowledging that a change in one constraint has had an impact on the other constraints of the project. Almost any change in a constraint requires decisions and actions to adjust the project and keep it viable.

A Change in the Time Constraint

The time constraint usually changes because of a change in the business environment that was driving the original deadline. Of the three constraints, this is the one that is the least likely to change. Once set, the deadline usually remains intact. However, if it changed, it is most commonly pulled in, shortened. It rarely is extended without a compelling reason. If the time constraint is shortened, it will require one of two possible actions actions in order to meet the new deadline:

- More resources will be required to meet the output requirements for the project. This may not mean that you need to add people to the project.

Remember that the currency of most projects is people's time. It may simply mean that you need more time from the people already working on the project.

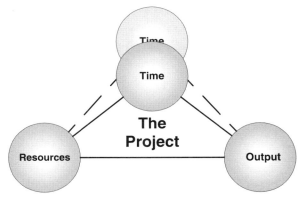

- The requirements for the output will need to be adjusted to compensate for the reduced time available to deliver. This one can be tricky. Changing the output of the project usually requires negotiation with the customer to determine which features can be left out or delayed until after the new deadline.

The most common reaction to a reduction in the time available to complete the project is to apply more pressure to the resources assigned rather than to add resources or reduce output. This the "blood from a rock" approach. Squeeze the resources still on the project to get more output rather than add additional people or reduce the output requirements. This is where overtime comes from. Within reason, this will usually work. Where it starts to fail is when the time reduction is too extreme and there simply isn't enough time to get the work done.

> **PROCESS TIP**
> **Why the Time Constraint may change**
> A change in the time constraint usually occurs as a result of a change in the circumstances that caused the project to be undertaken. If this is what has happened, you need to know what has changed. This can give you the information you need to build the case for increasing resources or reducing output. But, if you don't know the reason for the shift, you can't respond to it intelligently. Ask questions about "why" the deadline has been moved.

A Change in the Resource Constraint Of the three constraints, this is the one that most commonly changes enough to cause a problem. Losing resources can occur for a variety of reasons, but the most common is a change in the priority status of the project. As the business goes through its normal cycles, the importance of the projects being done changes. What was critical yesterday may only be important (or even only "interesting") today. Changing the resource constraint (which usually means losing resources, usually people, but also money or any other budgeted resource) will require:

- More time to meet the output requirements. When resources are lost, additional time is needed in either the form of a delayed deadline or more time committed from the remaining resources. In either case, this negotiation should include everyone who has a stake in the project.

- Adjusting the output requirements to compensate for the lack of resources. The real danger in this one lies in the skills of the people remaining on the project. If you lose a person with a critical skill set, the whole project may be in jeopardy.

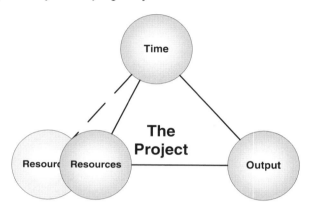

Unfortunately, the knee-jerk response to this problem is the same as the response to a change in the Time constraint — squeeze the remaining resources harder. While this may work in some cases, as a standard response it is dangerous. The greatest danger lies in situations where a critical resource has been lost — when a unique skill set is lost to the project.

PROCESS TIP
Why the Resources Constraint may change
The most common reason for the Resources constraint changing is a shift in priorities. There is little that can be done to protect a project against this problem unless the project is a "life-or-death" activity for the organization, in which case it will probably take precedence over just about everything. In those cases where it isn't life or death, doing a very good job on the stakeholder analysis and project pre-work can go a long way. This will help ensure that you have the information necessary to build a strong case for keeping (or recovering) the resources needed for your projects. See information in "Stakeholders in the World of Projects" in this chapter and all of Chapter 2.

A Change in the Output Constraint Of all of the constraints around a project, output is the one most likely to shift at some point in the project. Virtually all projects are subject to some degree of change in the Output constraint. This is partly due to the fact that most projects are not as well defined on the front end as we might like. If the original definition of the output is not complete or not clear, the chances that it will change as the project unfolds are almost 100%. This is sometimes known as "feature creep," "creeping functionality," or "scope creep." By whatever name, it is a problem that almost every project will encounter at some point. The good news (if there can be good news in having your work redefined while you're doing it) is that most Output changes can be absorbed with minimal impact on the overall project. The changes that you need to be watching for are those that significantly impact your ability to complete the project within the time-frame utilizing the available resources. Changing the output constraint (which usually means adding functions or capabilities to the project's output) will require:

- More time to develop, test, and add the new functions. It is important to remember that projects do not usually fall behind schedule because of a single, major change. Projects get behind schedule in small increments — little changes that, in and of themselves, don't have much impact but, when taken together, can seriously impact the overall schedule.

- Increasing the resources (people and/or money) to compensate for the additional work. When new features or requirements are added to a project, somebody has to be sure they get included. This takes somebody's time.

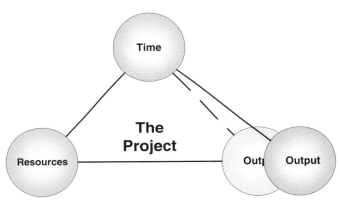

Once again, we have the same knee-jerk reaction as before — squeeze the resources to produce more output in the same time-frame. Small changes can usually be dealt with by the existing staff. It's the big changes or those that fundamentally change the project that require a serious look.

PROCESS TIP
Why the Output Constraint may change
Output changes are almost guaranteed to happen. Most of them will appear to be (and may, in fact, be) minor. However, keep careful track of even the smallest changes to output requirements. It is not the impact of individual changes that cause the major problems. It is *the cumulative effect* of several small changes that does the damage.

While the most obvious impact will generally be on the project's schedule, don't ignore the impact output-requirement changes may be having on the way in which the project needs to be done — changes in the actual content of the work. There will be much more on this in the Change Control section of Chapter 5: *Project Implementation*.

"Trade-off" is the name of the game in dealing with changes to any of the three major project constraints. There are trade-offs inherent in virtually every change in a project. Being able to negotiate these trade-offs is one of the marks of a good project leader. It is also a major responsibility.

The lesson here for in-house project leaders is:

> *You may not have the authority to make every decision required by your projects, but you do have a responsibility to get the necessary decisions made.*

The Characteristics of Effective Project Leaders

> Any leader worth following gives credit easily where credit is due. He does not take someone's idea, dress it up and offer it as his own. He offers it as theirs. Otherwise, ideas will cease to flow his way. He plays fair with everyone and recognizes the strong points in people as well as the weak ones. He never takes advantage for his own selfish purposes.
>
> **Franklin J. Lundling**
> Lawyer

Like projects, effective project leaders share some specific characteristics. The list below is by no means definitive, but the most effective project leaders seem to share most, if not all, of these traits. In combination, they are a powerful mix of skills and attitudes that foster the teamwork and commitment among the project team necessary for leading projects to successful conclusion. They also foster confidence on the part of the organization that you are the person for the job. The most effective project leaders are:

- "People" people
- Good planners
- Good problem-solvers
- Goal-driven
- Action-oriented
- "Business-aware"

"People" people

> I not only use all the brains I have, but all I can borrow.
> **Woodrow Wilson**
> 1856-1924
> 28th President of the United States

Plans do not accomplish project goals. Schedules do not deliver project output. Monitoring systems do not get anything done. Project management software does not manage projects. People are required for every activity connected with a project. People do the work, accomplish the goals, deliver the results, monitor the progress, manage the activities.

In order to be an effective project leader, you must first be an effective "people" person. This does not necessarily mean you must have experience as a people manager. It does mean you must have the ability to be, or to become, an effective leader of people.

Most successful project leaders do not rely on organizational authority (the authority which comes with positions or titles). They rely on their own personal power to motivate and inspire.

Another dimension of being a "people" person is respect. I know of at least one very successful project leader who has been overheard making the following statement more than once:

> "I assume every person I meet and work with on a project is a genius. I assume that they are on my project because they can do things that neither I, nor any other person on the team, can do. I try to make this clear to them from our first meeting and this is the way I treat them until they prove me wrong. And, you know what? I'm rarely proven wrong."

Being an effective "people" person does not mean spending all your time making sure everyone is happy. It means treating people with respect — respect for them as individuals — as intelligent, competent, valuable members of the team. If you really don't like people and have no respect for what someone else can do or contribute, find something else to do. Project management is not for you.

Good Planners

The will to win is important, but the will to plan is vital.

Joe Patemo
College Football Coach

The bulk of a project leader's job revolves around planning (and re-planning). Logic skills, problem-analysis skills, a "big-picture" view — all are manifestations of good planning skills. In addition, good communication skills are needed to convey the details and requirements of project plans to those who must implement them.

Good planners have a methodology they use to do their planning. As you gain experience with planning and managing projects, your own personal planning methodology will evolve. It may be highly complex and detailed or it may be loose and flexible. Whatever the methodology, it should be applied with the same rigor to each and every project you undertake.

Effective project leaders walk a thin line between the macro and micro activities of a project. One of the most dangerous traps a project leader can fall into is that of becoming too involved in the details of some part of the overall project. Good planning and effective monitoring of the plan provide excellent guidelines for when to "get buried in the details" and when to "stick to the big picture."

Good Problem-Solvers

Never go out to meet trouble. If you will just sit still, nine cases out of ten, someone will intercept it before it reaches you.

Calvin Coolidge
1872-1933
30th President of the
United States

Effective project leaders get problems solved. They do not necessarily solve every problem that comes along. Rather, they empower members of the project team to solve the problems they discover.

To the effective project leader, a problem is a challenge to be met in the most efficient manner possible. They recognize that problems are inevitable and that, in most cases, the person closest to the problem is the person best suited to solve it. Therefore, when someone comes to them and says, "I have a problem," their initial response is not, "Leave it with me and I'll take care of it." Rather, they respond with, "What do you think we should do about it?" In many (if not most) cases, the person bringing the problem to your attention has already thought about it and has probably thought of at least one or two possible solutions. What they may be asking is not, "Will you solve this problem for me?" but rather, "Which of my solutions should I try first?" In some cases, it's even more basic. They may really be asking, "Do I have your permission to solve this?" When these situations arise, pick a solution or grant permission. There is only one caution that goes with this: Never forget to close the information loop. The last thing you need is to have problems identified and not know whether they have been effectively dealt with or not. Always finish these conversations with something like, "Try this approach and let me know what happens." It is also a good idea to attach a time-frame to the request for a response such as, "And let me know by tomorrow afternoon." Then, follow up to be sure it worked.

Some problems are really the project leader's responsibility. They are outside the bounds of what the team member can do or they require access to resources the team member can't draw on. When appropriate, the leader should take on the problem. The good news is that, in some cases, you can pass the problem on to someone else more qualified to solve it.

Remember the earlier discussion about decision-making: You're not responsible for making every decision, but you are responsible for seeing that necessary decisions get made. Problem-solving is the same: You are not responsible for personally solving every problem. You are, however, responsible for seeing that the problems get solved. Effective project leaders also recognize that not every problem can be solved by team members or even by themselves. When a problem like this occurs, they will see that the people who must solve the problem are aware of it and will do what is necessary to get the problem solved at whatever level is appropriate. Effective project leaders don't solve every problem; they see to it that the problems get solved.

Goal-Driven

Men, like nails, lose their usefulness when they lose direction and begin to bend.
Walter Savage Landor
1775-1864
English Poet and Writer

Projects are implemented to accomplish some specific goal. The project plan is based on doing the work necessary to deliver the output of the project. Once the planning is done, effective project leaders tend to be very focused on the accomplishment of that goal. They look at every activity and task, every problem, every deliverable in terms of how it will affect the accomplishment of the project goal.

Decisions are made, contingency plans are implemented, work breakdowns are revised in order to more effectively and efficiently accomplish the goal of the project.

This would be easier if project goals would stay put once they are set. In reality, however, they have a tendency to "drift" or get redefined along the way to their accomplishment. In some cases, this results from an intentional change in the requirements for the output. In other cases, it results from discoveries made as the project unfolds requiring a change in one of the constraints.

Regardless of its stability, the project goal is the target at which all work on the project is aimed. Effective project leaders never let that target out of their sight, no matter how it shifts.

Action-Oriented

Don't wait for your ship to come in, swim out to it.

While effective project leaders recognize the importance of detailed planning, they also recognize the need to "get it off the drawing board" and get the project underway. Once project planning is complete, everything centers on the implementation and completion of the activities of the project.

Activities are tracked very carefully and decisions are made which will move the project ahead. Problems are addressed as soon as they appear. Resources are allocated where they will do the most good. Contingency plans are implemented without waiting for a situation to reach the crisis stage. All activity is aimed at accomplishing the project goal within the time frame of the project.

Projects develop a kind of internal momentum as they unfold. They usually start slowly, and build in terms of both activity and speed as they develop. Managing this momentum requires careful monitoring of both the work being done and the people doing it.

The one thing that most project leaders want to avoid is a "stall-out" on their projects. As anyone who's ever worked on a project that got stalled for any significant period of time will tell you, after a certain point, you might as well start over. Oddly enough, a stall does not have to be terribly long to cause problems. Four to six weeks is enough for many projects to require significant restarting. In the best cases, you simply need to review, in detail, all the work that was done before the stall. In other cases, you need to actually redo the work. Once a project gets moving, do everything you can to keep it moving.

"Business Aware"

The creative person wants to be a know-it-all. He wants to know about all kinds of things: ancient history, nineteenth-century mathematics, current manufacturing techniques, flower arranging, and hog futures. Because he never knows when these ideas might come together to form a new idea. It may happen six minutes later or six months or six years down the road. But he has faith that it will happen.

Carl Ally
Founder, Ally & Gargano Advertising

Unless a company has hired people specifically as project managers — with training and experience in managing projects in a variety of disciplines — project leaders are most likely to be individuals who are selected based on some technical expertise deemed necessary to the completion of the project at hand. This has inherent pitfalls.

There is a natural tendency on the part of many technically competent people to work within their personal "comfort zone" which may be too deep in the details of the project. That is, after all, where their expertise lies. Effective project leaders, with technical backgrounds, are able to separate their technical expertise from their project leadership duties. They do this by being "business-aware," that is, being constantly aware of the larger context in which the project is being undertaken. They maintain a clear understanding of how the project fits into the context of the entire business, not just the area in which it is being implemented.

Business awareness is difficult to teach and is usually the result of simple curiosity — some individuals are just more interested in "how it all fits together." It is this orientation on the larger context that helps effective project leaders keep their projects in the proper organizational perspective. There are benefits to developing your business awareness. For one thing, you are likely to be able to find and utilize resources outside your own area, if you know what else is going on in the company and who's doing it. For another, if you are aware of the goals and objectives of the organization, you can link your project closely to one or more of those goals, and thereby gain additional support for your work.

Another aspect of business awareness is being able to tell whether a particular project is appropriate for the organization to undertake. For example, in most medium to large organizations, you would likely be able to find a group of people with the basic expertise and possibly the experience to design and build a racing yacht. The question is not whether the organization could build a racing yacht but whether it should. Unless the organization is in the business of building boats or boating-related products, at the very least, someone should ask the question, "Should we really do this?"

The linkage or connection between a project goal and some other goal or objective of the organization is a critical source of support in the ongoing struggle for resources, assistance, expertise, time, and commitment. If you can draw a clear line between the accomplishment of your project's goal and some other goal of the business, your ability to argue effectively for needed resources and support is greatly improved. Obviously, the higher the goal you can connect to, the better for your project. But, even linking it to a simple workgroup goal will help. If you can also connect it clearly to a department goal, so much the better. If you can draw that line from the project through the work group, through the department and into the level of divisional, corporate, or organizational goals, your chances of getting and maintaining support for your project improve even more.

In fact, if you can't find a clear linkage between your project goal and some other goal of the organization, you should ask why the project is being undertaken. If there is no connection between the expenditure of resources on the project, and the furthering or accomplishment of some organizational goal, why should the organization support the project? In fact, the answer is, it probably shouldn't.

Stakeholders in the World of Projects

> The people you want to reach, whether they're your co-workers, your boss or an organizational president, should be viewed as distinct target audiences that require different approaches and strategies.
>
> **Jeffrey P. Davidson**
> Marketing Consultant

There are several individuals and groups who can have a significant interest in you and your projects. Not all projects have highly defined roles but there are aspects of each of these roles on virtually every project:

- The project's sponsor
- The project's customer and other interested parties
- The project team

Identifying these players early in the project is important to planning. The roles outlined here may be shared by a single person or group or they may be spread among a large number of people and groups. For example, the project's sponsor may also be the project's customer.

Every organization implements these roles differently. In some, the roles are clearly defined with a clear set of responsibilities outlined for each. In others, the roles may not even be explicitly acknowledged. In all cases, however, these roles exist to some extent.

What we're talking about here is doing some "stakeholder analysis." Determining, up front, who the stakeholders are and what they want and expect from the project will go a long way toward helping you deliver a satisfactory output. It will also help you address all requirements and many of the desirable additional features or characteristics of the output. It will also help ensure that the project fits within the overall priorities of the organization.

Stakeholder analysis can be detailed or superficial or anything in between.

This form covers the basic steps in the process. The level of detail you go into should be appropriate for the culture of the organization and the needs of the project at hand.

Stakeholder Analysis Worksheet

Fill in the appropriate project information

Identify the Stakeholder and indicate their current perceived stance about the project: Supportive, opposed to it, or undecided or unsure.

Identify the features or characteristics of the project that you believe would be of interest to them.

Identify the benefits these features or characteristics are expected to deliver.

Identify the value you believe these features and benefits have for the Stakeholder.

Develop a strategy to ensure continued support, overcome or circumvent opposition, convert the uncommitted.

Project:		Date:	
Project Leader:			
Project Sponsor:			

Stakeholder:		☐ Supports ☐ Opposes ☐ Unsure/Undecided	
Features	Benefits	Value	

Strategy:

Project Sponsor

There are two slightly different definitions for the Sponsor's role. In both cases, the key is managerial authority:

- The person who initiates the project, whether this is the customer or not, and who will be the main source of management decision-making and resource assistance throughout the project.

- A person, usually in management, who will act on behalf of the project when issues exceed the project leader's authority or responsibility. This person may or may not have been the initiator of the project.

Most projects need a sponsor. Due to how project leaders are selected in most organizations, the full range of managerial authority is rarely granted along with the assignment. At some point, outside assistance with decision-making, resource acquisition, or intervention is likely to be needed. Knowing who to go to for this help is important to the continuation and success of the project.

The Fried Egg Model

In every person's job there is an area that is completely under the control of the individual. Within this area, the person can make decisions and take actions without consulting anyone else. For every person reading this book, that area of control is likely to be a different size. Think of this area of control as the yoke of a fried egg. Unfortunately, your projects will rarely, if ever, fall within the area over which you exercise complete control.

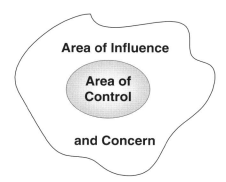

Around this yoke of control is an area over which you can and should exert influence and about which you will have concerns. Think of this as the white of the fried egg. This is where most projects occur. And, this is also the area where you will need the assistance of a Sponsor. Ideally, your Sponsor's "yoke" should encompass your "white" — their area of control should encompass your area of influence and concern.

The person in the Sponsor's role has certain responsibilities. They should:

- Support the project, the project leader, and the project team in their efforts to complete the project successfully

- Provide advice and assistance as needed

- Act as an advocate for the project, the project leader, and project team

- They should intervene on behalf of the project in situations that are outside the span of authority and control of the project leader, or where outside support is required

PROCESS TIP
Project Sponsors

Identifying a Sponsor for your project should be one of the early activities you undertake. In many cases, the Sponsor will be the person who initiated the project, frequently you manager. In those instances where you or someone other than your manager initiates the project, consider who has a vested interest in the success of the project and recruit them as the Sponsor.

Formalizing the Sponsor relationship is not always necessary. However, you should at least have a conversation with your Sponsor to discuss the project and the role you expect them to play in its completion.

The Project's Customers   A customer is anyone who receives and uses the output of the work you do.

The project's customer is the recipient of the output of the project — the deliverable handed over at the end. Knowing who your customers are is an important key to defining and delivering an output they can use.

It is also important to recognize that most projects have multiple customers. For example, if your project is to develop a piece of accounting software for internal use, the customers might include: The accountants, the accounting manager, the accountant's customers (those who use the information the accountants produce), and possibly even vendors to and customers of the company. However, none of these are the primary customer — the individual who will receive the project's output first. If you develop a piece of system software, you will most likely give it to a system administrator who will load it on the company's computers, test it, and deploy it to the accounting users. If that individual cannot do the job of loading and deploying the application, no one else in the customer chain will be able to derive the benefit of the new program.

In many instances, a project's customers are others inside the organization. They are members of the same work group or a related work group. Or they may be a work group that you and the project team members support in some way as part of your jobs. In these cases, it is easy to speak directly with them and to enlist their input and aid in defining and reviewing the work being done.

Even when the project's customer is outside the organization or otherwise not directly accessible, it is important to consider their needs and situation when developing the project.

With internal customers this is fairly easy — you can go talk to them. With external customers this usually requires either someone who is in contact with them or someone who can effectively represent the customer's interests. Product development projects frequently have representatives from the Marketing or Sales function on the team to act as the customer's stand-in.

Most projects will touch more than just the project's immediate customers. Others within the organization will be impacted by either the development of the project or the delivery of the project's output. Identifying who has an interest in your project is an important part of the definition and planning process.

Take, for example, a project to develop a new manufacturing process. The obvious customers for this project are the manufacturing people who will use the new process to do their work. Others who are likely to be impacted by this project include:

- The people who will be responsible for maintaining the process once it is up and running. This may include one or more members of the project team that developed the process. It is important to recognize that ongoing maintenance of a process is not part of a project to build or implement the process. Even though the same people may be involved in maintaining the process once it is in place, this is not part of the project.

- The people in the process that precedes the new process in the manufacturing flow, since the requirements for what they provide may change.

- Production or plant management since they will be responsible for managing the new process.

- Production planning since they will need to plan work for a new process.

- Material control since they will be supplying material to the new process.

- Whoever receives the output of the new manufacturing operation.

Others who could be impacted might include: Design engineering, manufacturing engineering, packaging, shipping, accounting, and marketing.

Projects do not usually come into being in isolation. They are most often initiated to solve an organizational problem. Their output is usually intended to become an integral part of the ongoing operation of the business. Identifying who has a stake in your projects will help, both from the point of view of gaining and maintaining support, and from the point of view of creating a project output that has been carefully thought out and can be effectively integrated.

The Project Team   You may have an actual "team" devoted to the project on a more-or-less full-time basis. Or, you may have a flexible group of people working on the tasks of the project when they are available. The latter is more likely but, whatever the case, the people doing the work have the highest level of need-to-know next to you as the project's leader.

The people doing the work should be involved in designing the work to be done. They should be included in the planning of the project, if possible. They need to be kept informed of progress on the project; problems or opportunities encountered and what has been done about them; changes in project plans or schedules; implementation of contingency plans; etc. In short, they need to know almost as much about what is going on with the project on a daily basis as you do.

Chapter 3: *People Skills for Project Leaders*, covers a variety of topics related to working with people in a project environment. Chapter 4: *Project Planning*, outlines a group-centered project-planning process.

Three Broad Categories of Projects

While the overall flow of project activity is essentially the same regardless of the project being undertaken, there are some unique characteristics which emerge depending on the type of project.

Basically, projects undertaken within a business fall within three broad categories:

- Process projects are usually internally focused on development or enhancement of a process, technique, or method of accomplishing work.
- Product- or service-development projects are usually externally focused on developing and/or providing a product or service to the customers of the business.
- Software development projects can be focused on development of software for internal use or for sale to the company's customers.

Major facilities projects (such as the construction of a new facility, renovation of an existing manufacturing plant, or the construction of a retail outlet) are a combination of internally- and externally-focused projects.

These three broad categories are by no means all-inclusive. There are projects that don't really fit nicely into any category. However, for our purposes here, these will allow for discussion of some unique issues.

Process Projects   The customers of internally-focused process projects are those who will be asked to use the new process once it is developed and implemented. They are your co-workers in the company.

Process projects rarely have huge budgets, are limited in their scope and impact, and are usually completed with little involvement of outside vendors (with the exception of those who provide equipment required by the new process).

Internal process projects are by far the most common type of projects undertaken in business today. Much of the driving force for process projects is provided by the need to respond to changes in both the internal and external environments of the business.

Product/Service Projects   The customers of externally-focused product or service development projects are a combination of internal and external: Internal customers are those who will be asked to manufacture the product or provide the service, and external customers are the customers of the company who will purchase the final product or service.

Externally-focused projects tend to receive more attention than internally-focused projects. They tend to have larger budgets and greater access to diverse resources both inside and outside the company. There is usually heavy involvement on the part of the marketing arm of the company and, if carried out in a truly customer-focused manner, a strong dependence on customer input and customer interaction with at least some members of the project team.

Gaining commitment and assistance for an externally-focused project is usually fairly easy due to the fact that these projects are generally intended to generate income and it is easier to show the benefits to the company as a whole.

Software Projects   Software development projects are usually a unique type of project. On most other types of projects, there are physical components that are developed and delivered throughout the life of the project. Even if the project is canceled before completion, there are usually some physical items that show what was done. For example, pieces that could be sold or disposed of by some means to help recover some of the resources expended during the project. (Some examples include: Prototype or "first-run" products, land or building materials from a construction project, machinery or equipment from a process project.)

Software is a unique product in that its component parts (the actual lines of computer code) have little, if any, value until they are all integrated into the final program. In fact, they rarely have physical existence as anything other than binary instructions stored on magnetic media. This characteristic makes tracking, monitoring, and managing a software development project a unique challenge.

Much of the tracking and monitoring of project activity relies on the delivery of a physical output at various milestones. Software milestones are generally met when certain functions become usable or when a certain proportion of the final code is written. The deliverables of software projects are frequently demonstrations of functionality or printouts of lines of code.

Complex software development projects require extensive focus on the issues surrounding the integration of the component parts of the program into a complete, functional package. They also require careful coordination of technical and non-technical activities (such as the development of documentation to support the software).

A Generic Picture of Projects

The illustration which follows shows the elements of a fairly "normal" project. Every project is unique, but the majority of them will contain most of the steps shown in this illustration.

The remaining sections of this book provide details of the activities commonly occurring throughout the project planning and implementation process.

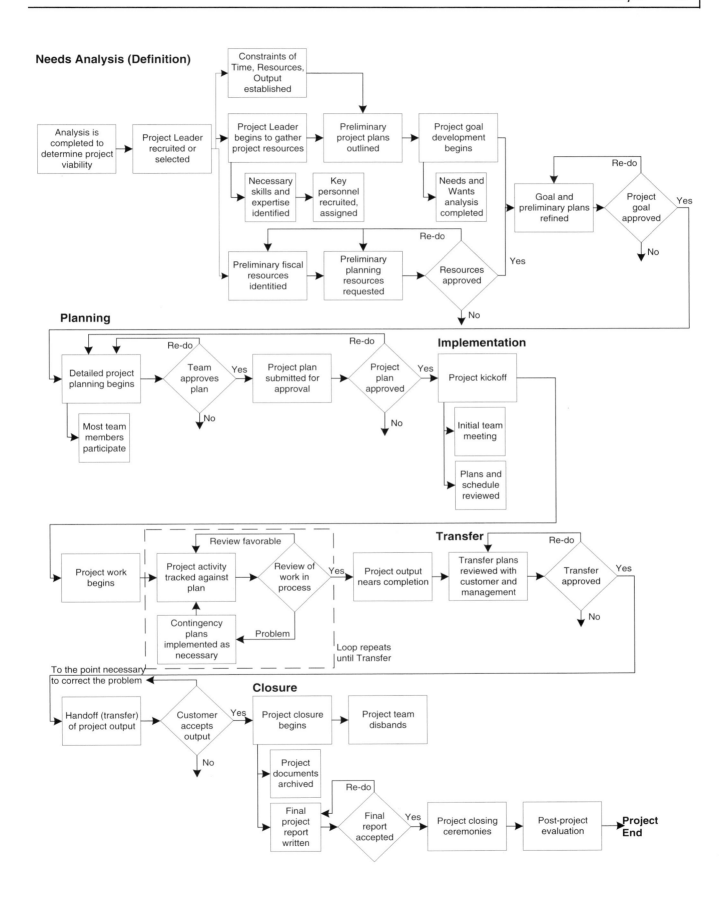

2

Project Pre-Work

Introduction

This first stage of project work is frequently a jumble of activities that are all going on simultaneously. There is no absolutely "correct" order for doing this work. For example, you might:

- Begin by developing a project goal statement that defines the need for the project. (A goal-development process is described in this chapter.) This would allow you to verify that the proposed solution fits the problem or opportunity to be addressed. You might then use the goal statement to gain agreement about the requirements of the output. (A Needs-and-Wants-identification process is described in this chapter). You might then use your list of Needs and Wants to help identify stakeholders and gain their support. With stakeholders clearly identified and "on board," you might ask one of them to be the project sponsor.

Or, you might:

- Begin with a careful definition of the problem or opportunity to be addressed by the project. From this you could complete the Needs and Want process for the project. The resulting list of Needs and Wants could help define the project's goal statement and the goal statement could be used to identify stakeholders and recruit a sponsor.

Or, in still another scenario, you might:

- Be assigned to the project by the project's sponsor. The assignment might come with a fairly clear statement of the project's goal. Using the provided statement as a starting point, you might complete the Needs and Wants process based on the characteristics implied by the goal. Identifying who needs to agree with the list of Needs and Wants would help identify stakeholders. A final project goal statement could be crafted from the approved Needs and Wants.

Or, you could follow the pattern in this book:

- Develop an understanding of the context of the project (how the project "fits" in the organization) and the problem or opportunity to be addressed by it — basically, a problem or opportunity statement. Complete the Needs and Wants process based on that understanding and use the list to help clarify and prioritize the requirements and characteristics of the proposed project output. Identify stakeholders and a sponsor based on what you know about the project at this point. With a clear idea of the output required (the approved list of Needs and Wants), write and circulate for approval a project goal statement that captures the essence of the project.

There is really no essential difference among these various approaches. The essential steps are completed in all of them. Only the order of completion changes. The order of completion is most often dictated by the specific circumstances surrounding a particular project. In some cases, plenty of information is available at the beginning to do a comprehensive Needs and Wants analysis and develop a goal statement. In other cases, the context of the project and what it should accomplish is so vague that a great deal of research is needed to simply determine whether the project should even be done.

Getting Started

Before a project begins, the context of the project should be clearly understood. This is a bit more than simply understanding why the project is being undertaken. It also includes understanding how the project "fits" in the larger scheme of things in the organization. Without a clear picture of what needs to be done to meet a specific need and how that need relates to the rest of the business, activity is likely to be unfocused and could result in lost time, false starts, and confusion.

Project pre-work is a form of problem-solving. In order to solve the problem, you must first define it and clarify what is desired of the solution. In most cases, an uncovered need is the reason why a project is undertaken in the first place. Someone has discovered they need something they don't have. This could come from virtually anywhere inside or outside the organization:

- From inside the organization it could be a need for an improved method of working. It could be a new manufacturing technique or process. It could be a new piece of software to automate a task. It could be a consolidation of two or more operations into a single process. It could be a need for a training program or a complex piece of documentation.

- From outside the organization it could be a request from a customer for an improvement to an existing product. It could be a request for a new product or service. It could be an idea from an employee for a product or service he or she believes has market potential. It could be an idea seen in a competitor's operation that could be adapted to the organization's needs.

However a project idea originates, simply being aware of the need is not the same thing as really understanding it. Projects have come into being and lasted for months (or even years) without producing anything significant in the way of output. This can happen because the exact nature of the need to be addressed was not clearly understood before project work began. This is an example of the "Ready! Fire! Aim!" mentality that is still more prevalent than it should be in business. The tendency to shoot without aiming is dangerous (and potentially very expensive) especially if you shoot without clearly understanding what (and where) the target is.

PROCESS TIP
Get help with your Needs Analysis
Try to enlist other people to assist with your analysis. Look for people who may be likely to work on the actual project. You can start building your "core team" even this early in the process.

In the pre-work to the project planning process, several questions should be asked to help define the need and the response to it that will be the project:

- What is the problem or opportunity to be addressed?
- What should be done about it? How should it be addressed?
- Who are you doing it for? Who is the customer of the project?
- Who should do the work? Who do you need on your project team?
- When should the final output be delivered?

Answering these questions will not only help clarify the context of the project, it will also help to define the constraints of:

- Time
- Resources
- Output

In this chapter, you will explore several aspects of project pre-work. You will look at a process for developing an understanding of the need for the project and for developing information about the best response to that need. You will also examine the importance of having a clear project goal and look at a simple process for developing one. Next, you will be presented with a simple tool for defining the skills needed to do the work of the project and for linking the individuals to those skills. Finally, you will be given some basic things to consider when developing or recruiting members for the project team.

Researching the Need

A problem well stated is a problem half solved.
Charles F. Kettering
1876-1958
American Electrical
Engineer and Inventor

Whatever approach you choose to take (or whatever approach is dictated by circumstances) is appropriate as long as it allows you to reach some level of understanding of each of the issues listed above. You should realize, however, that you will probably end up with an imperfect understanding of one or more of them. This is, unfortunately, the nature of many in-house projects — you must begin (and, in some cases, complete) the project with one or more of the major issues undecided. The goal here is for you to develop the best understanding circumstances will allow.

The following process is designed to provide a structure for project pre-work. Some situations are very straight-forward and do not require extensive pre-work analysis. Others are ill-defined, poorly thought out, or more complex. Yet others have numerous possible solutions or outcomes, any one of which might address the issue. This pre-work process will guide you through defining the problem and some of the requirements of any solution to it, and assessing overall project risks. In addition, for those projects with multiple possible deliverables, there are three optional steps you can complete to help with developing options and alternatives, analyzing which option will best solve the problem, and assessing overall project risks.

Many in-house projects are the result of someone (inside or outside the organization) expressing a desire to have something developed that will make their lives easier. This may seem like a simplistic view of the situation but, when all the fancy language and specifications are stripped from many project requests, they sometimes boil down to, "If I had this, I could do my work better, be more successful, have more free time, make my boss happy, etc." These are the projects that usually fall into the "problem" category. People are usually looking for a personal benefit from the project. They want the problem solved. In these cases, you can look for the benefits they expect and develop a project that will provide them.

In other cases projects result from a desire to take advantage of an opportunity rather than solve a problem. Most product-development projects fall into this category as do many technology upgrades and a fair number of the "quality of work life" projects such as employee-benefit program upgrades, some training-development projects, etc. Oddly enough, most organizations are more willing to do a more thorough job on the pre-work for "opportunity projects" than on "problem-solving" projects.

Some organizations seem to have an aversion to going through this process for either type of project. They would rather see something get started rather than spend time trying to detail "why" and "how" it should be done. If yours is such an organization, getting the answers to some of these questions may be difficult. However, just because it isn't easy doesn't mean you should skip it. Get as much of the information as you can and think through the rest — from the customer's point of view. The structured process described here should help you through this activity.

This project pre-work process involves five "required" steps and two "optional" steps. The two optional steps come into play when you have a project with several possible answers and need some help determining which option to pursue. The steps are (the optional steps are indented):

- Define the problem or opportunity
- Determine Needs and Wants
- Rank Wants according to their importance and gain agreement among stakeholders
- Write the project goal statement
  - Develop options to deliver the desired outcome
  - Compare options to Needs and Wants
- Assess overall risk

Define the Problem

Understanding the problem or opportunity is the first step. You must understand, as thoroughly as possible, the situation to be addressed by the project. Some helpful questions to ask at this stage include:

- What are the observable conditions that call attention to this situation? What can be seen and measured to demonstrate that the problem or opportunity exists?

- What brought this situation to your attention? What has happened to make this a priority?

- What is the history of this situation? How long has it been around? Has it gotten worse or better recently?

- What are the consequences of not addressing this situation? What is its impact in terms of cost, time, productivity, frustration, lost revenue, etc.?

- Why hasn't this been addressed before? Why is it a priority now?

> **PROCESS TIP**
> **Problem-definition is best done by a group**
> Problem-definition is another place where many heads are far better than just one. If you have been able to recruit assistance from some of the people who will likely work on the project, involve them in this activity as well. This is really a brainstorming activity and should be treated as one. Review the descriptions of Brainstorming techniques in Appendix D: *Problem-Solving Tools* and use the technique that seems best suited to the situation and the group.

"As Is" and "To Be"   A good tool for describing a problem or opportunity situation is the "As Is" and "To Be" approach detailed in the structured problem-solving process described in Appendix A. The problem-solving process is included in this book as an additional tool for use when there is no readily apparent solution to a problem. It is a data-intensive process that can be quite time-consuming to complete. Therefore, it is not suggested for every problem that you encounter. Unless a problem is extremely serious, most organizations will not spend the time to really do this whole process correctly. Save it for when you really need it.

Having said that, however, there are a couple of aspects to the process that are easily transferrable to general project pre-work. The definition of an "As Is" statement of the situation and a "To Be" statement of desirable out come works very well.

The first step is to describe the current situation — the "As Is" statement. Try to define this in terms that describe the observable situation rather than terms that imply either cause or effect. Be as factual as possible. Some examples of "As Is" statements are:

- Information about customer opinions regarding service, product quality, and price is perceived as incomplete

- Current products, in terms of performance and price, are aimed exclusively at the professional wood-worker (carpenter) market.

- Accounts Payable check-writing is a manual process.

Each of these statements describes an existing situation that is observable to anyone who wants to look at it. Even the first one, which really deals with an opinion about information, can be verified by asking some questions of the people who use the existing data. In none of these statements is there any indication of the reason for the current situation nor is there any implication of an answer. The answer is described in the "To Be" statement.

Once a good "As Is" statement has been developed, it's time to develop the "To Be" statement that describes the "ideal" change in the situation. For example:

- Information about customer opinions regarding service, product quality, and price will be described as useful, comprehensive and useable for decision-making.

- Viability of our products in the consumer market will be determined.

- Accounts Payable check-writing will be automated.

As with the "As Is" statement, it is important to keep this statement limited to observable conditions. This is usually harder than it seems. For instance, in the first case it would be tempting to say that "A customer feedback system will be developed that will produce information about our customers ...." In the second instance, it would be tempting to pick a product or two to develop for test marketing. And, in the third instance, it might be tempting to state that the automation of the process will be achieved by purchasing new Accounts Payable software that includes the check-writing functions.

However, to be really useful, this statement needs to simply convey the conditions that should exist when the changed situation is in place.

Developing a good "To Be" statement may require doing some additional data collection or research in order to develop a clear picture of the situation and the desired response to it. The project's customer — whoever will receive the final deliverable from the project — is likely your best source for this information. It is, after all, probably their situation you are being asked to address. The project's sponsor is also a good point of reference in this process.

Determine Needs and Wants

When talking with the project's customer and sponsor about the history and background of the situation to be addressed, you can also explore their ideas about what they think you should do about it.

There is a major caution that goes along with this:

Customers in particular can frequently tell you what they want but they may not be able to tell you what they need. Your job is to find out what they need.

As a starting point, you should ask most of the following questions:

- How do you see this problem or opportunity?

- What are your ideas about possible ways to address it? Why do you think that would adequately address it?

- Can you see other alternatives that might also address the situation?

- How will you measure the success of the solution?

- What are your major requirements for a successful solution?

Armed with this basic information, you can begin to develop a list of Needs and Wants. There is a distinct difference between a "Need" and a "Want:"

- Need — a requirement that must be met by any solution implemented in order for the solution to be viewed as minimally successful.
- Want — a desired outcome of the solution that, while it may be important, is not critical to success.

Using these definitions, it should be clear that Needs are very black and white; they are mandatory for success. If these results are not achieved, if these resources are exceeded, if these policies are violated, etc., the solution is a failure. Needs are either addressed by the solution, in which case the project meets the minimum requirements for success or, they are not and therefore the project fails to meet the minimum standards of success.

In defining the Needs and Wants, remember to try to state them in measurable terms. You will need some means of determining whether you have met the requirement or not. Try for the most quantifiable measures you can develop. When you are faced with a Need that does not lend itself to easily quantifiable measurement, such as "satisfaction" or "ease-of-use," develop a solid set of criteria for determining whether the Need has been met.

It is difficult to overstate this point: If something can be misinterpreted, it probably will be. As an example, let's say you indicate that the project "needs" to result in a decrease in processing time but don't state by how much. The chances are almost 100% that someone will interpret your statement to mean at least twice the decrease you intended. Having a number in your head does not communicate it to anyone else. Be as clear and specific as you can be about how you plan to measure whether you have met a Need or Want.

PROCESS TIP
Brainstorm Needs and Wants
Brainstorming Needs and Wants is another good place to involve your support team. In this case, an actual structured brainstorming session is in order. Try this technique: Hang a sheet of flip chart paper on a wall or use the actual flip chart. Discuss, with the group, the evolving project. Capture ideas about possible Needs and Wants on individual self-stick notes such as Post-It® Notes. (The 3" X 5" size works well for this.) Write only one idea on each note and randomly stick it to the flip chart. This is a variation on the Slip Method of brainstorming. This Process Tip deals with the first step in this activity. See the Process Tip in the next section for the next step.

Let's take a look at some examples of Needs and Wants for the three example projects described in the discussion of "As Is" and "To Be" situation descriptions.

Customer Information Process

As Is: Information about customer opinions regarding service, product quality, and price is perceived as incomplete.

To Be: Information about customer opinions regarding service, product quality, and price will be described as useful, comprehensive, and useable for decision-making.

Possible Needs and Wants (unsorted):

- Provide weekly reports
- Capture responses about service, quality, price, etc.
- Capture written comments
- Capture verbal comments
- Capable of producing ad-hoc reports
- Telephone interviews
- User-friendly
- Both statistical (scaled response, multiple choice, etc.) and open-ended
- Max: 3 minutes to complete
- Prefer less than 90 seconds to complete
- Document trail for follow-up
- Built-in alert system for problems that need immediate attention

Hardware Product Market Feasibility

As Is: Current products, in terms of performance and price, are aimed exclusively at the professional wood-worker (carpenter) market.

To Be: Viability of our products in the consumer market will be determined.

Possible Needs and Wants (unsorted):

- Test product: Carpenter saw
- Less expensive version
- Same dimensions as professional model
- Same tooth count
- Aimed at mid- to upper-level home user
- Minimum 20% lower manufacturing cost
- Desired: 30% lower manufacturing cost
- Maximum 70% current model hardness and edge hold
- Lower grade steel
- Plastic handle only if significant cost savings
- Prototype available for August National Hardware Show
- Manufacturing samples available for August National Hardware Show

Accounts-Payable Check-Writing Automation

As Is: Accounts Payable check-writing is a manual process.

To Be: Accounts Payable check-writing will be automated.

Possible Needs and Wants (unsorted):

- Upgrade existing accounting software
- Purchase upgrade package from vendor if available
- Develop application internally
- Check printing uses current printers
- Check blanks procured through current vendor
- Check application must link to all current tracking functions
- Include "sundown" date alert for uncashed checks
- Maintain existing security
- Improve security
- Capable of "one-off" check writing
- All fields searchable
- Integrate with existing accounting database

Rank Wants and Gain Agreement Among Stakeholders

The next step is to sort the Needs from the Wants. Some projects have only Needs — no Wants at all. There are no "optional" features or characteristics. For these projects a comprehensive list of Needs is all that you will develop.

On the other side, not all projects have Needs as defined here. There are projects that are not driven by absolute necessity. In these cases, you may end up with a long list of Wants. But even these projects have "requirements" that, while not essential, are nevertheless desirable. These are Wants, and they usually vary in their degree of importance to the project. Therefore, we need an additional classification system for Wants. For example, I want an Italian sports car. But I need reliable transportation. The difference between the two is in the neighborhood of $130,000 and a live-in mechanic. If the project delivers what I want, it will not only likely be way over budget, it may not actually meet the Need for "reliable" transportation. (Italian sports cars are not noted for their reliability — that's why I may need the live-in mechanic.)

In order to be useful, a Want should:

- Be stated as an outcome or result.
- Cover one, and only one, aspect of the developing solution. Avoid letting your Wants get "fuzzy" or complex. Try to avoid the word "and" in any Want. If you have two aspects you want to record, record them as separate Wants. Keep Wants simple and clear. Do not mix short-term and long-term Wants.

A simple and effective means of distinguishing the relative importance of Wants is ranking: Indicating relative importance on a scale of 10 to 1. The Want that is the most important is designated a 10. All other Wants are assessed and ranked relative to that benchmark. A Want assigned a rank of 5 has half the influence of a Want with a rank of 10. In some cases, two or more Wants will be determined to be of equal importance. Assign them the same ranking.

PROCESS TIP
Use your Post-It® Notes to sort Needs from Wants
Hang the flip page with the collection of Post-It® Notes on a wall. Hang an additional flip chart page next to it. Label one sheet "Needs" and the other sheet "Wants." Discuss with the group and sort the various ideas into categories of Needs and Wants. One way to determine if an item is a Need is to ask: "If the final output doesn't contain this (do this, have this, etc.), is the project a failure?" If the answer to this question is "Yes," the item is a Need. It must be included in the final output in order for the project to be seen as minimally successful. If the answer is "No," the item is a Want.

Assigning ranks to Wants is a subjective process. Several people evaluating the same set of Wants may well give them very different ranks depending on the judgement, experience and the understanding they bring to the process. For this reason alone it is good practice to involve several people (preferably people who are either identified stakeholders or potential project-team members) in the development of the initial list and ranking.

PROCESS TIP
Use your Post-It® Notes to rank the Wants
Sorting Needs and Wants is one activity where using Post-It® Notes really comes in handy. Ask the group to "Identify the most important item on the Want list." This should be the one Want that is so important that it is almost a Need. Place this Note at the top of the Want sheet. Then ask, "Are there any other items that are of equal importance?" If there are, place them at the same level. In most cases, these will be your #10-level Wants. You should do everything possible to include these in the final output of the project. Once the group has agreed on the #10 items, sort the remaining items in order of importance under them. Remember, you can have multiple items at the same level. Rank each item according to its relative importance in relation to the #10-level Wants. Give each Want a specific numerical value. (Try to stick to whole numbers. There are ten levels of importance in this scale. You shouldn't need to resort to 8.75 as a value. If that's what someone wants to rank it, make it a 9.)

You are not trying to fill every available space between 10 and 1. It is quite common to have a cluster of items in the upper third of the list (the 10 - 7 range), perhaps a 6 or a couple of 5s, and a cluster of 3s and 2s down at the bottom of the page. These rankings become more important as this process continues to be as realistic as possible.

Once you've developed and ranked your Wants, it's helpful to step back and review them. Make sure the Wants all pertain to the problem. The complete list should be stated clearly so that Needs are measurable and Wants are well defined, ranked, and measurable.

Even if you've involved some of the appropriate people in the development, it is still a good idea to pass your list by others who were not involved for their input and comment. This list of requirements and desirable features will become one of the key measures of success for the project. It is also a great tool for resolving conflicting expectations about the project.

The list of Wants has another, less obvious, purpose: It is a predefined "editing" list for project output. When you read breaking news (the events that are happening right now as opposed to feature articles that are not time-sensitive) in a daily newspaper, you'll notice that all of the information critical to understanding the story is usually in the first three to five paragraphs. Everything that comes after that is elaboration or restatement of the original information. This is because, when the story is being written, the writer has no idea how much space will be devoted to the story when the newspaper is finally assembled and printed. You see, contrary to popular belief, what you're reading is not really a "news" paper. It is really an advertising paper with news included. Most daily papers devote about 30% to 35% of their total available printing space to news. The rest is advertising (including the classified ads). It is the advertising, not the newsstand price, that pays for production and distribution of the paper.

It is therefore somewhat understandable that the advertising is put in place in the layout first. The space that is left over is knows as the "news hole" and it will vary in size from edition to edition. With limited space available and a large number of stories to be included, something has to give. That something is usually the end of the story that the reporter wrote. Having the less important information at the bottom of the story allows editing to be done quickly and efficiently. This is what you are trying to develop for your project: An editing list of features and characteristics that will allow you to "edit" pieces off the project when resources and/or time gets short.

Another way to look at this is to identify those features or characteristics that are important enough to devote time and resources to, and those that are still desirable but only if they are relatively easy to accomplish.

> **NOTE:** This is also a good point to document and solicit agreement about any assumptions you and the team have made about the project. This can include assumptions about availability of resources, the portable output of the project, priority within the work load of the participants, etc.

PROCESS TIP
Transfer your lists to a Comment Form for routing
Transfer your sorted, ranked list to a more manageable format, such as the Needs and Wants Comment Form. Circulate the list among stakeholders and gather their feedback. You're looking for two things:

1.   Is the list complete and sorted correctly? Is there general agreement that what you've identified as Needs are Needs? Did you miss any? Are all the Wants really Wants? Did you miss any?

2.   Are the Wants correctly ordered and ranked? Is there general agreement that the relative importance placed on each Want is correct?

Also include any assumptions you have used to help make decisions.

Needs and Wants Comment Form

Fill in the appropriate project data. Include the date by which comments must be returned.

Project:	Date:
Project Leader:	Date Comments Required:
Project Sponsor:	Comments by:

These instructions tell the commentor what the information is and what is being requested of them.

The following is a list of the Needs and Wants identified for this project. A Need is defined as: "a feature or characteristic that MUST be part of the final deliverable in order for the project to be seen as minimally successful." A Want is defined as: "a feature or characteristic that should, if possible, be included in the final deliverable, but is not essential for project success." Wants are ranked according to their importance using a scale of 1 = low importance to 10 = high importance. Needs, being absolute requirements, are not ranked.

This list is being circulated for comment and input. The Needs and Wants and the ranking given to each Want are a "first cut." Your input and comments are being solicited. Please review, comment, and return this form by the date indicated above.

List any assumptions about the project that are known at this time.

Project Assumptions:
1.
2.
3.

List Needs in the first column.

This column is for commentators to use to indicate a suggested change in the position of an item. They can shift a Need to a Want or shift a Want to a Need.

List Wants in order from most important to least important.

Indicate the ranking given to each Want.

This column is for commentors to suggest different rankings for Wants.

Needs (Absolute Requirements)	Shift (Need to Want -> <- Want to Need)	Wants (Desirable, but optional feature. Importance ranked 1=low to 10=high)	Rank	Alternate Rank

Additional Comments:

Additional comments can be included here.

You will probably not get universal agreement about this list. What you're looking for is a strong enough majority (or agreement from the most important stakeholders) that the list is correct enough to proceed with the project. The main parts of this form are shown here. Examples of completed forms follow.

Continuing with our example projects — the Customer Information Process-Development project, the Hardware-Product Development project, and the Accounts-Payable Check-Writing project — the following pages show how the Needs and Wants Comment Form is used to show the edited, sorted, and ranked lists for each one. Following each example of the form is a discussion of the contents that helps illustrate how the information was developed and some of the reasoning that went into the selection and ranking of the items on the form.

Customer Information Process

Needs and Wants Comment Form

Project: Customer Information Process	Date: 10/10/00
Project Leader: Bob Lindstrom	Date Comments Required: 10/16/00
Project Sponsor: Carl Haskins	Comments by:

The following is a list of the Needs and Wants identified for this project. A Need is defined as: "a feature or characteristic that MUST be part of the final deliverable in order for the project to be seen as minimally successful." A Want is defined as: "a feature or characteristic that should, if possible, be included in the final deliverable, but is not essential for project success." Wants are ranked according to their importance using a scale of 1 = low importance to 10 = high importance. Needs, being absolute requirements, are not ranked.

This list is being circulated for comment and input. The Needs and Wants and the ranking given to each Want are a "first cut." Your input and comments are being solicited. Please review, comment, and return this form by the date indicated above.

Project Assumptions:
1. We need a pro-active process to solicit, capture, organize, and analyze customer feedback.
2. At least initially, the process should allow customers to complete a feedback form.
3. A possible extension of this process is to actively pursue customer input through telephone follow-up.

Needs (Absolute Requirements)	Shift (Need to Want -> <- Want to Need)	Wants (Desirable, but optional feature. Importance ranked 1=low to 10=high)	Rank	Alternate Rank
Provide automatic weekly reports of all customer feedback		Capable of producing ad hoc reports	10	
Capture comments about product quality		Preferred specifications for a customer-completed instrument: - Maximum size: 5.5" x 8.5" - Single-sided - 4 scaled questions	10	
Capture comments about price		Built-in alert system to call attention to immediate problems - triggered by more than three comments about the same issue in any 24-hour period	9	
Capture written comments		Capture open-ended responses (if this feature is added, include one open-ended question in preferred specs)	9	
Allow for statistical (scaled, multiple choice, etc.) responses		Possible to complete in less than 90 seconds	6	
Maximum time required to complete: 3 minutes		Capture verbal comments in all categories	4	
Provide a document trail for follow-up		Useable for telephone interviews	4	
Maximum specifications for a customer-completed instruments - 8.5" x 11" paper - Single-sided - 6 scaled questions				

Additional Comments:

- The first assumption states that the preferred solution is to develop and implement a "formal" customer-feedback process. This narrows the options of how to do the project.

- Note how the assumption that this will be a paper process, completed by the customer, is included. This will minimize the chances that someone will assume that this will be a computer-based collection process. This potential is included in the third assumption where the possibility of making this an even more pro-active process is mentioned. The items related to this (open-ended questions, verbal comments, and telephone interviews) were moved to the Wants category where they will remain unless the project definition is changed to require developing this expanded process.

- The item originally identified as "user-friendly" has been broken into two much more measurable pieces (the items identifying specifications), one in the Needs list and the other in the Wants list.

- The built-in alert system for problems that need immediate attention is more specific now with the addition of the criteria for triggering the alert. This criteria could be changed in the review.

- The issue of statistical versus open-ended responses was separated into two issues.

- Two of the items related to the expanded project definition are at the bottom of the Wants list. This includes that they are the pieces most likely to be left undone unless their ranking is changed.

Hardware Product Market Feasibility

Needs and Wants Comment Form

Project: Hardware Product Market Feasibility	Date: 10/10/00
Project Leader: Lana Kelly	Date Comments Required: 10/16/00
Project Sponsor: Paul Jarvis	Comments by:

The following is a list of the Needs and Wants identified for this project. A Need is defined as: "a feature or characteristic that MUST be part of the final deliverable in order for the project to be seen as minimally successful." A Want is defined as: "a feature or characteristic that should, if possible, be included in the final deliverable, but is not essential for project success." Wants are ranked according to their importance using a scale of 1 = low importance to 10 = high importance. Needs, being absolute requirements, are not ranked.

This list is being circulated for comment and input. The Needs and Wants and the ranking given to each Want are a "first cut." Your input and comments are being solicited. Please review, comment, and return this form by the date indicated above.

Project Assumptions:
1. A single product may not be sufficient to gauge market feasibility.
2. Extreme care must be taken that the existing brand and products are not negatively impacted by the introduction of a lower-grade product.

Needs (Absolute Requirements)	Shift (Need to Want -> <- Want to Need)	Wants (Desirable, but optional feature. Importance ranked 1=low to 10=high)	Rank	Alternate Rank
First test product: Carpenter Saw targeted to the mid- to upper-end consumer		Manufactured samples available for Hardware Show	10	
At least three additional, related products to be considered		Separate brand name/product line to avoid diluting current professional brand recognition	10	
Can be up to 2" shorter than professional model		30% lower manufacturing cost - all consumer-grade products	8	
Same tooth-count per inch as professional model		Three other products available in prototype for Hardware Show	8	
Minimum 20% lower manufacturing cost - all consumer-grade products		Suggested retail no more than 75% of professional model	7	
Prototype available for National Hardware Show		Lower grade steel should reduce cost and degrade performance enough to prevent confusion with professional product	3	
		Plastic handle will help differentiate from professional product - should also result in lower cost	3	

Additional Comments:

- There are two items that are considered 10-level Wants: First, having a manufactured product (as opposed to prototype samples) for the National Hardware Show, and second, clearly differentiating between the company's line of professional products and the proposed consumer versions of the same products.

- Another issue that is fairly important is having more than one product available for the show. There is no attempt to identify what products these would be. This is a pivotal issue for this project. At this point in this project, the issue of whether these products also need to be "manufactured samples," or whether prototypes would suffice, is left open. If the decision is made that they need to be manufactured samples, the scope of this project increases by about three-fold. It would require significantly more resources to complete the work under the rigid deadline of the national trade show.
- The minimum cost savings required is stated as a Need while the desired target is stated as a Want. Also, the minimum target is set as a baseline for "all" products.
- The two material items that were in the original list (lower-grade steel and a plastic handle) are included as low level Wants. Technically, these two items don't really qualify as Wants but they are listed here to demonstrate some of the trade-offs that will be made in order to produce a consumer-grade version of the professional product.

Accounts-Payable Check-Writing

Needs and Wants Comment Form

Project: Accounts-Payable Check-Writing Automation	Date: 10/10/00
Project Leader: Ken Sukahara	Date Comments Required: 10/16/00
Project Sponsor: Juanita Lopez	Comments by:

The following is a list of the Needs and Wants identified for this project. A Need is defined as: "a feature or characteristic that MUST be part of the final deliverable in order for the project to be seen as minimally successful." A Want is defined as: "a feature or characteristic that should, if possible, be included in the final deliverable, but is not essential for project success." Wants are ranked according to their importance using a scale of 1 = low importance to 10 = high importance. Needs, being absolute requirements, are not ranked.

This list is being circulated for comment and input. The Needs and Wants and the ranking given to each Want are a "first cut." Your input and comments are being solicited. Please review, comment, and return this form by the date indicated above.

Project Assumptions:
1. Accounts-Payable check-writing functionality is a necessary enhancement to the accounting software. At this point, it is not known whether our software vendor has an upgrade available that will meet the functional requirements.
2. If our vendor does not have an upgrade available, the functionality must still be developed and implemented. This could be developed in-house or through a contractor. This decision has not been made at this time.

Needs (Absolute Requirements)	Shift (Need to Want -> <- Want to Need)	Wants (Desirable, but optional feature. Importance ranked 1=low to 10=high)	Rank	Alternate Rank
Link to all existing accounting tracking functions		Purchase an upgrade from current vendor	10	
Maintain existing levels of security		Check printing functions should use existing printers - no new hardware	9	
Integrate with existing accounting database		Complete by end of current accounting quarter	8	
All check fields searchable		Capable of "one-off" check printing	5	
Upgrade existing accounting software - new software is not an option		Improve security	4	
		Check blanks (for printing) available from our forms vendor	3	
		Include "sundown" date alert for uncashed checks	2	

Additional Comments:

- In this project, four of the seven Wants are relatively unimportant items. If possible, they should be included in the output but, they probably don't justify a significant expenditure of either resources or time. This could be particularly true if delivering on one of these negatively impacts delivering either a Need of one of the three high-level Wants. The Needs and the top three Wants really set the parameters of this project. None of them are particularly difficult but if any one of them is not done, the whole project falters.

- The highest-level Want (Purchase an upgrade from current vendor) is an acknowledged unknown in the project at this point. If it turns out that the current vendor cannot supply the necessary upgrade, the upgrade still needs to be produced. This project then becomes a "design, build, and implement" project rather than a "specify, purchase, and implement" project. If this should happen, it would be a good idea to redevelop this list and recirculate it because these two projects are quite different.

PROCESS TIP
Choosing what gets planned, what needs more study,
and what gets dumped from the start

If you would like a "system" to help make some initial decisions about what the ranked Wants are telling you, try this as an approach for making a first cut.

If an item ranks at 10, 9, 8, or 7, plan it into the project from the beginning. These Wants are important enough that every effort should probably be made to include them. You can treat them like Needs. These items are only candidates for elimination if something severe (usually a significant loss of resources) hits the project.

If an item ranks at 6, 5, or 4, you and the team may need to do some additional thinking about what will be required — in terms of time and resources — to include them. These Wants, while possibly desirable, don't have enough strength to make it into the plan without some consideration of the effort and time needed to include them in the final output.

If an item ranks at 3, 2, or 1, dump it unless it's "free." By "free" I mean requiring minimal time and resources to include it. If the commitment of time or resources is even slightly significant, including these Wants buys you little and could cost you much. Do not, however, dump these without thinking about them first. These low-level Wants can sometimes be nice little "Wow" features that will make the final output more attractive. If they can be included with a minimal expenditure of time and resources, consideration should be given to leaving them in. Just realize that, if things get tight at some point in the project (usually toward the end), these are the first candidates

Build the Project Goal Statement

Any company needs a strong, unifying sense of direction. But that need is particularly strong in an organization in which tasks are differentiated and responsibilities dispersed.
Chris A. Bartlett
Harvard Business School

The first three steps of this process should yield sufficient information to allow you to develop a preliminary statement of the desired outcome of the project, at least in general terms. This is the first step in developing the Project Goal statement.

Project goals need not be complex, excessively detailed, or long. They should, however, clearly state the desired outcome of the project in a way that can be used to guide and drive the project.

The whole pre-work process is, in one form or another, a series of negotiations with management and various stakeholders in the project. You are trying to gain agreements and commitments from those most affected by or concerned with the project. What you need to know is that what you propose to do, how you propose to go about it, the criteria for success, the resource requirements, and the time-frame for completion are all acceptable.

A great tool for these negotiations is the project goal statement. Setting a clear project goal is a critical activity at the beginning of a project.

In setting a project goal you are trying to do two things:

- Focus yourself and your team on the target.
- Create commitment to, and agreement about, that target.

Frequently, project leaders complain that they cannot get good direction from management: "They can tell me what they don't want but not what they do want." This is one of the reasons for going through the previous three steps in the needs analysis process. Clear goals are the result of a process. It is a process that takes time, energy, and dialogue. It is a process of going back and forth with other people, working toward clarity of direction for the project — in short, it is a process of negotiation.

Since projects tend to be somewhat unique, it can be difficult to be clear on a goal from the very beginning. Goal setting is a process of dialogue, it can start from either end:

- Management can tell you what they see as the project goal.
- You can tell management what you see as the project goal.

It is usually easier to edit than it is to create. So, develop a draft goal statement. Take it to one or more of the project's stakeholders and say, "Here, this is what I think the project goal is." This gives them the option to say, "Yes, that's the goal. Proceed." or "No, that's not what I meant. Here's what I meant." You go back and forth as you move closer to achieving clarity about the direction and the expected end result of the project. If you've done a good job of developing and circulating the Needs and Wants list, you should be pretty close to agreement by the time you get to this step. This may simply be a process of agreeing on how to state the agreement.

One fairly useful way to look at a project goal is as a statement of project output: How will we know we are finished? What will the end result look like? Try to put the goal in the customer's terms. Who is the customer of your project's output? What does your customer — client, user, manager — want from you? What does the customer say you are supposed to be doing?

A customer doesn't care that you are trying to produce a new accounting system. The customer cares about obtaining certain information about inventory and sales at the end of the day. Providing a system that meets the customer's needs is your goal; designing a new accounting system is how you will deliver that capability. Putting yourself on the customer's side improves your chances of hitting the target.

Effective project leaders always try to include the customer in the definition of the project, or at least to imagine the user's point of view.

SMART Goals

Fixing your objective is like identifying the North Star — you sight your compass on it and then use it as the means of getting back on the track when you stray.
Marshall E. Dimock
Author

One of the largest projects in human history was undertaken based on one simple statement:

"I believe this country should dedicate itself to the task, before this decade is out, of sending a man to the moon and returning him safely to earth."

President John F. Kennedy, 1961

The scope of activity this simple statement created is almost unprecedented in human history. Whole industries came into being as a result of this goal statement and the subsequent project.

While most of your projects won't result in the level of national activity that Kennedy's statement caused, you should give it a great deal of thought. A good goal statement makes the rest of the project planning process, and the actual work on the project, much easier to manage.

Good goals are SMART goals. In addition to being established in terms of the user, an effective project goal has five characteristics. The acronym SMART captures the characteristics of a goal that is likely to provide focus and create commitment. SMART goals are:

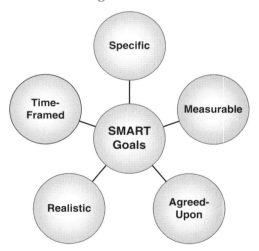

- Specific
- Measurable
- Agreed-upon
- Realistic
- Time-framed

Specific

Your goal should be so specific, so well defined, so clear that anybody with some basic knowledge of the project area can read it, understand it, and know what you are trying to accomplish. You could leave the company tomorrow and somebody else could pick up the statement of your project's goal and know exactly what to do.

This is the statement of Output from the triple constraint. As clearly as possible, it should state exactly what will be delivered at the end of the project.

Measurable

If you can't measure it, you can't manage it. To manage a project to successful completion, you have to be able to measure the goal. It's been said — wrongly — that some project goals cannot be measured. Of course, some goals can be measured more easily than others, but all goals need to be measurable. In fact, developing clear measuring standards for the most ambiguous and fuzzy kinds of goals is where you should spend the most time. Without measurable goals, project team members cannot get any sense of direction, and they wind up shooting at the wrong target. Project participants need to work on measurable activities, even if the measures are crude, in order to know what to do. And you need a measurable goal if you are to manage it.

Give people a target they can aim at. They should also be able to measure their own progress. Having clear measurement criteria is a vital part of the process of setting good goals.

Avoid vague terms like "quicker," "cheaper," "more productive." Use quantifiable measures like, "reduce process time by 18%"; "reduce cost by 21%"; "improve productivity by reducing rework by 80%, increasing output by 20%, and reducing scrap by 90%."

Even the fuzziest goals should have measures. Customer satisfaction and employee-morale goals may seem hard to measure but there are ways. For example, customer satisfaction can be measured by tracking complaints and compliments, returns, warranty claims, service calls, etc. Employee morale can be measured by surveys and interviews. Find the measures that will allow you to determine your success at meeting the goal and include them in it.

Agreed-Upon

There must be agreement about the project's goals. The end user, be it a customer, upper management, or a subordinate in the organization, must agree that the achievement of the project's goal is necessary and desirable. Stated differently, the project leader and the project's stakeholders must agree that the end result should solve the problem or respond to the need that led to the initiation of the project. The more people agree and have clarified the goal up front, the easier it will be to develop a viable plan for the project. This agreement will make it easier to respond to changes that may require modifying the goal as the project unfolds. Agreement is based on sharing information, and it builds commitment toward the project.

As stated in Chapter 1, the connection of the project's goal to some other goal in the organization is a critical element for gaining the necessary support. The clearer the connection between the project goal and the organizational goal, the better. This also makes negotiation about the project much easier since you already have common ground on which to build.

Realistic

You cannot seek for the ideal outside the realm of reality.

Leon Blum
1872-1949
Premier of France

Project goals must be realistic. Realistic is not a synonym for "easy." Most projects will challenge the participants. The project may well require that they do things they've never done before; think more creatively than usual; experiment with new approaches, techniques, and ideas. This does not mean accomplishing the goal is impossible — just more difficult than doing an everyday task. Even though the project is unique and different from what may have been done before, it should not be totally alien to project personnel. If it is, you are asking for trouble.

There is a significant trade-off in a project where there is a steep learning curve. You will need to set aside time for research and learning, or perhaps engage consultants or hire new project team members or even delay the project. You should not get trapped into doing things you know little about, unless you love the smell of your own adrenaline or don't mind failing. This is the wisdom of "stick to your knitting," which successful companies follow. Do the things with which you have some experience. The goal-setting process should help you clarify this issue.

It is important to recognize that projects can be a great teaching tool. Most projects could be characterized as "everyday work in a pressure cooker." Including someone on the team in order to fast-track their learning is a perfectly legitimate decision. However, it is also important to realize that the person in the learning mode will not be as productive as an experienced person and they will require more time to understand and complete tasks. If these issues are considered up front and the decision is made to go this way, the project timeline should be adjusted accordingly.

Realism also includes the resources available for completing the project. All too often project leaders agree to goals that are impossible to achieve, given the resources, knowledge, and time available. These project leaders are setting themselves up for frustration and failure. How many times have you been assigned a project and a deadline before the goal is clarified, only to find out that the project cannot possibly be completed on time? One of the benefits you derive from dialogue in the goal-setting process is determining whether you are talking about a goal that is realistic, given your time and resources. You have to question this assumption explicitly. Don't just say, "Sure, we can get that done." Discuss resources, personnel, and timing to determine how realistic the goal is. Making it realistic may mean adjusting the goal, the deadline, the resources, or possibly all three.

Time-Famed

The ultimate inspiration is the deadline.

Nolan Bushnell
Founder, Atari

Finally, you need a clear time frame for the goal. How much time do you have to accomplish this project? Is there any flexibility in the deadline? Is there any flexibility in the resources available for the project? This goes back to looking at what is actually attainable. You want a deadline that is reasonable, given the resources available and the knowledge and experience you have with this type of project.

This is the piece of the goal that is most likely to be dictated by circumstances that are out of the direct control of the project team. This does not mean that you shouldn't take a very careful look at the deadline in light of the project as it stands at this time.

Testing the Goal Against the Criteria

Writing is easy. All you have to do is sit staring at a blank piece of paper until the drops of blood form on your forehead.

Gene Fowler
American Writer

Let's look at the Kennedy goal statement in the light of the SMART criteria.

"I believe this nation should commit itself to achieving the goal, before the decade is out, of landing a man on the moon and returning him safely to the earth."

President John F. Kennedy
Speech to Congress, May 25, 1961

Specific:

- Send a man to the moon
- Return him to Earth
- Alive
- By the end of the decade

Measurable:

- Man arrives on the moon
- Man returns to earth
- Man is still alive upon landing
- Done by the end of the decade

Agreed-upon:

There are several factors that impacted this criteria with regard to the Apollo project. First of all, there was never universal agreement that the moon landing was a necessary or desirable goal. There was however, sufficient agreement among the primary stakeholders — the military, the Washington establishment, the major contractors who would develop and deliver the hardware, and the scientific community — to carry the day. Among the population at large, enthusiasm and agreement varied widely. The portions of the population that agreed were very vocal in their support. The portions that disagreed, while they outnumbered the supporters by a significant margin, were disorganized and unfocused. In addition, all the other things that were going on in the "sixties" took the public focus off this project: The assassinations of John Kennedy, Martin Luther King, Jr., and Robert Kennedy; the "war on poverty;" the civil rights movement; the counterculture revolution; and that little trouble spot known as Vietnam. All of these kept the space program somewhat in the background except when there were major accomplishments to be announced.

Another set of factors that had a significant impact on the acceptance of this goal was the world political situation. In October, 1957, the Soviet Union launched Sputnik I, the first artificial satellite. Just one month later, November, 1957, the Soviet Union launched Sputnik 2 which remained in orbit for six months. Sputnik 2 carried a dog, Laika, who was kept alive for seven days before being put to sleep. The U.S. followed in January, 1958 with Explorer 1. In March, 1958, the U.S. launched two more satellites, Explorer 2 (which failed to reach orbit) and Vanguard 1 which transmitted signals for three years. In September, 1959, the U.S.S.R. landed (well, crashed, actually) the first spacecraft, Luna 2, on the moon. Both the U.S and the U.S.S.R. continued to launch, with varying degrees of success, various space vehicles.

Then, on April 12, 1961 the Soviets sent the first man, Yuri Gagarin, into space. He orbits the earth once. On May 5th, 1961, the U.S. launched the Mercury Freedom capsule carrying John Glenn into a suborbital flight and he became the first American to orbit the globe. There is one central theme through all of this. It is embodied in the phrase "...the U.S. followed...." This was a situation we, as a nation, were not happy about. We did not deal well with being Number Two. Particularly not behind the Soviet Union. This situation, coupled with the general paranoia about what the Russians would do if they got to the moon first, provided most of the impetus needed to push the Apollo project forward.

Realistic:

Much of the technology needed for the moon shot existed in 1961. We had the rocket and basic guidance technology to get a ship to the moon. By 1961, we had sent up and retrieved several satellites and had proven that a man could survive lift-off, orbit, and re-entry. Some of the problems that still needed solving included the part about a soft landing on the moon's surface and that sticky problem of lifting off and returning to earth. Kennedy's science advisors were convinced that, with enough money and manpower, these problems could be solved, and so the Apollo project was launched.

Time-framed:

By the end of this decade. Not only did we meet this deadline, we actually beat it by several months — Apollo 11 lifted off from the Kennedy Space Center on July 16, 1969. The lunar landing occurred on July 20, 1969. Astronauts Neil Armstrong and Edwin Aldrin remained on the lunar surface for about 21 hours, collecting rock samples and planting an American flag before lifting off to rendezvous with Michael Collins in the Apollo command module that had remained in orbit around the moon. They splashed down in the Pacific Ocean on July 24, 1969.

PROCESS TIP
A Project-Goal-Development Process
If you've ever tried to just sit down and write a goal statement, you know that it is not all that easy. Some people agonize over them for days. At this stage of the project, you don't need a goal statement that will win an inspirational literature prize. You need a working statement that can serve as a solid starting point.

If you are fortunate enough to have access to some of the people who will ultimately work on your project, try the following process and see if it doesn't help speed up the process of developing a draft goal statement.

Bring the group together in a room with a flip chart and a couple of pads of self-stick notes (such as Post-It® Notes from 3-M Corporation). Get the group talking about the project and what needs to be done. Don't try to guide the discussion too much. As people talk about what the project entails, capture key words and phrases on individual self-stick notes. When you've gotten several pieces, stick them randomly on the flip chart. Let the group go until they begin to run down.

When the flow of ideas starts to slow down, try arranging the words and phrases you've captured into basic pieces of sentences. You'll be missing most of the connecting words like "the", "and", "with", etc., and you can add these if you wish. Step back from your draft and ask whether it looks like a goal statement that could be used to get the project started. The answer will likely be that it doesn't really look like that yet, but most of the pieces are likely to be there as a starting point. From there on, it is simply a matter of refining and fine-tuning what you have as a beginning.

This process is a variation on brainstorming and, like brainstorming, a little practice and experience makes it easier to use. A few tips can make this process smoother:

- Keep in mind that your project will have a beginning, a middle, and an end. Try to arrange the pieces of your goal statement in that order. Start with the biggest pieces of the project and work toward the details.

- It is sometimes helpful to provide the opening few words for the developing statement such as: "Design and build...," or "Research, design, and implement...," or "Specify, purchase, and install...." This can get the group focused on the overall purpose of the project rather than all the details of doing it.

- Try several arrangements of the pieces. One of the advantages of using self-stick notes is that they are almost infinitely movable. Try grouping similar parts together and working on them as individual sentences within the overall goal statement. Try rearranging the order of words within your developing sentences.

- When reviewing the developing goal statement, read it out loud. You can add the missing conjunctions as you read it. This also helps people get a "feel" for the spirit, power, and effectiveness of the words being used.

- Don't throw away any of the notes until you're certain you won't need them. Simply remove them from the working page of the flip chart but keep them handy. You may find that you need them as the statement begins to get refined.

- Ask frequently if the statement is developing into some

> thing that could be used to drive the project. This helps keep the group focused on the purpose of the exercise and keeps the process moving. This whole activity should only take between ten and twenty minutes.
>
> When you and the group are satisfied with what you have developed, write it down and use it as your draft goal statement. If you feel it's needed, develop an "elaboration" of "detail" document to accompany the goal statement. This is where you put all the details that don't make it into the final goal statement.

To continue with our three sample projects, here are brainstormed lists of possible words and the goal statements and detail documents that resulted from each one.

Customer Information Process

Brainstormed List:

- customer feedback process
- develop
- weekly reports
- design
- quality
- price
- service
- implement
- two months
- train
- customer completes
- easy to use
- statistical information
- less than three minutes
- ad hoc reports
- document trail
- comment card
- written comments

Goal Statement:

Design, develop, and implement a customer feedback process that captures input about product quality, price, and service. Minimum process output includes a weekly report of feedback, serious-problem alert, and problem-resolution tracking. Ad hoc reporting will be developed if feasible. Employee training will be developed to be implemented by the Training Department. Project delivery two months from start.

Additional Details:

- Development of training is part of this project. Delivery of the training is not. Training will be delivered by our Training Department once the process is operational.
- Initial specifications for the input instrument are:
  - Maximum: 8.5" X 11", single-side paper or card with up to six scaled questions.
  - Targeted: 5.5" X 8.5", (half-sheet), single-side paper or card with up to four scaled questions.

○ Possible: Inclusion of one open-ended question.

Is it Specific?

Yes. The action words that will help drive this project are: design, develop, and implement. The deliverable of the project is a customer feedback process. Features of that deliverable are: That it captures input, provides weekly reports, has a serious-problem alert feature, has problem-resolution tracking, has ad hoc reporting, and includes employee training. The deadline is stated as: delivery two months from start.

Is it Measurable?

Yes. The same words provide the measures of success. Some of them are shorter-term such as design and develop, while others are more final-product-oriented such as captures input and weekly report.

Will it be Agreed-upon?

Probably. This goal should be agreeable, at least in its broadest sense, to all the stakeholders in this project. Keep in mind that many of the pieces that didn't make it into the final statement can be included as additional detail or supporting information. Not everything needs to be in the goal statement itself. In this case, notice that many of the output specifications are not included in the goal statement. They are measures that can be applied to the project but are really too fine-grain for the goal statement.

Is it Realistic?

It should be. In terms of being realistic, this goal is not out of the realm of possibility for almost any business. It's something any business should be able to do.

Is it Time-framed?

Yes. The time-frame is established at two months from the start date. This is probably not an unrealistic deadline. The project is not all that complicated as it is stated. It might become a bit more difficult to meet the deadline if the telephone follow-up piece gets incorporated into the project. If that happens, it would be a good idea to revisit this.

Other issues:

• The "easy to use" phrase was not included because it isn't measurable as stated. The three-minute completion requirement made it into the final statement as a baseline requirement. The Want of "less than 90 seconds" didn't make it into the final statement because it may not be achievable.

• The whole issue of telephone follow-up is ignored since it is not, at this point, part of the project. If it becomes part of it later, the goal statement will need to be rewritten to reflect the change.

PROCESS TIP
Don't forget to include the creation of Training and
Documentation in your project plans
This discussion of the Project Goal is an appropriate place to discuss a relatively common project problem. If the project output includes training, support, long-term evaluation, or some

other on-going activity, give very careful consideration to excluding that activity from the project itself. The development of the training materials, the process, even an initial pilot delivery to make sure everything works, etc., can all be part of the the project, but the on-going delivery should be considered a post-project activity. The same is true of support activities and long-term evaluation of the project implementation. Both of these need to be considered part of operations, not part of a finite project. If you don't do this — make this clear distinction between the project activities and on-going or operational activities — it will be very difficult to close out the project. The end date just got extended indefinitely. Projects with these types of activities in them have a real tendency to take on lives of their own. They really want to become careers. This is a picky distinction but it is an important one: On-going activities — whether performed by members of the project team or not — that become part of continuing operations should not be considered part of the project.

Hardware Product Market Feasibility

Brainstormed List:

- hardware show
- prototype saw
- cheaper
- less expensive
- shorter
- same tooth count per inch
- new brand (marketing)
- 20% lower manufacturing cost

- three additional products
- drill
- screwdriver set
- mid/upper-end consumer
- manufactured samples
- plastic handle
- 30% lower manufacturing cost

Goal statement:

Design, develop, prototype, and transfer to manufacturing a carpenter saw aimed at the mid-to-upper-end consumer-market as part of a Marketing-driven, market-feasibility study. The product must achieve a minimum manufacturing-cost savings of 20%. Manufactured samples will be available for introduction, under a new brand identity to be developed by Marketing, at the National Hardware Show in August.

Additional details:

- In order to complete a valid market evaluation, it may be necessary to prepare up to three additional products, at least in prototype, for presentation at the National Hardware Show. If this is determined to be necessary, it is suggested that they be developed as separate projects.

- Some specific characteristics of the proposed product being considered at this point include: A shorter overall length maintaining the professional product's tooth-count, using a lower grade (lower hardness rating) steel, and making the handle plastic instead of wood. All of these will be decided in the design, development, and prototyping phases of the project.

Is it Specific?

Yes. In this one, the action words that will help drive the project are: Design, develop, prototype, and transfer to manufacturing. There are actually two deliverables in this project. The first is a ready-to-manufacture (designed and prototyped) carpenter saw. The second is manufactured samples of that saw for the Hardware Show. In addition, there is a tie-in to two other projects: The market-feasibility study and the development of a new brand identity, both being done by the Marketing department. There isn't much in terms of features in this one, mainly because most of the features of the product will be determined as the project unfolds through design, development, and prototype.

Is it Measurable?

Yes. There are two major measures in this one: The 20% manufacturing cost savings and the National Hardware Show deadline. Some other measures could include the mid-to-upper-end consumer target customer and the completion of each of the major activities (project phases) of design, prototype (and test), and transfer to manufacturing. The ones that got ignored are the higher cost-savings target (30%), the very specific characteristics of toothcount and length of the saw, and the plastic handle. All of these will be addressed by the project as it unfolds and may or may not be met. So, why have them in your goal statement (for which you will be held accountable) if you don't know if some of them are even valid measures as yet?

Will it be Agreed-upon?

Most likely. This one probably has an excellent chance of achieving agreement because the goal is very clear and the need for the project appears to be driven by some fairly strong business forces. The pitfall in this one is the issue of the additional products that have been mentioned as part of the final package for the show. As written, this goal statement ignores them completely.

Is it Realistic?

Probably, but it is by no means a no-brainer. This project is being done by a hardware manufacturing company with a full line of professional products already on the market. This fact could actually work against them in this project. Getting an organization to upgrade output quality is not all that difficult in most cases because the benefits can be very clearly stated. However, getting an organization that prides itself on producing a high-end, quality product to down-grade its quality standards in order to meet the needs of a less discerning market segment could be a real up-hill battle. In fact, it could prove to be a bad idea. The creation of a separate brand identity for the new line should help.

Is it Time-framed?

Tightly. There's a funny characteristic of things like the National Hardware Show; if your new product isn't ready, they won't delay the show until it is. Seems kind of rude somehow. This is a drop-deadline. If the product isn't ready, the premier showcase for new products in this industry will be missed. The consequences of this are significant.

Other issues:

- The biggest open issue in this project is the development of not just one but up to four new products. As stated before, if the additional products become part of the project, the impact on resources and output will be major. The temptation may very well be to expand this project to include the additional products but this is not the only approach that would work. The opportunity being addressed, in part, by this project is the possibility of expanding into a new market segment. In most businesses, this would be an effort driven by the Marketing department. Marketing already has two projects underway that relate to this opportunity and, therefore, relate to each other: The market-feasibility study and the development of the new brand identity. The saw project should deliver one tool to help with the analysis of the potential market. Each of the other new products would have the same relationship to the feasibility study. So, one way to approach this issue is to develop a project to manage and coordinate up to six interrelated projects: The market-feasibility study, development of a new brand identity, development of the consumer-oriented carpenter saw, and three additional product-development projects. And, lest we forget, there should be some serious coordination between all of these projects and the probable project to prepare for having a presence at the National Hardware Show for the company and all of its existing products.

PROCESS TIP
A reminder of the importance of understanding the connection between the project goal and other organizational goals
The above situation is an example of why it is so important to understand the relationship between a project and other things that are going on in the business. If it were assumed that the project to develop the saw was independent of everything else, the chances of making a major mistake would be almost 100%.

Accounts-Payable Check-Writing Automation

Brainstormed list:

- link to current tracking
- link to current database
- one-off check writing
- maintain existing security
- improve security
- end of next quarter
- "sundown" dates for uncashed checks
- upgrade existing software
- purchase a fix
- search all check fields
- build in-house
- use current printers
- blanks from current vendor

Goal statement:

If available, purchase and install an upgrade to the existing accounting software that allows for automation of the accounts payable check-writing process. If an upgrade is not available, develop the application in-house; test, document, install, and train users by the end of the next accounting quarter. Regardless of where the application comes from, it must merge with existing tracking and security systems, use the existing accounting database, and produce output using the department's current printers.

Additional details:

- Other desirable features include: Procurement of check blanks from our existing forms vendor, automating the "sundown" date notification that alerts accounting to uncashed checks over six months old, one-off check-writing capability, and search-and-sort capability for every field on an A/P check.

- If an appropriate upgrade is not available from our accounting software vendor, internal resources will need to be dedicated to this project in order to meet the deadline.

Is it Specific?

Yes. The scope of this project is quite clear. Whether the upgrade comes from the vendor or is developed in-house, it is to address a specific application — writing accounts payable checks. In addition, some of the more important functionality is included in the statement such as the necessary links to the existing software, the database, and the maintenance of existing security. The deadline is also stated.

Is it Measurable?

Quite. The first measure is the "make or buy" decision that determines the rest of the project. Regardless of the outcome of this decision, the must-meet measurement criteria for evaluating the software are included. Additional measures are included in the additional details section.

Will it be Agreed-upon?

Shouldn't be a problem if the vendor upgrade is available. However, if this is to be an in-house development project, there might be some resistance to committing the resources on short notice. This particular goal statement should probably only be circulated with the Additional details section clearly attached. The second point in that section (about needing dedicated resources if development comes in-house) is a very important issue and may need some discussion. This actually opens a third possibility that might come into play: Contracting the development to a third party. We'll look at all of these in the next section.

Is it Realistic?

Probably. Certainly if the vendor upgrade is available. Then the project becomes simply an evaluate, install, and test activity. If the development comes in-house, there may need to be some discussion about whether this is something the in-house IS/IT folks can or should do. That, once again, raises the possibility of farming out the development to a contractor. This may be a more "realistic" approach.

Is it Time-framed?

Yes, the end of the accounting quarter. This would seem to be a deadline based on wanting to incorporate new functionality into the accounting software at a natural break-point in the accounting cycle. It could be that if the deadline is missed, implementation may be delayed until the end of the next accounting quarter.

Other issues:

• This one is pretty clean. Except for the open question of whether the vendor has an existing upgrade, the features and functions of the output are relatively straight-forward and clear. However, the fact that there are multiple potential projects here suggests that, at least in this case, some additional steps are needed in order to complete the pre-work.

PROCESS TIP
The importance of the Project Goal

The project goal statement is a powerful tool throughout the life of the project. It is the benchmark against which every activity, every decision, every deliverable is measured. The process of gaining approval for your project goal is an excellent place to begin building the agreements and commitments that will be needed as the project unfolds. As you negotiate for goal approval, remember that it isn't just the approval of management that is needed. You need agreement and commitments from just about everyone who will be affected by the project. This can be a tedious process, especially on very large projects or on projects that have far-reaching impacts.

Most of the time, there is no simple way to achieve this commitment. It requires one-on-one discussions between the project leader and the individuals from whom the commitment is needed. There are two things to keep in mind when approaching people for commitment:

What's in it for them? If you are asking someone for support for the project (either through supplying resources or personnel, or by providing expertise), you should try to find some benefit for them which will help compensate them for their support.

What, exactly, are you asking them to do? Be as specific as possible. You are asking them to agree to some form of support. Be sure they understand exactly what that support is to be, when you expect it, how long you will need it, what you plan to do with it, etc.

The project goal is an excellent tool to use when negotiating support. If it is well defined, the benefits to the organization (and the individuals within the organization) should be fairly clear. There is more on the subject of Negotiation in Chapter 3: *People Skills for Project Leaders*.

Optional Steps   The next two steps are suggested as helpful when there are multiple possible approaches to addressing the situation. This may be as simple as having two or three possible vendors for a piece of equipment or as complex as two or three completely different approaches to the work. In any case, if you have multiple potential projects, it is a good idea to evaluate them up front to determine which one is most likely to produce the desired result, usually for the least cost in the shortest time.

Even for those projects where the approach is pretty clearly outlined from the beginning, it is a good idea to consider whether there are alternative ways the project could be done. If for no other reason than to reassure yourself that the chosen approach is the best available.

Develop Options   The first step in this sub-set of the process is to develop options for achieving the Needs and Wants of the project. We need a list of options from which to make our choice. In some situations you may be presented with a list of acceptable alternatives. At other times, you may have the responsibility for generating alternatives.

When we talk about alternatives, we're talking about significantly different approaches to the work, not just minor variations. For instance, let's say you have a project to put on a company picnic. You would probably have more than one location where the picnic could take place; say, two different public parks. You might also have two options for providing food for the event; say, catered food or do-it-yourself hamburgers and hot dogs.

In the case of the two different parks, choosing one over the other won't really affect the fundamental tasks and structure of the project. Either location must have a space large enough for your group, an area for eating, and restrooms. Everything else is details.

In the case of the choices between how to provide food, however, there is a significant impact on the project structure depending on which option you select. If the event is catered, the cost probably goes up; possibly by a lot. If the choice is the do-it-yourself approach, there are all the logistics of getting food, having (or bringing) the means to cook it, volunteers to do the cooking, set-up and clean-up, etc. This creates two very different projects, both of which will meet the basic Needs of providing a picnic. It's through the Wants that these two alternatives should be evaluated.

The way the project to develop the customer feedback process has developed to this point, there really aren't major differences in approach available. It's a pretty straight-forward project — build a paper-based, data-collection process and the supporting system to track, compile, analyze, and report on the data collected.

The same is true for the product-development project — get a new version of an existing product into manufacturing.

Among our example projects, only the accounting application-development project really has multiple approaches available.

In that example, the preferred approach is to purchase and install an upgrade from the software vendor. If this solution is available, other alternatives become unnecessary. Assuming that this option is not available, we have the following basic alternatives:

- Option #1:   Develop the application internally, using only in-house resources.
- Option #2:   Contract the development to an outside firm.
- Option #3:   Design, specify, and test the application in-house; contact the development and coding work to an outside firm.

Each of these alternatives has the potential to meet the Needs of this project. So, which one should you choose? In order to determine which alternative will best meet the highest percentage of Wants, we need to have a process for evaluating each alternative against all the other alternatives.

Compare Options to Needs and Wants For many projects, this step is an exercise in judgement rather than an exercise in empirical evaluation. Once options are identified, you need to see how they perform against the Needs and Wants. Base your assessment on the best available information about each option. In addition to known facts, this information may take the form of your best projections or the opinion of experts. The Needs and Wants serve as the guide for your data gathering. For each Need and Want, you should have the most complete information possible about how well each option meets it so that you can make a reasonable judgement. This is not always possible. Sometimes it just comes down to a"good guess."

Begin with the Needs. Use them to screen out those options that fail to meet these minimum requirements. When an option does not meet a Need, drop it as a possible choice. There is no point in considering it further. Remember, Needs are absolute — they must be met in order for the project to be viewed as minimally successful. (If your project is one of those with no absolute Needs, all options will be evaluated against the Wants.)

If all options are eliminated when compared to the Needs, you can choose to do one of several things. You can choose to develop additional options. You can review both the problem statement and Needs to see if a realistic choice is even possible. You can look at changing the requirements of the Needs or you can choose to broaden (or narrow) the scope of the project.

Assuming your options survive the Needs Screening, you can analyze which of them best satisfies the Wants. Again, to do this effectively, you should have quality information about each alternative. Because the comparison of options depends on your ability to accurately assess the information, you need to make every effort to ensure that the information is complete and correct. Even with the same data available, interpretations may differ based on people's different backgrounds, experience, values and responsibility in the project. Significant differences in viewpoint should be explored, since they most likely arise from unclear or inadequate information or a disagreement about the meaning of a Want.

PROCESS TIP
Rating Options

Options Rating Form

Project:		Date:	
Project Leader:			
Project Sponsor:			

		Options						
Wants	Rank	Score	Total	Score	Total	Score	Total
Total Points							

Complete the appropriate project information.

List the Options across the top.

List the Wants down the left.

List the importance ranking for each Want in this column.

Work across, evaluating each Option against each Want, one at a time. The question to be answered is: "How well does this Option address the requirements of this Want?" Assign a score reflecting how well each Option satisfies each Want. Use the 10-to-0 scale: 10 = addresses the requirements of the Want completely; 0 = does not address the requirements of the Want at all.

Multiply the score by the Rank for that Want and enter the total.

Total each Option column. The highest score will reflect the Option that best addresses the majority or high-level Wants.

NOTE: The downloadable version of this form is a spreadsheet with the calculations built in.

Rating options is another good place for group interaction. You can do this a couple of different ways. You can bring everyone together in the same room and do the whole process as a group activity. Or, you can have individuals fill out the form independently and then bring them together to iron out the inevitable differences in scoring. Either way, multiple heads are far better than one for this process. Because this is essentially an exercise in individual judgement about how well each Option will perform, some discussion about why people rate the options the way they do is almost essential. You want a variety of opinion as part of the evaluation process but you also want to come to some agreement (I hesitate to call it consensus) about the relative performance of each Option.

Since only one of the project examples really has optional solutions, let's take a look at a possible completed Options Rating Form for the accounting project. Notice that the highest rated Want from the initial list — "Purchase and upgrade from current vendor" — is not included since this Option has been eliminated as not available.

In this scenario, the second Option — "Contract all application development to an outside firm" — is a fairly clear winner. The main reason is the time. There is obviously a concern about the availability of in-house resources. This not only impacts the first Option — "Develop the application internally "— but also the third Option — "Design, spec, and test internally; contract development and coding." In both cases, in-house resources will need to be devoted to the project and their availability is of concern.

Options Rating Form

Project: Accounts Payable Check-Writing Automation		Date: 10/18/00			
Project Leader: Ken Sukahara					
Project Sponsor: Juanita Lopez					

		Options					
		#1 Develop the application internally; use in-house resources only		#2 Contract all application development to an outside firm		#3 Design, spec, and test internally; contract development and coding to an outside firm	
Wants	Rank	Score	Total	Score	Total	Score	Total
Check printing uses current printers	9	10	90	10	90	10	90
Complete by end of current quarter	8	5	40	10	80	8	64
Capable of "one-off" check writing	6	7	42	10	60	10	60
Improve security	5	4	20	10	50	7	35
Check blanks available through existing vendor	4	10	40	10	40	10	40
Include "sundown" date alert for uncashed checks	2	6	12	10	20	10	20
	Total Points	244		340		309	

Looking at each Want in turn, we see:

- "Check printing uses current printers." This is primarily a formatting issue that all of the Options could easily address.

- "Complete by end of current quarter." Here's the first place the resources issue becomes obvious. The score for the first Option shows a concern about being able to devote the resources required to get the project done by the deadline. There is even a concern about being able to devote the resources necessary to design, spec, and test the work of an outside developer.

- "Capable of 'one-off' check writing." Again, the resources issue comes up in the first option. The problem is not seen to be as severe as in the previous Want because this is a single feature that needs to be developed, not the deliverable as a whole. Development of this feature (which would require little in-house time to specify and test) could be made a requirement for the outside contractor so these Options score well on this Want.

- "Improve security." Another problem with internal resource availability. This time the concern is stronger since more work is involved in creating this type of feature. The second Option scores well since this could be made a requirement of the contract. The third Option again reflects concern about the availability of in-house resources to specify and test the work of the contractor.

- "Check blanks available through existing vendor." All Options could meet this Want fairly easily since it is mainly a formatting issue — not a lot of effort is needed to include it, specify it, or test it.

- "Include 'sundown' date alert for uncashed checks." Once again, the in-house resource issue comes up. Specifying and testing this feature would not require much effort and could be part of the contracted requirements for an outside developer. Developing it in-house would require the use of obviously tight resources.

Notice that this process tends to weight scoring in favor of the higher-level Wants. If Option #1 scored the maximum available on the bottom four Wants, the total score for that Option would still only be 300 — not enough to put it ahead of either of the other two Options. "Complete by the end of the current quarter" still drives the decision because of its relative importance to the perceived success of the project.

Most of the time, going through these two optional steps will yield a clear "winner" in terms of an Option that will best address all of the high-level Wants for a project. Even if you end up with a tie between two or three Options, you will have narrowed the list to a manageable number and completing the final step in the process should give you a preferred Option.

Assess Overall Project Risks

Jack the python got loose again. Don't go in there alone. It takes two to handle him.
Note on the front door of a hunter's cabin in the western United States

This is the final step in the process. This step should be done whether you have completed the previous "optional" steps or not.

Considering the risks associated with a project should become second nature. You should always look at what might impact your projects. This is not just looking at what could go wrong during its implementation. It is also looking at factors outside the project that could impact your ability to pull it off successfully. Draw on your own experience as well as the experience of others. In this step, you are trying to answer the questions: "What major problems might we encounter in doing this project?" and "What effects might these problems have on our ability to complete the project successfully?"

All projects have risks associated with them. The fact that you are undertaking something even slightly new or unique carries inherent risk. It is the type and severity of the risk to the project as a whole that you should be concerned with at this point. You will do another round of risk assessment at the end of project planning when you develop your contingency plans. That exercise is focused on the task-level risks that are always part of a project. This first pass at risk assessment is focused on risks to the project as a whole.

Risk can be defined as "exposure to the possibility of economic or financial loss or gain, physical damage or injury, or delay, as a consequence of the uncertainty associated with pursuing a particular course of action." Translation: Unexpected stuff happens.

Risk analysis can be a sophisticated process that involves a number of approaches to dealing with the problems created by uncertainty, including the identification, evaluation, control, and management of risk. It is, in fact, a discipline unto itself. This approach is not an attempt to deal with the subject at that highly sophisticated level. It is more of a means of stepping back from the project and looking at it in the context of the environment in which it will be done.

Significant Project Risks

Take calculated risks. That is quite different from being rash.

George S. Patton
1885-1945
General, U.S. Army

While all projects carry some level of risk, certain characteristics of either the project or the circumstances under which the project is to be completed increase the potential for severe adverse consequences. Risk increases significantly when projects involve:

- Large capital outlays. Expensive projects are risky projects. If the organization is going to expend significant amounts of money, the organization is probably going to expect significant return on that investment. As long as the need for the expenditure is clearly stated and understood at the outset, this risk is manageable.
  - Unbalanced cash-flow. This is another aspect of large capital outlays. Some projects require a large proportion of the total investment to be expended before any returns are obtained. New product development projects are excellent examples of this type of risk. In new product development projects, virtually all the development and start-up manufacturing expenses are incurred with the expectation that, when the product hits the market, these expenses (and a substantial profit) can be recovered. Impatience and "cutting corners to save money" are the greatest threats to these projects.
- Significant new technology. There are two aspects to this issue. The first is the most obvious: If you are among the first to adopt a new technology, you are at risk. You may be the one to discover the "fatal" bug in the technology. Being the Beta-test site for that new software may be fun and exciting but, if you need the software to be fully operational when you use it, waiting until it has been reviewed, revised, and reissued may be a better course of action.
  - The second aspect of new technology risk involves being the first in your organization to adopt a new technology. Even if the technology is not all that "new" to others, it may be very new to you and your organization. The learning curve on new technologies can be very steep. This must be factored into any plans to adopt a new technology. Any introduction of a "new" technology to an organization should be viewed as a potentially risky undertaking. Most of the time, with appropriate training and support, this risk is manageable. However, if you don't factor training and support into your project planning, you may find yourself implementing a "brilliant technological solution" that meets so much resistance that it fails.

- Stringent legal, insurance, contractual, regulatory, or licensing requirements. These usually involve constraints placed on the project from outside the organization.

  ○ In the case of legal issues, projects that butt up against copyright and patent issues are risky.

  ○ Insurance issues come in two basic varieties: Protection and performance bonds. In the case of protection, a project that requires special insurance to guard against loss or damage is more risk-prone than one that does not. In the case of performance bonds, if the project is not completed in conformance to the bond, the bond is forfeited.

  ○ Contractual issues can be as simple as "no delivery, no money," or they can involve penalties (sometimes into the thousands-of-dollars-an-hour range) for late delivery. It is also possible to have rewards for early delivery written into contracts but this is more rare.

  ○ Regulatory requirements are a common issue in government projects. Documentation and reporting requirements are frequently included in contracts issued by the government. Regulations can also involve most of the other issues in this list such as performance bonds and special insurance requirements. They can also include legal issues such as EEO (Equal Employment Opportunity and Minority Business participation) and ADA (Americans with Disabilities Act) compliance.

  ○ Another piece of the regulatory issue comes into play if your organization falls under the regulatory control of a government agency. In these cases, you may be required to include activities and deliverables in your project that have little, if anything, to do with the actual required deliverable for the project itself, in order to remain in compliance with the regulatory requirements of the agency. Pharmaceutical companies and those that manufacture medical devices fall under the watchful eye of the Food and Drug Administration. The maze of regulatory compliance requirements usually adds significant complexity to projects (particularly those involving new-product development) done by these companies.

  ○ Licensing issues are somewhat less common unless the project involves the use of someone else's proprietary property, such as the use of a patented product or process or use of copyrighted material.

- Sensitive environmental or safety issues. Both of these are common in construction projects. They may also be of concern in product or process development projects, particularly when the project involves the use of dangerous or hazardous materials or processes.

- Risks to internal (or external) relationships. This one came up at a recent workshop and, frankly, the question had never been asked in quite this way before. "What about the risks a project might pose to some of the relationships with people you work with all the time?" The resulting discussion came to the following conclusions. You should look at the impacts your projects may have on your (and your department's) relationships with other people and departments inside your company. It is very possible to have a project that will negatively impact some other group within the organization. These risks, while not as financially serious as some of the others, are just as great and can have long term impacts. As part of your stakeholder analysis, look for both positive and negative consequences to your projects. You need to address any potentially negative impact before the project gets underway. It may be enough to keep a project from being done as originally anticipated and could require rethinking the approach. Take care of the relationships you have developed (or want to develop) and include them in your consideration of the overall potential risk involved with a project.

In most cases, the risks faced by project leaders inside organizations are not of a catastrophic nature. You will probably run across an occasional "project killer", they really aren't all that common. This does not mean that risks do not exist, only that they are not generally of a magnitude sufficient to justify a full-scale risk-engineering approach to their identification and analysis. If you do run into one of the project-killer situations, bring it to the attention of the project's stakeholders and get some help with the decision-making that is needed — specifically the decision about whether to do the project or not.

What most project managers face are the risks associated with the inability to accurately and consistently forecast the future. It is difficult to anticipate every situation that may arise in the course of a project and it is not really necessary. What you must do, however, is to examine your projects for those situations which present greater than average uncertainty and to plan what you will do if the worst (or the very bad) happens.

To complete this discussion of overall project risk, we need to have some way of determining the potential impact of an identified risk.

For every risk you identify you need to consider and evaluate two conditions:

- The probability that an identified risk will materialize — that something will go wrong.
- The impact on the project if it happens.

Another way to say this is: How likely is it to happen and, if it does, how bad will it be?

The first part of this, the probability piece, is really a judgement call on the part of you and anyone you can rope into helping you figure it out. Use as much information as you can get your hands on about past projects with similar conditions but also rely on your "gut feeling" for how likely a potential problem is. The numbers in parentheses are used, in combination with the numbers from the Impact rating, for calculation of the overall risk.

- Very Low (1) — this event is very unlikely to occur. The chance is less than 10%.
- Low (3) – while possible, this event is still unlikely to happen. The chance is between 10% and 25%.
- Moderate (5) – this is in the 25% to 50% range.
- High (7) – this one is fairly likely to happen. The chance is between 50% and 75%.

- Very High (9) — at this level, it's probably going to happen. The chance is greater than 75%.

Probability Rating

Probability of Occurrance	Very Low 1	Low 3	Moderate 5	High 7	Very High 9
	Very unlikely to occur (less than 10% chance)	Possible but still unlikely to occur (10%-25% chance)	25%-50% chance of occurance	50%-75% chance of occurance	Greater than 75% chance of occurance

The second evaluation can be based on much more concrete information. What will it mean to the project if the problem occurs? How bad will it be? Can you recover from it? Will it kill the project? Will it require you to start over?

Rating impact requires looking at each of the three constraints of time, resources, and output separately. Again, the numbers in parentheses are used in the overall risk calculation.

- Very Low (1) impact on:
  - Cost or resources: The impact will be insignificant.
  - Schedule: The impact will be negligible.
  - Output quality or performance: Any impact will be barely noticeable.
- Low (2) impact on:
  - Cost or resources: A less that 5% cost increase or change in resource utilization.
  - Schedule: This will result in less than a 5% slippage in the schedule.
  - Output quality or performance: Only very demanding usage or applications will be affected.
- Moderate (3) impact on:
  - Cost or resources: Between a 5% and 10% increase in cost or resource utilization.
  - Schedule: An overall project schedule slip of between 5% and 10%.
  - Output quality or performance: This change in quality or performance requires customer approval.
- High (5) impact on:
  - Cost or resources: An increase in cost or resource requirements of between 10% and 20%.
  - Schedule: An overall project schedule slippage of between 10% and 20%.
  - Output quality or performance: The change in quality or performance is unacceptable to the customer and must be corrected.
- Very High (10) impact on:
  - Cost or resources: This will result in a cost increase of greater than 20% or a change in resource utilization of greater than 20%.

○ Schedule: This will result in an overall project schedule slip of greater than 20%.

○ Output quality or performance: If this happens, the project deliverable is effectively unusable.

Impact Rating

Impact on Constraint	Very Low .5	Low 1	Moderate 2	High 4	Very High 8
Cost or Resources	Insignificant cost increase or impact on resource utilization	Less than a 5% cost increase or 5% change in resource utilization	5%-10% cost increase or 5%-10% change in resource utilization	10%-20% cost increase or 10%-20% change in resource utilization	Greater than 20% cost increase or 20% increase in resource utilization
Schedule	Insignificant schedule impact	Less than 5% slipage in schedule	Overall project schedule slipage of 5%-10%	Overall project schedule slipage of 10%-20%	Overall project schedule slipage greater than 20%
Output Quality or Performance	Impact on quality or performance barely noticeable	Only very demanding applications are affected	The change in quality or performance requires customer approval	The reduction in quality or performance is unacceptable to the customer	Project deliverable is effectively unusable

To calculate the overall risk, multiply the Probability rating by the Impact rating. Find the total in the Probability/Impact Matrix below. The scoring scale is non-linear and weights toward high impact situations. The shading in the matrix indicates:

• Light grey = Low overall risk

• Medium grey = Medium overall risk

• Dark grey = High overall risk

Probability/Impact Matrix

Probability	Risk Score = Probability X Impact				
9	4.5	9	18	36	72
7	3.5	7	14	28	56
5	2.5	5	10	20	40
3	1.5	3	6	12	24
1	.5	1	2	4	8
	.5	1	2	4	8
	Impact				

Project Risk

☐ Low overall project risk   ▦ Medium overall project risk   ■ High overall project risk

A low overall risk score indicates a situation that can probably be ignored. This level of risk is almost always present in most projects. These risks can frequently be prevented with a little attention to the planning of the project.

A medium overall risk score is something to think about. The scores in this range are weighted toward those risks that threaten a high impact even though their probability may be low. Again, these risks can frequently be avoided (or reduced) by careful planning.

A high overall risk score must be addressed. The risks in this range pose a significant threat to the project. While planning can do a lot toward reducing or even eliminating these risks, it may be necessary to actually change the definition of the project in order to deal with them. Look first to the constraints that are most severely impacted.

If it is the cost/resource constraint, look for more resources or an increase in the budget.

If it is the schedule constraint that poses the potential problem, look for ways to move the deadline out. It may be possible to address this one by looking at resources as well — more resources, less time (in some cases).

If it is the output quality or performance constraint that is impacted, look to the requirements (Needs and high-level Wants).

The important thing is to identify and address these situations before too much time or effort is expended on a project that is likely to blow up.

In most cases, this first pass at risk assessment for the project as a whole will point out some issues that you should pay attention to but not necessarily loose sleep over. Let's face it, most in-house project leaders aren't going to be assigned to the major "like-or-death" projects that carry the level of risk that would qualify as a potential "project-killer." The issue here for most in-house project leaders is more one of awareness than anything else. You shouldn't undertake projects you haven't thought through carefully and examined from a variety of points of view. Risk assessment is one of those points of view.

Summary of the Process

Here's a quick review of the total project pre-work process:

- Define the problem or opportunity.
  - ○ State the problem in clear terms that define the situation and the desired response to it — "As Is" and "To Be" statements.
- Determine Needs and Wants.
  - ○ Identify those things that are absolutely required for success (Needs) and those things that would be nice, or even important, to include but that are not essential (Wants).
- Rank Wants according to their importance and gain agreement among stakeholders..
  - ○ Use the 10-to-1 scale (10 = very important; 1 = unimportant) to organize Wants and as a basis for discussion and negotiation among stakeholders.
- Write the project goal statement.
  - ○ Remember the SMART criteria: Specific, Measurable, Agreed-Upon, Realistic, Time-framed.
    - - Develop options to deliver the desired outcome.

> *   Identify the various ways the problem or opportunity can be addressed.
>
> -   Compare options to Needs and Wants
>   First, screen every option against the Needs. Any option that does not meet every Needs is discarded. Evaluate the remaining options based on how well they address each Want.
>
> • Assess overall risks.
>   ○ Look at both probability and impact.

Revist Your Stakeholders

You've completed your pre-work. You should be at a point where you're comfortable with your understanding of the project and its implications. Now is a good time to revisit your stakeholders and review and verify the agreements and commitments you have with them. Go back to your original Stakeholder Analysis forms and check to see if anything has changed now that you have a more clearly defined project. Specifically, look for changes in the commitment of time, resources, assistance, etc., that need to be acknowledged, verified, or possibly renegotiated.

The more of this you can do up front, the fewer problems you will encounter later in the project. If the agreements and commitments are clear; if everyone understands their roles in relation to the project; if the resources are committed early on; there will be fewer points of confusion as the project plan is actually implemented. Open, clear, concise, and fairly constant communication is a key component in managing or leading any project. It is the interface between the project and the rest of the organization and it must be carefully managed.

PROCESS TIP
Using the Commitment Form

Commitment Form

Fill in the appropriate project information.

Project:		Date:
Project Leader:		
Project Sponsor:		

List the individuals identified in the first column.

Indicate the commitment needed from each individual. Be specific aobut the commitment needed. If you need resources from them, list whom. If you need information, list what. Whatever you need, list it here.

Indicate your (or the team's) assessment of the individual's current stance about the project: For, Against, Unsure.

Individual	Commitment Needed	For	Against	Unsure

A Commitment Form is a variation of the Stakeholder Analysis Form. It is a simpler tool for outlining who supports, who opposes, and who is neutral about your project. It can also spur planning about how you will gain the commitment and cooperation of the various people connected with the project. It is a simple list of whom you need commitments from, what commitment you need from them, and where you believe they stand at the moment (for, against, or unsure).

This is not a "hard" scientific tool based on verifiable data. It is based on you perceptions of where specific people stand in relation to the project. It is also not necessarily a tool for publication. You may want to use it to simply identify who needs to support your project, in what way, and where you thing they stand at the moment.

This is a tool for developing strategy. How will you strengthen the commitment of those who already support your project? How will you convert the "unsure" into supporters (or at least keep them from going over to the "against" side)? What can you do to change the minds of those who are against it? Or, if you can't change their position, how can you minimize their ability to negatively impact the project?

Determining the Skills Needed for the Project

You can dream, create, design, and build the most wonderful place in the world, but it requires people to make the dream a reality

Walt Disney
1901-1966
American Film Producer

With the project pre-work completed, your should have a pretty good idea of the skills that will be needed to complete the project. Hopefully, you'll be able to have some influence over the selection of the people who will work on your project. It is important to acknowledge that this is not always (or even usually) the case. In many organizations, project team members are assigned right along with the project leader. In others, one is actually "assigned" to a project; you simply use whomever is available when you need to get some work done. In other organizations (unfortunately, still a minority or them), people are actually linked "officially" to projects and they are expected to stay with the project through completion.

Even in the most project-savvy organizations, when people are assigned to a project team they are frequently chosen based on some basic, general knowledge of the project work and, most importantly, their availability. That "availability" criteria does not always yield the people most qualified to do the work. It yields the people who aren't doing something else at the moment.

You should, to whatever extent possible, try to influence the selection of the people who will work on your projects. For some of you, this will be an easy task. For others, this will be very difficult. The important thing to keep in mind is that the overall success of the project is your responsibility as the project leader. You can't produce the best possible project without the resources to do the work. The better qualified the resources are, the more likely it is that you will produce a high-quality output. Exert what influence you can over the selection of project team members.

PROCESS TIP
Using the Skills and Influence Matrix
The Skills and Influence Matrix can be used to identify the skills needed to accomplish the work and show which team members have which skill sets. It can show when critical skills are duplicated in several team members. It can show when critical skills are missing completely. The second half of this tool, "Individuals to be Influenced," can be used to identify people outside the project team who need to be influenced in some way. This can include stakeholders and customers, key managers, etc. Identify the person to be influenced and connect them to team members who have access to, or influence with, them. This tool can be used in negotiations for people with necessary skills and contacts.

Skills and Influence Matrix

Project:	Date:
Project Leader:	
Project Sponsor:	

Potential Team Members

Skills

Individuals to be Influenced

Fill in the appropriate project information.

List Potential Team Members across the top.

List the specific skills needed for the project down the left. Be very specific about the skills. If you need a programmer who knows C++, that's what you should list rather than "programmer."

Connect the skills to the individuals. Look for both missing and duplicated skill sets.

List individuals to be influenced on the lower portion of the form.

Connect potential team members with the individuals they can or might be able to influence. Identify any critical individuals to be influenced who are not accessible to team members and develop strategies to influence them.

> Like most of the tools in this book, this one works best when it is used by the team rather than by an individual. Ask for input from team members about their strengths and weaknesses. You may find some surprising talents you didn't know were there.
>
> As a variation, you can assign "ratings" to indicate the level of skill a particular individual has. For example, 1 = low skill, 5 = high skill.

Assembling the Project Team

Very small groups of highly remarkable propensity to succeed.
Ramchandran Jaikumar
Harvard Business School

Assuming you can influence the selection of project team members (and even if you can't), there are some things you should consider when pulling your team together.

For one thing, most in-house projects are not staffed by "dedicated" personnel — people assigned full-time to the project. They tend to be staffed by "borrowed" personnel — people who still have other jobs and who work on the project in addition to other duties, and frequently, other projects as well. This creates a tendency toward "multiple loyalty" on the part of team members. People will tend to give more weight to the desires of those who can directly affect their careers, i.e., their managers.

This presents some challenges for most project leaders. Most projects operate, at least somewhat, outside the functional lines of authority and power of the organization. This means that most project leaders do not have direct authority over the individuals on the project team. They don't write their performance reviews, grant raises, etc. This puts the project leader in an interesting position when it comes to ensuring continued support and cooperation.

What we have here is another aspect of Stakeholder Analysis. After all, project team members and their managers are all stakeholders in the project. They just have a little different stake in it than some others.

Potential team members have a stake in the success of the project in that they will share in that success and, if you're a good project leader, in the rewards that come with it. Consider the following as some of the commitments and understandings you need from team members:

- A commitment to the goal of the project. If they are going to work on the project, they should be committed to its success. They should "buy in" to the goal and understand its implications and importance.

- A commitment to the tasks and activities for which they will be responsible. By assembling most of the team prior to beginning the detailed planning of the project, you have an excellent opportunity to build commitment through the planning process itself. People are more likely to commit and follow through on tasks they have helped design than they are on those that are simply assigned to them.

- A realistic assessment of the time that the team member can devote to the project. The key word here is "realistic." How much time can the person actually devote to the project, given all the other duties and responsibilities they have? There is a tendency for people to over-estimate when they are excited about a project and to under-estimate when they are not. You may need to do some verification of their estimates. There are some tools for this in the planning process in Chapter 4: *Project Planning*.

- An understanding of functional responsibilities that may cause scheduling conflicts with the project. You need to know those activities and tasks that are likely to require significant or recurring allocations of the person's time. These can be things like mandatory weekly staff meetings, daily or weekly tasks that must be done regularly, commitments to other projects, etc.

> **PROCESS TIP**
> **The value of involving team members early**
> If you can involve potential (or identified) team members in the development of the project goal and other pre-work, most of these commitments will come out of their participation in that process. People are much more inclined to be committed to, and to work hard to accomplish, work they have helped design than when a task is simply assigned to them. If at all possible, involve the people who will be doing the work in the design of that work.
>
> If you continue to involve them in the actual planning of the project (something that will be encouraged by the planning process presented in this book), most of the potential scheduling conflicts will be identified and can be resolved in the planning activity.

You also need commitments from the functional managers of the people who will be working on your project. Consider these as some of the commitments and understandings you may need from your team members' managers:

- A commitment to support the activities of his or her employees working on the project. This is important. There will almost certainly be times when the needs of the functional area and the needs of the project will conflict. The last thing you want to happen is to put the team member in the middle of this kind of conflict. A commitment of support up front goes a long way toward ensuring that these conflicts get resolved.

- An agreement that the project is important and that the employee's participation is required in order to accomplish the project goal. What you're asking for here is agreement about the project's goal. The more closely connected the project goal is to some goal of the managers, the better. This can also allow you to raise the issue of whether the person assigned to the project is the best person for the job based on the skill needs of the project (as documented on the Skills and Influence Matrix). The more important a manager sees the project as being, the more likely they are to offer up their best people to get it done.

- A realistic assessment of the time the employee can devote to the project and still perform his or her functional duties. This can provide the verification of what the employee estimated about their availability. If there is a big discrepancy between the two estimates (the employee's and the manager's), discuss it with the employee.

- An agreement about how conflicts between the needs of the project and the needs of the functional department will be settled. This is an acknowledgement of the fact that you know there will be times when the needs of the project and the needs of the functional group will conflict. The most common response from managers to this is, "We talk it out and reach a decision." This usually means the manager wins. This is actually how it should be in most cases. The needs of the functional operations of the business almost always supercede the needs of projects within those businesses. All you want to do here is acknowledge the probability of conflict and set the stage for bringing the discussion into the open.

> **PROCESS TIP**
> **The importance of verifying commitments**
> Whenever possible, you should try to actually have these discussions and develop these agreements. Ideally, you should have them with everyone who functionally manages members of the project team. Obviously, this will not always be possible. However, you should consider carefully who your key resources are and whether some sort of discussion with their managers would be beneficial. In most cases, going the extra mile in defining and clarifying roles on a project will prove to be excellent groundwork. It will come in handy when you're dealing with the inevitable conflicts between the needs of the project and the needs of the functional organization.
>
> And remember, if you are in the same boat — still performing functional duties in addition to your project duties — you should try to negotiate the same agreements with your manager.

Project Proposals

Ok. If you need one, now you can develop a Project Proposal for your project. Sounds a little late in the sequence for how things usually work, doesn't it? But, this really is the point at which the project proposal should be written — not way back there when you didn't really have a clue about what the project involved.

> **PROCESS TIP**
> **Project Proposals**
> Even if you aren't required to complete a formal Project Proposal, it's not a bad idea to use this tool as a means of summarizing a project. It can be used as a final check on the agreements and understandings you've built around the project. It can also serve as a quick way to explain the project to someone

unfamiliar with it. And, finally, it can serve as the official "approval" document that launches the project.

This example of a Project Proposal contains almost everything that could be included in one. Not every project needs this level of detail. When you create your own version of this form (or edit the form that is available online), add or delete information blocks as appropriate.

Project Proposal

Fill in the appropriate project information.

Project:		Date of Proposal:	
Proposed Project Leader:		Proposed Due Date:	
Proposed Project Sponsor:			

List any project that must be completed before this one can begin. List projected completion dates and people responsible.

List any projects that depend on this one being completed. List projected start dates and people responsible.

List any projects that will be done in parallel with this one. If there are interdependencies between projects, list them. Indicate projected completion dates and people responsible.

Related Projects

Preceding Projects	Completion Date(s)	
Succeeding Projects	Start Date(s)	
Parallel Projects	Completion Date(s)	

Project Description

Describe the problem or opportunitiy this project will address.

Explain the business purpose of the project.

Describe the expected impacts of the project.

List project deliverables.

List key milestones.

List constraints and assumptions.

List those things specifically excluded from the project scope.

List resources expected for this project.

Estimate person-hours needed to complete the project.

Estimate the cost of the project.

Indicate where to find additional detailed information in the "Detail" sections.

	Detail
Problem or Opportunity to be addressed by this project	Detail
Business Purpose of this project	Detail
Expected Impacts/Effects of this project	Detail
Project Deliverables	Detail
Key Milestones (based on deliverables)	Detail
Major Constraints and Key Assumptions	Detail
Items/Issues specifically excluded from this project	Detail
Resources Expected for this project	Detail

Estimated Total Person Hours	Detail	Estimated Cost	Detail

Deliverables at This Point

For most projects, there are several deliverables at this first milestone:

- The output of the pre-work (problem/solutions statements, Needs and ranked Wants, assessment of risks, etc.) with whatever support material is needed to justify your conclusions. Remember, it's a good idea to have this all reviewed by others to verify your findings and to clarify any unclear instructions.

- A good draft of the project goal statement with whatever supporting detail is needed.

- A list of potential team members (or at least a good idea of who they should be). If needed, the Skills and Influence Matrix is a tool for justifying your choices.

- A request for the resources needed to effectively begin planning the project. This can take the form of a "formalized" project proposal.

Issues by Project Type

There are some special concerns that surface depending on the type of project being undertaken. These are some of the issues the project leader should watch carefully during this period.

Process Projects

In process development projects (primarily internally-focused), most of the concerns at this stage involve clearly defining the impact of the proposed project on the total work flow of the organization. Specific issues include:

- Determining the actual process-needs to be addressed. This is accomplished by working closely with the ultimate users.

- Determining the potential impact of a process change on other processes. This involves working with both the ultimate users and representatives of all the areas that may be impacted by a change (those which precede, follow and work in parallel with the process being changed).

- Determining the input and output constraints involves careful "mapping" of the total system of which the process is a part.

- Determining the technical constraints around the process requires a solid understanding of the process and the system of which it is a part. You need to know how they work, what the lot-size requirements are, how they inter-relate, what limitations are placed on the process by the total system, new developments in technology which might help or hinder development, etc.

- Determining capital equipment and expense requirements and constraints involves working with various functional groups such as management, purchasing, production planning, facilities, etc., in order to develop a good "rough draft" or estimate of what capital investments will be needed.

- Obtaining agreement among all parties regarding the proposed process. It is very important that you involve everyone who will be affected by the process in the project to some degree. You will need their cooperation at some point and involving them early and allowing them to state their concerns can prevent massive headaches when it comes to implementation.

- Determining implementation impacts on existing processes. Involving all the players up front can uncover hidden pitfalls that would otherwise surface only after you tried to make the process operational. This can help you "map" the impacts of the process so you will know what to anticipate at later stages.

- Obtaining input regarding the timing of implementation, costs, training needs, documentation of the process, etc. All of this information is grist for the planning mill. It is the kind of information you will need in order to complete many of the detailed tasks involved in breaking down work into realistic chunks that people can accomplish in a reasonable timeframe.

Product/Service Projects

Product or service development projects are primarily externally-focused. They are directed at providing a response to a perceived need in the external markets of the company. As such, they require the participation of personnel from various internal functions and from the external customer base. (External customers can be represented by marketing and sales personnel from the company — just be sure their information is based on actual customer input, not just "hunches" about what customers want.) Specific issues include:

- Determining market need based on actual customer input can require conducting market studies, interviewing customers, analyzing competitive offerings, examining market trends, etc.

- Determining market size, competitive offerings, pricing constraints, delivery systems, etc., almost always involves direct contact with both the market and with various parts of the product or service delivery system. Some special expertise is required to gather useful data and, if not available internally, this expertise is usually hired from outside the company.

- Profit potential analysis is the process of forecasting the likelihood that the company will show a profit as a result of undertaking the project. This process yields many of the elements of the Triple Constraint by placing limits around the capital investment (and on-going production costs) that are realistic given the potential for profit. It also helps to specify the size of the "window of opportunity" that must be met to optimize profit.

- Establishing a connection between the proposed product or service and the current offerings of the organization. This is more important than it might seem on the surface. Companies get themselves into serious trouble when they "go too far afield" with new product or service offerings. If your business is hardware, expanding into painting supplies or building materials is a reasonable undertaking. Your existing customers are likely to believe that you have the expertise to market these products; you will potentially attract new customers for all your product lines since they are all inter-related. However, if your business is hardware and you expand into the fast food business, few will believe you know what you are doing; there is no reason to believe you can effectively operate in a market totally outside your proven expertise. There must be some realistic connection between the proposed product or service and the products and services you currently offer.

- Determining the technology constraints around the development process and the manufacturing or service delivery process should begin at this stage. It is unlikely that all the constraints will be anticipated, but a careful examination of probable constraints will set you on the right track for additional investigation as the project progresses.

- Obtaining agreement among all parties regarding the proposed product or service. Don't forget to involve customers (or representatives of customers) in this process. They are, after all, the ones who must purchase the product or service. Also, be sure to include everyone who must "handle" the product or support the service on its way to the customer.

- Determining probable production requirements. Include everyone, from purchasing and production planning to shipping and distribution, in this information-gathering activity. The last thing you want to happen is to get ready to launch the product and find that you forgot to have the packaging ordered or to notify distribution that there would be additional shipments coming.

- Determining the basic specifications of the proposed product or service. In most cases, this is an activity between the project team and marketing, but don't forget to include key production or support personnel in this development.

- Obtaining input regarding market-introduction timing, packaging, and distribution or service delivery, etc. Again, most of this involves marketing, but there are a significant number of other operations that should be consulted.

Software Projects Software development projects can be either internally- or externally-focused, i.e., development of a program for internal use (such as accounting or inventory-control software) or development of a program package for sale to industry or the public.

Software projects should be driven primarily by the needs of the end user and constrained by the limitation of the hardware systems on which they must operate. Specific issues include:

- Determining the actual need based on input from either the ultimate internal user or from potential customers. Internal users are much easier to find and a representative of the user group makes a good addition to the project team. Gaining input from external customers requires the same expertise and research outlined under the heading "Product/ Service Projects" development projects.

- Determining how the user will use the software is part of the basic development of the performance or quality portion of the Triple Constraint. In order to develop software that meets a specific need, you must understand what the user needs the software to do — how the software should make it easier for the user to do something.

- Analysis of existing offerings is an excellent starting point for much of this research. What do existing offerings do well? What do they do poorly? What features are missing? How much do they cost? Are they "user friendly" or do they require an extensive technical background in either computers or in the area the program addresses? All of these questions, and many more, will provide insights into how to meet the needs of a specific user group.

- Determining platform constraints is a critical early step in defining the project. Unfortunately (from the user's point of view) there is no "standard" operating system or common hardware. Decisions must be made early in the project about which hardware platform most potential users use. The software must then be developed with clear understanding of the operational constraints of that platform.

- Determining the programming language is a natural outgrowth of selecting a hardware platform and operating system. Each platform and language has its own set of limitations which must be taken into account in the development process.

- Determining the technical constraints of a software project is made more difficult by the constant (almost daily) technical advancements being made in the computer industry. This requires that project leaders on software development projects, and their technical counterparts, constantly research developments in the field.

- Obtaining agreement among all parties regarding the proposed software package. You should not only be concerned with the operational specifications of the software, but also with the training needs (internal) and the documentation required to make it useful. Should there be a demonstration program? Does it need a tutorial? How about after-sale support? What will you do about updates, etc.?

- Determining probable programming requirements in terms of number of hours, lines of code, etc. The best sources for this information are the people who will actually write the software. Actively seek the input of the people who will do the work and of the people (or their representatives) who will use the program.

- Determining the limitations of the proposed software. Set the boundaries of the product. Be very clear about what it must do, what it should do, if possible, and what it does not need to do. Pay particular attention to defining what it doesn't need to do. The biggest pitfall in most software development projects is adding "bells and whistles" that don't need to be there.

People Skills for Project Leaders

Introduction

Managing requires setting aside one's ego to encourage and develop the work of others. It requires a "big picture" and team perspective rather than an individual-achiever perspective.
Sara M. Brown
President, Sara Brown & Associates

People are the key to any project. People will make the plans, perform the work, solve the problems, track the progress, deliver the output. Some skills in working well with people are critical for any successful project leader. So, before getting too deeply into project planning and implementation processes, a discussion of working with people on the project team and others within the organization seems appropriate.

In-house project leaders usually work with borrowed resources — people who are already scheduled by their managers to do something else — almost always something unrelated to the project. In most cases, the people working on your project will not report to you in the sense of being your subordinates. You don't manage them. You don't write their performance reviews. You can't grant them raises, bonuses, or promotions. They work for someone else. You only have them on loan.

In situations like this, you can't manage people in the traditional sense of telling them what to do and expecting that they will do it. You need to lead them. You need to get them to perform through influence rather than authority.

The material in this chapter covers a wide range of "people" topics. Not all of them will apply to every situation. However, the chances are quite good that you will eventually use all of them sometime during your career as a project leader.

In this chapter, we will look at several aspects of working with people, individually and in a project environment. There are six topics that will be discussed:

- The Development and Use of Power and Authority
- Motivation
- Leadership
- How Teams Grow and Change Over Time

- Negotiation
- Communication

The Development and Use of Power and Authority

Everyone wants power. Few people have enough of it — particularly project leaders. Most of us believe our situations would be better if only we had more power.

We associate power with authority and with one's location in the hierarchy of an organization — position power. This limited view of power assumes that power is a fixed-sum commodity and that there is only so much to go around. Effective project leaders understand that power is dynamic, and like electricity it's all around us and almost limitless in its potential. The challenge is to tap into this energy and channel it to your purposes. Like money in a bank, power is a source of credit that expands with use and makes other people feel stronger and richer.

The word "power" means "to be able." Making something happen arises at least as much from personal competencies as it does from authority associated with a particular position. Professor Michael Badawy states in *Developing Managerial Skills in Engineers and Scientists* that, "Of the two types of power, positional and personal, the project leader's authority is actually based on power which largely stems more from his personal abilities and less from his position." In effective project management, power is based on an understanding of the reciprocal relationship between leaders and their followers.

Personal power is a set of skills and abilities. It refers to the ways we work with and respond to others in face-to-face situations. It doesn't come from an office. It travels with an individual.

Where Power Comes From

In some of the literature about the subject, power has been viewed as coming from one or more of five sources. It is important to recognize that every one of these descriptions includes some form of the words "perceive" or "belief." In almost every instance, one person's reaction to another is based on their "perception" of the situation and the person, and our "belief" about how we are supposed to react. So, most of the time when we talk about power, we're really talking about the "perception" of power.

Reward Power is based on our perception that another person has the ability to reward us or to grant us something that we desire. This is about one-third of the types of power most people associate with managers. This is the power to write good performance reviews; grant raises or promotions; parcel out the best work assignments; etc.

Coercive Power is the flip-side of reward power. It is based on our perception that another person has the ability to punish us or to withhold something we desire. The same manager who can write a good performance review can write a bad one. He or she can withhold a raise (or grant a smaller one than we think we deserve), give us the worst work assignments, etc.

The third leg of the managerial stool is what is commonly called Legitimate Power. This is based on our internalized belief and perception that another person has the legitimate right to request certain types of actions of us. It is further reinforced by the belief that we have a social obligation to comply with their requests. This gets into the whole area of the social contracts that (explicit or implicit) exist within almost every organization. Legitimate power plays into the managerial equation as the natural reaction to comply with a request from someone in a superior position in the organization. Legitimate power is often called "institutional power" or "formal authority."

There are examples of legitimate power all around us and most of them are based on this whole social contract idea. For example, most of us will obey the road worker holding up the "Stop" sign and "Slow" sign at a road construction site. Within the narrow confines of that situation, our general social contract says we should comply with their request to either stop or drive slowly through the construction zone. Would we automatically comply with a different request from the same person in another situation? Maybe not. But in that specific set of circumstances, we believe we have an obligation to do so. This form of power is usually quite limited. It only applies in certain situations and under specific conditions. Would we be as likely to comply with some manager's demands in a social situation? Probably not.

Referent Power is much more subtle. It is based on our desire to identify with another person. It manifests in our desire to comply with their requests and our belief that in doing so we will facilitate a favorable interpersonal relationship and foster mutual respect. This one probably needs a bit more explanation. Referent power comes into play in very personal situations — usually between two people. A good example of referent power at work is the mentor relationship. In a good mentor relationship, the person being mentored is probably looking to "be like" their mentor.

The mentor is the provider of information and guidance. They are the one to be looked to for information, suggestions, and assistance. Their input is based on their experience but it is the interpersonal relationship that is the basis of successful mentoring. The other half of the relationship, the person being mentored, is usually willing to go along with what the mentor suggests. For most, the underlying hope is probably that what they have been told is true. But there is a more subtle aspect to most good mentor relationships. From the mentored person's point of view, there may be a real hope and expectation that by going along with the mentor's suggestions, they will foster a better and closer relationship with the mentor.

Referent power stems from other people's desire to work with us. To get to know us. To gain something from their relationship with us. It is the strongest form of personal power there is.

The final form of power is Expert Power. This is based on our perception that the "expert" has some special knowledge, information, or ability relevant to the task or problem at hand. Of all the forms of power, this is the narrowest. It only applies to the area of expertise. Expert power doesn't buy a thing in any arena outside the area of expertise. Now, if you truly are an expert at something, this can be a very significant form of power. But, don't try to use your expertise as a computer programmer to get people to listen to your ideas about marketing. It won't fly.

The first three sources, reward, coercive, and legitimate power, form the basis of position power or organizational authority. They are directly connected to the position that a person holds within the structure of the organization. If the person in the manager's office changes, the power remains essentially the same. The power is in the position, not the person.

The last two, referent and expert power, are personal power. They reside in the individual regardless of their position. There are limits to the amount of position power that you can hold. There are no limits to your personal power. Most of us know someone who is not in a position of organizational authority but who still manages to exert significant influence over the actions and behavior of others. This is an example of personal power at work.

How Power is Distributed

Researchers have found that the differences in effectiveness between two similar operations within a business can be linked to the distribution of power. They have consistently found that managers in the under-achieving areas hoard power. In the high-performing areas, the managers share power. As a result, the people at every level on the high-performing area feel that they can, and should, be responsible for the area's effectiveness. Contemporary management thinking has found the old saying "Power corrupts" to be untrue. In fact, it is now believed that "Powerlessness corrupts." And it can corrupt in a more damaging way — when people feel they have power, they feel that they can make a difference and productivity improves.

A study of project leaders reported several significant relationships between overall project performance and the use (or attempted use) of various types of power. For example, the less project personnel perceived project leaders as using position power and the more they perceived them using personal power, the greater the levels of involvement and openness of upward communication. Also, the higher the productivity of the project team. Openness of upward communication is critical to a project leader. Without open, honest communication about what is happening at all levels of the project, a project leader cannot possibly be effective. Similar findings emerge from other studies of such diverse occupations as sales personnel, college teachers, insurance underwriters, postal service carriers, and assembly line workers.

Guidelines for Developing and Using Power

Power does not kill; it permits suicide.
Earl Shorris
Manager and Writer

People respond in one of three ways when you use power:

- They may show commitment to your request by enthusiastically doing what you've asked.

- They may simply comply. They may go along with your request because they feel they have to, but they do not do anything beyond the minimum required.

- They may resist by failing to follow through or even by pushing back.

Obviously, you need to understand how the various power bases can be used to generate commitment or, at the very least, willing compliance, rather than resistance to your requests.

Referent Power

The key to successful leadership is influence, not authority.

Kenneth Blanchard
University of Massachusetts

We'll focus on the strongest and most flexible power source first — referent power. You develop referent power when others on the project team respect and admire you personally. This source of power is almost solely determined by the way you treat people. Showing consideration for their needs and feelings, dealing with each person fairly, and standing up for the group are ways to increase referent power. Face-to-face interaction with each individual is essential.

Another way you create referent power is by setting an example. You've probably heard about the importance of "modeling" the behavior you want to see from those around you. Well, it's true. If you want your team to perform in a certain way, you must provide the pattern for that behavior. You should intentionally set an example of what you expect and want from others. For example, if quality is important, you need to emphasize quality in all you do, from the work products you produce to the correspondence you send out. (And, yes, this means you should run your e-mail through the spell-checker before you send it.)

If schedule is the most important thing, you need to be sure to deliver everything you do on time, show up for meetings on time, and adjourn your meetings on time. Show that you value everyone's time.

If it's resources that are key, you should remember to continually verify that the appropriate people are working on the tasks, that they have the tools and information they need, and that they are being appropriately recognized for their efforts.

> ### PROCESS TIP
> ### In meetings and discussions, focus on the "driving" constraint
> One good way to demonstrate which of the three constraints is most important (and one of them will always be the driver) is to make it the first thing that comes up in any discussion about the project. For example, if quality is important, make it the first item on the agenda of every team meeting and the first question you ask when reviewing individual progress. The same goes for schedule or resources. Focusing your attention on an issue will tend to focus everyone else on that same issue.

Expert Power

One accurate measurement is worth a thousand expert opinions.

Grace Murray Hopper
1906-1992
Admiral, U.S. Navy

You cannot influence other people just because you think you are (or may actually be) the technical expert. Remember, the effective use of power depends on whether others believe we have it. Others must recognize that you have the expertise and that you are a credible source of information and advice.

Several things can influence how your expertise is viewed by others. For example, if others are aware of your formal education or training they will be more likely to believe you know, at least somewhat, what you're talking about. However, you shouldn't begin every conversation with a recitation of your curriculum vitae. Having a good list of relevant work experience also helps. In this one, remember, the experience must be relevant to the task at hand. Also, having been recognized for some significant accomplishments never hurts — as long as they relate to the current situation. You also need to stay current and up-to-date in your area of expertise. The closer you are to the "bleeding edge" of a technology, the more important current knowledge becomes. You cannot maintain an image of expertise unless you keep up with the developments in your field and remain professionally active.

Expert power can be undermined by relying too much on logic and rationale as persuasion tactics. The perception of arrogance can also weaken your position. Dictating or imposing your views on others will usually get someone's back up. One-way communication often leaves others feeling backed into a corner and trapped. This is not a good way to build relationships. Two-way communication, in which you uncover the feelings and concerns of others and deal with them in making persuasive arguments is much more effective.

> ## PROCESS TIP
> ### Develop your skills at asking questions that lead others to the answer
> One way to work around the problem of simply telling people the answer is to develop some skill with what is called the "Socratic Method." Socrates, the Greek philosopher, rarely gave an answer when asked a question. He would, instead, ask questions designed to lead the other person to the correct answer. This doesn't always work, particularly when the other person doesn't have the necessary knowledge, but it can be a way to guide discussion to an agreement rather than a pronouncement.
>
> Also, people usually react negatively to someone who flaunts his or her greater expertise and experience. It is usually counterproductive to try to convince others by belittling their arguments or making them feel stupid. This will happen if you are perceived as treating their objections, concerns, or suggestions as unimportant, trivial, or insignificant. Recognizing the contributions of others, respecting their self-worth, and incorporating, when possible, their ideas into action plans encourages their perception of your expertise and your good sense.

Legitimate Power

Control freaks don't grow good companies.
Jeffrey A. Timmons
Babson College

You are exercising legitimate power when you make a legitimate request — one that is within the scope of your authority. You will encounter less resistance if you make it easy for others to comply with your request. The simplest way to do this is to be polite when making your requests. This usually means including the word "please." This is especially important for project personnel who are likely to be sensitive to status differences and authority relationships, for example, someone older or with more seniority than you or someone with multiple supervisors.

Finally, it is helpful when project personnel understand that your requests are within the scope of your authority. Linking requests with official documentation such as written rules, policies, contract provisions, and schedules is one way to do this. It is not sufficient to just say, "Trust me." It helps when people perceive that higher authority is on your side.

> **PROCESS TIP**
> **Make it easy for people to comply by explaining the reasons behind a request**
> Another way to make it easy to go along is to explain the reasons behind the request. Others are more likely to go along with your requests if the see them as consistent with agreed-upon task objectives. It can be helpful to review the decision-making process with the team. This can be a variation on the Socratic Method mentioned above. Take the time to lead them through the process step by step. Show them why the decision was made and why other alternatives were rejected.

Reward Power

The most important words in the English language:
5 most important words:
    I am proud of you.
4 most important words:
    What is your opinion?
3 most important words:
    If you please.
2 most important words:
    Thank you.
1 most important word:
    You.
                Anonymous

The most common way of using reward power is to offer tangible rewards to people if they go along with your requests. Unfortunately, the ideal conditions for using reward power seldom exist. Most project leaders lack access to and control over attractive tangible rewards. Project participants often have interdependent tasks that make it difficult to use individual incentives. (And one of the most destructive things you can do is single out one person for recognition when there were several people equally involved in the success.) In addition, objective indicators of performance are not available for many kinds of tasks and a person's behavior is not often easily observable.

There are other problems with relying too heavily on rewards as a source of influence. You may win compliance but you are unlikely to win a person's heart or commitment. When people perform tasks to get a promised reward, they are likely to see their behavior as a means to an end. This may tempt them to take shortcuts and neglect less visible aspects of the task in order to complete the assignment and get the reward. Few internal incentives are generated to motivate the individual to put forth any effort beyond what is required. There is little incentive to demonstrate any particular initiative in carrying out the task. Consequently, over time, their relationship with the project leader will tend to be defined in purely economic terms. Special rewards come to be expected every time something new or unusual is required. Even when they have access to them, most managers run out of tangible goodies, especially as expectations escalate. In addition, using reward power can lead to resentment and resistance because people feel they are being manipulated by the contingent ("I'll do this if you do that") nature of the relationship.

It is important to remember that not all rewards are financial. Many times, the most effective rewards are what are sometimes called "psychic" rewards — recognition, appreciation, rewarding relationships, etc. These are the types of rewards anyone can give out. They don't cost anything and the response to them is usually completely out of proportion to the effort needed to provide them. Consequently, rather than using rewards as explicit incentives, effective project leaders use them more subtly to recognize and reinforce desired behavior. They focus on rewarding intrinsic needs like recognition, self-esteem, and future opportunities for growth and challenge.

> **PROCESS TIP**
> **Use your ability to "reward" to support your referent power base**
> The use of reward power should supplement and strengthen your referent power base. Give rewards, psychic or otherwise, in a way that expresses your personal appreciation for efforts and accomplishments. People come to like people who repeatedly provide these subtle rewards. Interpersonal relationships are more satisfying when they are viewed as an expression of mutual friendship, respect, and loyalty rather than an impersonal economic exchange.

Coercive Power

The emphasis in sound discipline must be on what's wrong, rather than who's to blame.

George S. Odiorne
1920-1992
American Educator and Business Writer

Here again we have the flip side of reward power. As a general rule, coercive power should be avoided except when absolutely necessary. And it is rarely absolutely necessary. Its use can create resentment and erode your referent power base. With coercion there is usually no chance of gaining commitment. Even willing compliance is difficult to achieve.

For most in-house project leaders, this issue is somewhat moot. For the most part, you won't have the authority to administer discipline. Under most circumstances, you'll need to pass the problem to someone in a position of true managerial authority.

Coercion is most appropriate when it is used to stop a behavior detrimental to the organization or the project. For example, theft, sabotage, violation of safety rules, or blatant insubordination. "Positive discipline" is a term used to describe strategies that are directed toward encouraging others to assume responsibility for helping to resolve discipline problems. This tends to be much more effective than threats or sample doses of punishment. The following are some guidelines for using positive discipline. This list may look like something you'd expect to see as a guide for grade-school discipline but, frankly, most of the things that work on school children also work on adults even though we probably don't like to admit it. One advantage you may have with adults that you may not have with very young children is that, with most adults, logic and reason can have an impact whereas with some children it is a bit more of a behavioral modification exercise. Come to think of it, that's the case with some adults.

- Be sure people know the rules and the consequences of violations. If there are specific behavioral requirements, state them explicitly. Don't be vague.

- Administer discipline consistently and promptly. This sounds like training a dog but it's still true. The closer the consequences are to the act, the more likely it is that the connection will be made.

- Provide sufficient warning before resorting to discipline. It's up to you to set the number of strikes but there should almost always be an opportunity provided for someone to "clean up their act" before the ax falls.

- Get the facts before using reprimands or discipline. This is very important. Not only should you get the facts, you should also take the time to check them to make sure they're correct.

- Stay calm and avoid appearing hostile or vindictive. If you become emotional, you lose. Remain firm in your stance but stay focused on the behavioral issues and avoid, at all costs, bringing personality into the discussion.

- Make the consequences appropriate. Minor infraction, minor consequences. Major infraction — major consequences. If anything, you should probably err on the side of letting someone off a little lightly rather than ruining a career over something not all that important.

- Administer warnings and discipline in private. Never — repeat, never — discipline someone in front of others. The damage you will do if you make this mistake is enormous. Not only will you embarrass the person being disciplined, you will also embarrass everyone who witnesses it. And, you will have seriously damaged your own reputation. Justified or not, almost everyone who witnesses this kind of public humiliation will wonder if and when it could happen to them.

PROCESS TIP
Coercive power is not all negative but use it sparingly
Not all coercive power results in career-limiting consequences. Like reward power, coercive power can be exercised through non-material means. For example, you can show your disappointment in someone's behavior or performance through words and actions just as well as through sending them to the manager's office. It is important to remember that you can only exert this kind of power over someone if your opinion matters to them. If they don't respect you in the first place, your displeasure won't have much effect.

Whatever your ability to exert coercive power — positional or otherwise — use it sparingly and only after careful consideration of all the other possible alternatives. Of all the forms of power, coercive power is the one that must be exercised the most carefully. Abuse of this form of power has the most severe consequences to the wielder.

Motivation

Contrary to some popular beliefs, you can't motivate anyone to do anything. All you can do is create a set of circumstances in which they can motivate themselves. Motivation is purely internal. You can provide an opportunity for someone to obtain something they desire (see Reward Power in the previous section) and hope they want it enough to do what you've asked. But that's about all. If they want the reward (are motivated by it), they'll likely comply with the request. If they don't, they likely won't.

Abraham Maslow, a research psychologist, made a study of motivation and created a model of motivational factors that sums this up nicely. (Remember that psychology class from college?) According to Maslow, we, as human beings, are all motivated by predictable, fundamental needs. These needs can be grouped into five categories that form a pyramid.

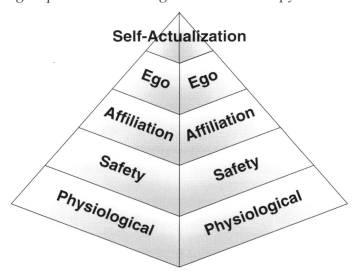

The basis of Maslow's theory is that a "met need no longer motivates." That is to say, once a need has been met, it no longer has the power to motivate us to do those things that led to its fulfillment. This is a key concept when trying to create motivational situations for people. The motivator must be something they want in order to be effective.

According to Maslow's theory, the two bottom sections of the pyramid are the most basic needs. The physiological needs — food and water — are the basic drivers. We can't survive without them. If these are threatened, everything else goes on hold until they are met. Once these needs have been met, the Safety needs come into play. If we have sufficient food and water to become comfortable we will no longer be content to simply be fed. We will now work toward assuring our safety, through shelter and clothing, ensuring our own protection, etc.

These two are the most basic needs we have, and they are the needs that can most easily be met with money. With sufficient funds, we can buy food and guarantee shelter. Most people in today's workforce have these needs met adequately. Therefore, their power as a motivator is significantly weakened. It isn't eliminated but the strength of the motivation dwindles as we begin to realize that more money only buys more of what we already have.

Keep in mind that different people have vastly different levels of "perceived need" connected to the two basic levels of this model. For some, a good sense of security can be achieved with a much lower level of income than others. However, the basic premise still applies — once these needs are met to our satisfaction, they no long have the power to motivate.

Once our Safety needs have been met, we move on to meeting our need for companionship — Affiliation. In modern society, these needs are met by family, friends, and co-workers. This can be a very strong motivator in most work situations. We spend a significant portion of our waking life in the company of our co-workers. If we like them, enjoy their company, and get pleasure from being with them, continuing those relationships and strengthening them can be a powerful motivation to perform well on the job.

> **PROCESS TIP**
> **Stress some of the relationship aspects of the project**
> Consider the possibility of stressing the relationship aspects of your project teams. The chance to work with new people (or the same people in a different context) can be an exciting prospect for some people. Most of us enjoy the chance to meet a challenge with people we like and respect. For many teams, the relationships that were forged or strengthened in the course of a project are more lasting than the immediate rewards of getting the project done.

After our Affiliation needs are sufficiently met, we move on to gratification of our Egos. Ego needs include enhancing our sense of self-worth, status, and gaining the respect of others. This, too, can be a powerful motivator for people. The chance to "show what we can do" is very appealing to most people. And projects usually offer this chance to some degree. The more challenging the project, the greater the opportunity to shine.

Some egos are much larger and require much more attention than others. But everyone has one. This need can easily be met through recognition of individual and group accomplishments. Never miss an opportunity to recognize someone's success.

> **PROCESS TIP**
> **Look to yourself for clues aabout what is likely to motivate others**
> Think about what motivates you, personally. How different are you from your peers — really? Probably not all that much. Look for things that you would like to receive as a result of your involvement in the project and try to find ways to make the same things available to your team members.
>
> Personal attention and sincere appreciation are probably the most powerful motivators you have at your disposal. And, the beauty of it is, they're free. It doesn't cost anything to pay attention to someone nor does it cost to thank them for a job well done.

These two sets of needs — affiliation and ego — are the primary motivators for most people in a business setting. Unfortunately, most of the reward and recognition systems out there focus on the first two levels of need rather than these two. In survey after survey of the factors that motivate employees, managers consistently rank things like salary, benefit package, and job security at the top of the list. Employees, on the other hand, consistently rank things like recognition and a sense of accomplishment, interesting or important work, good co-worker relationships, and a chance to have some control over their work life as the most important. While the managers' response leads to a focus on monetary rewards, the employees' response leads to a focus on relationships, recognition, and appreciation. Here's the good news: you don't need a budget to hand out these rewards.

The last step in Maslow's hierarchy is Self-actualization. In this stage, only after all other needs have been met, can we begin to focus on realizing our full potential as human beings. This is the level that rarely gets satisfied at work. This is an intensely personal quest for meaning and fulfillment. It is also almost totally focused inward — on our innermost being. There is little in the way of external conditions that can affect this one.

Just to restate the basic point of this section, most people in business are in the middle of Maslow's Hierarchy — in the Affiliation and Ego areas. Therefore, those things which fulfill Affiliation needs, such as cooperative relationships, involvement, participation, etc., and those things that satisfy Ego needs, such as praise, recognition, respect, etc., are the things that will provide the means for their motivation.

Leadership

Think of yourself as a leader rather than a manager. Even if you are a manager, in most project situations, it will be your leadership skills, not your organizational power base, that will generate the results you need.

Conventional wisdom says that, in general, managers "do things right" and leaders "do the right things." Much of a manager's job is ensuring that the "rules" are followed; that things are "done the right way." Much of a leader's job, on the other hand, is ensuring that the proper things are being worked on; that the focus of the effort is in the right areas and leading toward desirable goals. You can certainly be both a manager and a leader but the activities and the focus are different depending on which role your fulfilling at the moment.

Effective leadership depends heavily on personal power — mainly Referent power — and your ability to provide the motivators your people want and need. It is based on providing an inspiring vision of what needs to be done and providing the environment in which it can be accomplished.

The characteristics of effective leaders, as discussed here, are not in themselves either positive or negative. Throughout history there have been some very effective leaders who were, by most modern measures, thoroughly evil.

What People Want From Their Leaders

- Advice (from kindergarten) for managers:
- Share everything.
- Play fair.
- Don't hit people.
- Put things back where you found them.
- Clean up your own mess.
- Don't take things that aren't yours.

Remember, in all the descriptions of the various kinds of power, the most important factor in having any form of power work is "in the eye of the beholder" — what counts is what others perceive. The way you handle yourself, your team members' interactions with you, your managerial and leadership style, etc., all influence people's perception of your power and hence the effect you have on their behavior.

This point is important enough to merit restating. Most of the people on a project team do not require management. Management is ensuring that things are done correctly, that the proper protocols are followed, that things are done according to the rules, "that all of the 'i's' are crossed and all of the 't's' are dot-

- Say you're sorry when you hurt somebody.
- Wash your hands before you eat.
- Flush.
- Warm cookies and cold milk are good for you.
- Live a balanced life — learn some and think some and draw and paint and sing and dance and play and work every day some.
- Take a nap every afternoon.
- When you go out into the world, watch out for traffic, hold hands and stick together.
- Be aware of wonder.
Robert Fulghum

ted." Management is a function of hierarchical authority. Most in-house project leaders have little, if any, hierarchical authority.

What project team members usually need is leadership. They need to know that someone is keeping watch over the "big picture," that someone is taking care of all of the interconnections throughout the project, that someone is dealing with all the issues that arise between the project and the rest of the organization. In short, they usually need you to be much more of a leader and much less of a manager. For some, this is a natural condition. They are "natural" leaders. For others, being an effective leader requires some conscious effort. Whichever you are, the characteristics of effective leaders are something you should be aware of and think about.

So, what do others want from you as a leader? What do people expect from their leaders? Numerous studies, involving thousands of managers, have singled out four personal characteristics that people admire, look for, and expect most from those they are willing to follow. As you read this, think about how you believe you would measure up in the eyes of your project team.

Honesty

The most frequently mentioned characteristic is honesty. People want a leader who is truthful with them and can be trusted. People judge your honesty by observing your behavior. Do you do what you say you are going to do, or not? Being honest is a game involving some risk. The leader must be the first to ante up.

A further refinement on the idea of honesty is not holding back. Contrary to the way many businesses are run, people aren't afraid of the truth, even if it's bad news. Most people would rather be told the business is in trouble than told everything is going well one day and be laid off due to a loss of business the next. They'd also like to be told what they, personally, can do to help get it out of trouble. In companies that have taken this approach rather than trying to cover it up for fear "our employees will panic and that will just make things worse," the response has been incredible. Case after case can be cited where employees, when told the true situation, rallied behind the tough decisions, closed ranks and forged ahead to success. Do some panic and jump ship? Sure. So what? Let them go. In a crisis situation, you need committed people not nervous ones.

> **PROCESS TIP**
> **Consistency is important**
> In meeting the honesty requirement, you need to be consistent and even-handed. It does no good to be enthusiastic and upbeat one day, and depressed and convinced the world is coming to an end the next. Learn to treat every situation as an opportunity to move ahead. Don't look for the down side of every problem, but, at the same time, don't sugar-coat a situation that is truly serious.
>
> Consistency is extremely important. Studies have shown that consistency of leadership behavior is one of the major fac-

tors in determining work-group effectiveness. Groups whose leader is a wildly swinging pendulum — good mood, positive outlook, supportive behavior one minute; depressed, angry, negative, and vindictive the next — have the lowest levels of performance effectiveness. Groups with a consistently positive leader perform the best, but, perhaps surprisingly, groups led by jerk who is consistently a jerk out-perform groups led by inconsistent leaders. People know what to expect from the latter two. The only thing from the first one is the unexpected.

So, if you want to be a jerk, go ahead. Just be a consistent jerk, and you'll still get better performance than if you bounce around all over the place.

Competence

The second most desired characteristic is competence. Before they will follow a leader, people like to believe that the person knows what he or she is doing. This does not necessarily involve functional or technical abilities. The specific kind of competence followers look for is affected by many factors, including the person's position in the hierarchy and economic condition of the company. As a project leader, you must also be willing to demonstrate your ability to recognize the competence or expertise of those around you. In doing so, you demonstrate your trust in others, not unlike the kind of trust you want others to feel toward you.

PROCESS TIP
Demonstrating competence is an on-going process
You must demonstrate your competence throughout the project. You need to demonstrate your competence as a planner, as a problem-solver, as a decision-maker, as a guide and mentor, as a collaborator, and, probably, as an expert in your own field of knowledge as it relates to project work. In all cases, your competence will be judged based on your actions and behavior far more than on your words. Be conscious of this fact and think about how your actions will be perceived.

Another aspect of Competence is your ability and willingness to take "acceptable risks." This means that you are perceived as being someone who is willing to try something new — within the limits of what is acceptable in your organization. It means you are perceived as being conscious of the fact that risk-taking is a part of most projects and you are willing to step up and take a chance. It does not mean that you are a maverick who takes unreasonable chances and thereby puts the project and the team in jeopardy. Everyone has different level of tolerance for risk-taking. You need to be aware of your own level of risk-tolerance and work on it if you discover it is either tool high or too low for your particular circumstances.

Direction

The third most frequently mentioned characteristic is a sense of direction. This trait should be natural for project leaders. The whole point of most projects is to go in a particular direction to achieve a specific goal. Leaders are expected to be forward-looking, to know where they are going and to be concerned about the future of the enterprise. People want to have a feeling for the destination the leader has in mind. The project leader's clarity about the target and the project objectives are akin to magnetic North on a compass. They pull the project team forward and keep it on course.

Of course, magnetic North tends to move around a bit on most projects. This doesn't change the importance of keeping the project pointed toward wherever "North" happens to be at the moment. Remember to keep team members appraised of changes in direction. This won't lessen their confidence in you. It will strengthen it because you're still providing the sense of focus they need to keep working.

> **PROCESS TIP**
> **Use the project goal as a focus for direction**
> Develop a habit of restating the project goal whenever you have a chance. If and when the goal changes, make the change clear and then continue to restate the new goal as long as it is valid. This makes a good opening for team meetings and discussions with individual working on the project. It also reinforces your personal focus on the final outcome of the project and shows a commitment to accomplishing the goal, whatever it is. In addition, restating the goal regularly reinforces your consistency.

Inspiration

Finally, people expect their leaders to be inspiring. It is important that the project leader be seen as enthusiastic, energetic, and positive about the project. Apple Computer manager Dave Patterson put it this way: "The leader is the evangelist for the dream."

Nora Watson, an editor, offers this view: " I think most people are looking for a calling, not a job. Most of us have jobs that are too small for our spirit." This is a reminder that you must help people on your project team find a greater sense of purpose and worth in their day-to-day life on the job. Effective project leaders inspire confidence in their project teams about the correctness, validity, and value of their projects. They do this by their personal conviction and commitment to the project and by their actions.

> **PROCESS TIP**
> **A little inspiration can go a long way**
> Not every project can be as inspiring as the moon landing. However, most projects do have some significant value that can be exploited. Look for anything that can be used to provide a sense of purpose larger than the personal agendas of team members. If you can't find anything, fall back on the fact that

> everybody, at one time or other, listens to WII-FM (What's In It For Me?)
>
> Even if you can find an overriding inspirational "hook" for your project also look for personal benefits for team members involved in it. This can be as personal as a sense of accomplishment or as mercenary as the chance at a promotion as a result of being able to demonstrate competence. Whatever the reason, finding a personal "win" for team members can be very inspirational.

Honesty, competence, and being forward-looking and inspirational are the essence of credibility. When you are perceived as trustworthy, as knowing what you're doing, as dynamic and sincere, and as having a sense of direction, others will see you as credible. When you have credibility, people are likely to follow you. They're even more likely to demonstrate a sense of commitment in their follow-through regardless of the power source you tap into. Both you and others will feel empowered.

A Little Leadership Theory

Over the last century, there have been a number of theories about leadership. We seem to be fascinated by the idea of "leaders" and are constantly seeking to understand what makes a good, or even a great, leader.

This, however, is a book on project management and not a book on leadership. So, this brief side trip into leadership theory is just that, a side trip

The "Great Person" Theory

During the first half of the twentieth century it was generally accepted that some people had innate characteristics which caused them to be great leaders. The emphasis of this way of thinking about leadership was on the character of the leader. The theory also stated that these characteristics were "inborn" and that environmental factors could cause them to surface but could not instill them in someone in whom they did not already exist. Early studies into leadership behavior, however, demonstrated that only a small percentage of leaders fit this stereotype and this particular theory has pretty well been discarded.

Theories X, Y, and Z

Showing up is 80 percent of life.

Woody Allen
Actor, director, comedian

Two conflicting theories did battle in the middle of the twentieth century:

- Theory X assumed that people are inherently lazy. They dislike work, avoid responsibility, and require and desire direction and control. This was the prevailing theory at the time. Unfortunately, this one still persists in far too many organizations. This is the "manager-as-dictator" approach that says that employees "check their brains at the door because, once they get to work, everything they do will be dictated by a manager or supervisor." Some organizations still hire for "sitability" — the ability to sit in one place and do the same mindless task over and over.

- As a counter to Theory X, Theory Y came along. It assumed that people are internally motivated to achieve goals that they find meaningful, view work as being as natural as play, and can accept responsibility for providing their own direction.

Theory Y relied heavily on the work of Abraham Maslow on motivation (described earlier in this chapter). Theory Y stressed the need to find the motivators that would encourage the behaviors desired.

There was even a Theory Z, developed by William G. Ouchi, that explored the differences between Japanese management styles and American management styles as they related to productivity.

Task vs. Relationship Behavior

> If you aren't fired with enthusiasm, you will be fired with enthusiasm
>
> **Vince Lombardi**
> 1913-1970
> American Professional
> Football Coach

Robert Blake and Jane Mouton developed their Managerial Grid theory to try to gain an understanding of why some individuals seem able to encourage and maintain high performance from their subordinates and peers, and others do not. The Grid is a means of displaying the characteristics of leadership behavior that influence the behavior of others.

- A leader with a high degree of emphasis on production, tasks, and control was said to have a directive leadership style.

- A leader with a high degree of emphasis on people development, relationships, and supportive environment was said to have a participative or supportive leadership style.

The Grid is arranged on two axes: Concern for People (the vertical axis) and Concern for Production (the horizontal axis). An individual's placement on the grid is indicated by a pair of numbers (from 1 to 9) indicating the strength of those two major concerns. The range runs from a 1,1 individual who has a very low concern for both aspects to the 9,9 individual with a high-level of concern for both.

Transactional (Situational)

> Different leadership situations require different leadership styles.
>
> **Paul Hersey and Kenneth Blanchard**
> Authors

We'll go into this one a bit more than the others. According to Paul Hersey, "The most effective leader is one who can participate in a leadership transaction, and flex their own style to fit the requirements of the subordinate and the situation."

The Situational Leadership model, first developed and presented by Paul Hersey and Ken Blanchard in 1969, has been updated to reflect new thinking about the relationship between the Style of the leader and the Development of the follower(s).

According to Blanchard and Hersey, three factors influence situational leadership:

- The leader's personal style as applied to a given situation.

- The situation in which the leadership transaction takes place.

- The development level of the follower. This is viewed in terms of his or her competence in relation to the situation at hand and their commitment to it. Commitment is defined as a combination of their confidence and motivation.

The descriptions of leadership styles are similar to those of Blake and Mouton in the Managerial Grid. They classify leadership behavior as either Directive or Supportive. Directive behavior is characterized as structured, controlling, and supervisory in nature. Directive leadership is defined as the extent to which the leader:

- Engages in one-way communication.
- Spells out the follower(s) role.
- Tells the follower(s):
  - What to do.
  - Where to do it.
  - When to do it.
  - How to do it.
- Closely supervises performance.

Supportive (participative) behavior is characterized by praise, the extensive use of listening skills, and facilitation. Supportive behavior is defined as the extent to which the leader:

- Engages in two-way communication.
- Provides support and encouragement.
- Facilitates interaction.
- Involves the follower(s) in decision-making.

The situation is the second factor that impacts leadership style. This includes both the climate of the organization and broad personal-development issues. Organizations have personalities. In some, participative behavior is not only encouraged, it is valued and rewarded. In others, directive behavior is the norm. The type of organization in which they find themselves will impact a leader's ability to use a range of leadership styles to full effectiveness. Within the larger organization, the ability and commitment of the work group affects the reaction to a particular situation, as does the type and degree of difficulty of the task at hand.

The third factor impacting leadership style is the needs of the follower. Things that will impact these needs include the follower's degree of:

- Need for independence.
- Need to participate in decisions.
- Identification with company goals.
- Personal commitment and motivation.

The Situational Leadership model goes on to describe four basic styles of leadership:

- Directing: Providing detailed instructions and watching to see that they are carried out.
- Coaching: Providing some instruction but mainly encouragement.
- Supporting: Providing mainly support.
- Delegating: Providing very little in the way of either instruction or support.

All of these factors are combined with the recognition that individuals will exhibit varying levels of competence and commitment in different situations. The two factors that the Situational Leadership model focuses on are:

- Competence, defined as the person's current skill, not their potential to develop a skill.

- Commitment, defined as a combination of confidence and motivation. This is the person's self-assuredness, their belief that they can do the task well without supervision coupled with motivation — their interest and enthusiasm for doing the task.

As with leadership styles, Situational Leadership recognized four levels of follower development. Each of the levels requires a different leadership style.

If the follower's development level is low competence but high commitment, the leader needs to provide direction — the Directing style.

If the follower's development shows some competence and a low level of commitment, the leader needs to provide both direction and support. This is the Coaching style.

If the follower's development demonstrates a high degree of competence but the commitment varies, the leader should provide support to bolster the commitment — the Supporting style.

If the development level shows both high competence and high commitment, the leader needs to provide very little direction and support. This is the Delegation style.

The key point of the Situational Leadership model is that the leadership needs change from situation to situation, even though the same people may be involved. A simple example of this might be someone who is extremely competent in a particular area. As long as the work requires that skill, the leader can delegate the work with a high degree of confidence that it will be done well. This same individual, however, placed in a situation that requires other skills, knowledge, and abilities may be on the bottom of the scale of development and require a highly directive leadership style.

How Teams Grow and Change Over Time

> The whole object of organization is to get cooperation, to give each individual the benefit of the knowledge and all the experience of all individuals.
>
> **H.M. Barksdale**
> Management Executive
> Committee, DuPont

Maintaining the project team as a team is a significant part of the project leader's job. So is dealing with conflicts and problems between team members and between the team and other functional areas. And so is ensuring that individual issues do not prevent progress on the project. This responsibility is actually a significant part of your overall project leadership responsibilities. Understanding how groups grow over time and ultimately (given enough time and shared experiences) develop into teams can be helpful in dealing with this.

One thing to keep in mind here is that many projects are completed by ad hoc groups that do not develop into "real" teams. These groups are made up of individuals that come together on a task-by-task basis rather than for the entire project. These groups rarely exhibit true team behavior. Becoming a "team" requires that the group have the time to develop some level of interdependence and trust. This can only happen when the group spends time together.

The Team Growth Model

Project teams are task teams. They exist to complete a task, and, once that task is completed, they disband. This task-orientation can create some problems on the interpersonal level. This may be particularly true on highly technical projects with technically-oriented team members.

Most ongoing teams, such as work groups or work teams, will develop a style and procedures for dealing with interpersonal problems and conflicts.

These procedures usually have, as a primary element, the continuing "health" of team members and of the team as a whole. Task teams frequently suppress interpersonal problems in favor of the task. This can lead to serious problems over the life of a project.

As the project leader, you have responsibilities for both aspects of the team — task and interpersonal — and a model of how teams develop and change over time can be helpful in fulfilling these dual responsibilities.

There are several models of how groups develop over time. Most illustrate a series of stages that groups pass through on their way to maturity. The model shown here is a combination of several group-growth and development models and shows specifically how group development will impact a project team. This model is a combination of elements from the work of George O. Charrier (Cog's Ladder), Bruce W. Tuckman (Tuckman's Model), Robert S. Blake and Jane S. Mouton (The Managerial Grid), and numerous other professionals concerned with the developmental sequence of small groups. These models have all been tested over several decades and with thousands of groups in virtually every culture. The models have proven to be valid regardless of the cultural surroundings and regardless of the purpose of the groups.

There are four stages in this model based on Tuckman's Model:

- Forming
- Storming
- Norming
- Performing

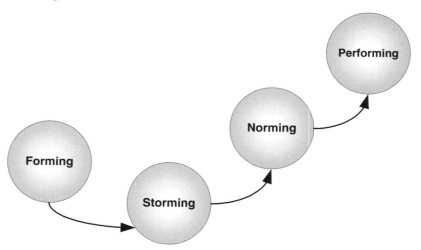

Each stage is characterized by specific behaviors. It is these observable behaviors that are the leader's clues about where the group is on the model, and about how to help the group progress to the next stage in its development.

The model looks at two basic, and broad, behavioral dimensions: Task and personal interaction. Using these two dimensions, it looks at how individuals on the team and the team as a whole behave in each of the four stages of the model.

The task dimension is concerned with how individuals and teams focus and perform on the tasks set before the group. It is concerned with the behaviors that move the group toward achieving its goals and accomplishing its tasks in each stage.

The interaction dimension is concerned with how individuals and the team perform on the interpersonal level. It is concerned with the behaviors that are directed toward building and maintaining the group as a working unit and with achieving and maintaining member satisfaction.

Each stage is characterized by its own distinctive behaviors. It is these behaviors that the project leader can affect by adjusting his or her own behavior to meet the leadership needs of the group. (See the discussion on Situational Leadership in the previous section.)

Another characteristic of the stages is the range of the level of participation by team members — at some stages, participation is fairly even by everyone; at others, the gap between high participators and low participators is much greater.

The descriptions of behavior at each stage are probably overstated for most in-house project groups. They're based on the assumption that the group members do not really know each other when the team comes together. However, there will be some similarity to almost every project team, if for no other reason than that the unique task of a project will impact the interplay among the members.

Participation Levels at Each Stage

"Involvement" in this context differs from "commitment" in the same sense as the pig's and the chicken's roles in one's breakfast of ham and eggs. The chicken was involved — the pig was committed.

Anonymous

This figure illustrates how the range of participation changes at each stage of the model. In the first stage (Forming), participation is fairly even by all participants. As the group moves into the second stage (Storming), the gap between high and low levels of participation expands greatly with some individuals almost dropping out of the group and others taking a very strong role. As the group progresses through the last two stages, the range of participation narrows until the team reaches its optimum range of participation.

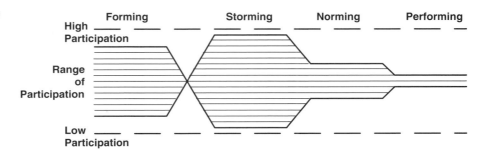

Forming

We are, by nature, a tribal people.

Linda Ellerbee
Broadcast journalist

There are two aspects to the Forming stage. In the first, the group is created. The members come together for the first time in the context of the project. This stage usually occurs during the pre-work and planning activities of a project. The team meets for the first time. They spend some time getting to know each other — introducing themselves and describing their backgrounds and reasons for being there. The second aspect comes into play when the group actually starts to focus on the task. The project goal gets identified and clarified. Major tasks and responsibilities get described. This group is not a team. It is still a collection of individuals or small groups. They are dependent on the leader for direction.

In the first aspect of the Forming stage, members are trying to determine "how I fit into the group." They may tend to be somewhat closed about feelings and reluctant to share concerns or fears. In many cases, they also do not share their questions about the task.

Typical behaviors in this aspect of the Forming stage include:

• Members relying on broad stereotyping to help categorize each other: Engineers, salespeople, accountants, etc.

• Cliques and sub-groups may form around individuals with similar interests, professional credentials, etc. These sub-groups, if they form, become important in later stages.

• Hidden agendas tend to remain hidden. Individuals keep their personal desires for the group to themselves.

• The need for group approval is strong. This is a normal social need most people feel in new situations. Most of us don't go into a new group intending to be rejected by that group. We tend to put on our "Sunday manners" until we figure out how we fit and whether we want to stay.

• The need for group identity is low. There is no real sense of "team." The group is not a team and it has little sense of being a team.

• Members participate actively and conflict is usually either absent or very superficial. At this stage, people have little stake in the team and are more concerned with being accepted as individuals.

PROCESS TIP

T-Shirts and coffee mugs don't make a team

Some companies are famous for their T-Shirt wardrobes. They attempt to "force" a team into being by bringing everyone a t-shirt at the first meeting. All this does is create a bunch of people in the same shirt. It has no effect on the group becoming a team. Teams develop over time. You can't force the behaviors by dressing everybody alike. You can certainly talk about becoming a team but don't try to shortcut the development process. It will backfire. The development and adoption of an identity symbol or name is a late-stage Norming or a Performing stage activity. Wait until you get there.

The second aspect of the Forming stage is the definition of why the group exists. As the group moves past the initial "getting acquainted" activities, the reason for the group's existence becomes the focus. This is where the involvement of the team in the planning of the project can be of great benefit in helping the individuals begin to become a team. As they work on the project pre-work and planning, they will help develop the group's goals and objectives.

Task-oriented groups spend more time at this stage while social groups spend very little.

This activity will almost inevitably lead to the second stage of development, the Storming stage. This is a part of the natural evolution of a team. It may not be the most fun thing a group can go through but it is necessary. The groundwork for the Storming stage is laid in this part of the Forming stage.

- The cliques and sub-groups that formed around similar interests will begin to wield influence. As the group's purpose is discussed, the stakes go up and sub-groups will begin to jockey for positions of influence over the group's direction and purpose.

- These sub-groups will likely flow and merge as they find shared purposes. Alliances will begin to form as the struggle for control escalates.

- Hidden agendas begin to emerge as individuals and sub-groups try to verbalize group objectives that are most satisfying to themselves.

- At this stage, group identity is still low. At this point the group is still a fragmented collection of individuals and small groups, not yet a team.

- The need for approval declines as members begin taking risks by stating positions and opinions and by displaying commitment.

- There is usually fairly active participation by all members.

The time spent in this phase varies widely. The easier the objectives are to define, the faster the group will move through this phase. When the purpose comes from outside the group (e.g., a project team with an assigned goal), the group will still discuss it in order to gain understanding and build commitment. Trying to impose a goal without allowing for discussion only puts off the inevitable. Allow for this discussion time and make any minor (or major) adjustments to the goal that are needed. The group also needs to know that the purpose agreed upon is important within the framework and nature of the group.

PROCESS TIP
The leadership style required at the Forming stage
In order to assist the team to move from one stage to the next, the leader must focus on certain mixes of behavior at each stage. As the team moves through he various stages of development, the leader should keep focused on where the group should be headed — not on where they've been.

In the first two stages, the team will expand a great deal of energy on the task aspects of relationships and therefore the leader should focus on the interaction aspects.

In the last two stages, the team will be more interactive and will require less assistance on that front. The leader should keep a "weather eye" on the interactions but should mainly focus on helping the team stay focused on its tasks.

During the Forming stage, the leadership style is primarily directive. Not in the sense of being a dictator but more in the sense of providing a set of guidelines. Consider the following suggestions for helping the group work through the Forming stage and the transition.

- Provide time and a structure in which the group can get acquainted.

- Introduce the task and guide the discussion about how it should be done.

- Be ready to clarify misconceptions about the task and to lay out your vision of the roles, responsibilities, and division of the overall project into specific tasks.

- Constantly test for agreement as the discussion progresses, begin to build the parts of the common vision.

- Seek input from individuals and groups about how they view their roles, their contribution, and their estimates about time and resources necessary to complete their activities.

- Restate agreements, check for hesitation or uncertainty.

There are a couple of fairly common problems that can occur at this stage.

- The trust level is low, members are too quiet, fail to share or ask questions. If this appears to be a problem try allowing extra time for socializing, schedule pre-meeting meetings, talk with members individually, structure sharing activities, and model the desired behavior.

- Members fail to fully understand the mission, task, role relationships, and leader expectations, and don't ask questions about them. If this happens, try putting this information in writing, display it, act as a teacher, and meet one-on-one to solicit reactions and questions.

Storming

A little rebellion now and then is a good thing.
Thomas Jefferson
1743-1826
Third President of the United States

This is the most uncomfortable stage in the group's life. Task-oriented groups may tend to try to ignore the interaction aspects of this stage. They may try to subordinate everything to the task. This can greatly prolong the time a group spends in this stage.

Members vie for influence. Conflicts occur. Confusion about roles and role boundaries may surface. Members may jockey for power over the group's actions. Disagreements with the leader and with other members are common and can range from issues regarding goals, methods, resources, and priorities to standards, values, and personal style.

Group-building and maintenance roles are important. The harmonizer looks for ways to defuse or at least de-personalize conflicts, the compromiser looks for common ground among differing ideas, the gatekeeper tries to maintain a balance between the needs of individuals and the needs of the group.

Some of the characteristics of the Storming stage are:

- Activity is usually characterized as competitive. Individuals and sub-groups compete for control with each other and with the leader. A member may try to rationalize his or her own position and to convince the group to take the actions he or she feels is appropriate. Other members may come across as closed minded and they may be accused of not listening.

- Conflict is at its highest level during this stage.

- A struggle for leadership (or for influence over the direction of the group) usually occurs that involves all cliques or sub-groups.

- Typical attempts to resolve the conflicts include voting, compromise, and seeking arbitration from outside the group. Consensus is the last thing on anybody's mind.

- Very little, if any, team spirit is present.

- Some members, who contributed willingly in the Forming stage, remain completely silent during this phase. Other members, who may have been quiet earlier, relish the opportunity to compete and attempt to dominate the group. This is the point where the widest range of participation usually occurs — some are in the thick of it and others are on the sidelines.

- Hidden agendas become public. As individuals and groups compete for control, their interests become more obvious.

- Feedback can be stinging. Criticism, which may have been completely absent in the Forming stage, now emerges as a major force. It can get quite personal. This is one thing you, as the project leader, need to monitor quite closely. If things start to get too personal, you need to step in and re-focus the group on issues and away from personalities.

- Creative suggestions for compromises or solutions tend to fall flat. They may be seen as a bid for recognition and power. Very little constructive work is accomplished during this stage. The group must resolve these issues before they can actively focus on getting anything done.

- There is still no strong group identity. Instead, there may be several small groups, each with its own identity.

- The need for structure is stronger at this stage than at any other. The leader must lead. Process is important. Use the planning tools as a means of focusing the group.

Groups that never get past this stage may still be able to fulfill their task, but the work that comes out of Storming-stage activity is usually not very good.

PROCESS TIP
The leadership required in the Storming stage
During the Storming stage, the leadership style is primarily one of coaching. You can't smother the conflict but you can help the team work it out.

First of all, expect Storming to occur. It is a perfectly natural part of a group's development. One of the reasons primarily social groups rarely accomplish much of real worth in terms on tasks is that they try to avoid the "unpleasantness" of this stage. As a result, they rarely make it to the next, more productive stages.

Storming is the group's "de-bugging" mechanism. One of the best things you, as a leader, can do is to reassure the team that this is a natural part of becoming a high-performance team.

• Work on bringing the reasons for conflict to the surface. Whether this is done in the context of the group individually with members is the leader's choice. Be aware that some people simply cannot deal with conflict publicly.

• Always go for the underlying issue in a conflict, not the surface symptoms.

The most common problems in this stage are:

• Members are fearful of conflict and resist sharing openly, yet hidden conflicts and agendas block the group. If you see this one, try working individually with members to deal with reasons for conflict. Raise issues on agendas: "Fuzzy role boundaries cause confusion."

• Highly-charged emotional confrontations make the group very tense and uncomfortable; negative feelings block task achievement. If this happens frequently, try to separate the emotional and the substantive conflict issues. Act as a "third party" to mediate disputes. Move the discussion into the negotiation arena and search for workable solutions.

Norming

> Make it clear that everyone is on the same team. Avoid practices that make it clear that some are on the first team and others are part of another.
>
> **Paul S. George**
> University of Florida

This is the end of the line for most short-term project teams. The transformation from a Norming stage team to a Performing stage team usually requires more time and intensity of involvement than occurs on most in-house projects. In the Norming stage, members are willing to change preconceived ideas or opinions on the basis of facts. Individuals actively ask questions and team spirit begins to build. These groups have resolved most of their interpersonal issues and have many of the characteristics of a real team. Members are mutually supportive and team spirit is evident. Many groups stabilize at this stage and maintain their performance over a long period of time. The transition from Storming to Norming comes about as a result of the resolution of conflicts in the Storming stage. This means agreements are being made — either explicit or implicit — and norms are being established.

Members begin to feel increasingly comfortable with each other. The team begins to behave like a team. Expectations are clearer and energy begins to focus almost exclusively on the task.

Some of the characteristics of the Norming stage are:

• Perhaps the most notable is that an attitude change takes place. Members give up attempts to control and substitute active participation toward achieving group goals. One of the most obvious signs of this is usually an increase in listening and a decreasing in the strident stating of positions and opinions.

- Real progress toward the goal becomes evident as the energy of the group shifts from power struggles to task. Now the real work can be done.

- Leadership will tend to be shared. Leadership is more of a function than a role. The person with the expertise to solve the problem at hand becomes the de facto leader. New problem, new leader. The group is likely to use the talents of any individual who can contribute. Practical creativity is high and creative suggestions are solicited.

- Group identity begins to become important. The members begin to think of themselves as part of a team. The range of participation also narrows and a better balance is achieved.

- Conflict is dealt with as a group problem rather than a win-lose battle between individuals.

- An optimum solution or work product can result from Norming-stage activity.

Exercises that enhance cooperation are very helpful in this stage. Those that enhance competition tend to disrupt and push the group back. At this stage it may be very difficult to integrate a new member without sending the group backward along the development path.

PROCESS TIP
The leadership required in the Norming stage
During the Norming stage the leadership role is primarily that of a developer. The individuals and sub-groups have resolved the majority of their interaction problems. Now they need help getting the work done.

- Help the team stay focused on the task. The project goal statement will help with this as will other project control tools.

- Formalize the agreements between individuals and groups which will assist in accomplishing their parts of the task.

- Help resolve task-related problems. Technical issues, resource issues, schedules, and alternative approaches to problems are the focus of the group's energy. Provide the assistance needed to resolve them.

- Barrier-bashing is the project leader's main job. The team is performing well on the task, your job is to get the road-blocks down so they can continue.

The most common problem in this stage are:

- If a new member is introduced into the team, this will usually upset the agreed-upon norms. This problem is fairly likely if only part of the team was brought together for the planning activities and the remaining team members are being added after planning is completed. The introduction of a new member is the most common reason for disruption in a team. The leader must take an active role in integrating the new member into the team. Treat this situation as normal and expected. Help the new member to find his or her place and assist members to adjust roles and responsibilities as needed.

Performing

> When a team outgrows individual performance and learns team confidence, excellence becomes a reality.
> **Joe Paterno**
> College Football Coach

This is as good as it gets for a team. The overall feeling in this stage is that, "We don't always agree on everything but we do respect each other's views and we agree to disagree."

The norms developed in the previous stage become very strong and binding. Members are seldom distracted from the task. Individually, and collectively, members are highly productive and are able to quickly resolve problems and disputes when they occur. Goals are achieved and the group makes rapid progress toward desired ends.

Some of the characteristics of the Performing phase are:

- There is usually a high level of group morale and loyalty. The team has become more important than the individuals. Members tend to think of themselves in relation to the team.

- Relationships are empathetic. Individual members are more aware of, and therefore more willing to understand, each other's problems as they relate to the task. Performing-stage teams can sometimes look a little like a support group. Members tend to have a high level of personal commitment to each other and it may well extend beyond the confines of the task.

- The need for group approval is absent since all members accept and approve of all others. This is the "they may be a weirdo but they're our weirdo and we like them just fine the way they are" attitude. This can allow some teams in this stage of development to tolerate some fairly outlandish behavior on the part of their members. Both individuality and creativity are high. Members actively support each other and contribute willingly to problem-solving efforts.

- Sub-groups are absent. The barriers between individuals that were mostly based on areas of expertise have been essentially removed.

- The group may create an identity symbol. If it's going to happen, this is where it will occur.

- Participation is as evenly balanced as it will ever be. Not only is it balanced, it is also as effective and efficient as it will get.

- The need for structure depends on whether the group is task or learning oriented. Learning groups at this stage have no need for formal structure. Task groups at this stage usually operate within a very loose, informal structure.

At this stage the group is strongly "closed." If a new member is introduced, the feelings of camaraderie and esprit de corps will be destroyed since the group must regress to an earlier stage and then grow again to the performing stage, bringing the new member along with them.

PROCESS TIP
The Leadership required in the Performing stage

The leadership style for the Performing stage is that of a consultant. The leader steps in when asked or when a problem becomes evident.

- Watch for breakdowns in spirit, goal-clarity, and cohesion. These are the areas where "burnout" is most likely to appear first. The more task-driven the individuals, the more likely some burnout symptoms will appear.

- Keep the team "tuned and energized." A little cheerleading never hurts. In this stage, it is a major leader activity.

- Protect the team from, or help them deal with, distractions that originate form outside and hinder performance. At this stage, much of the project leader's time is spent running ahead of the team getting things out of their way.

A couple of the more common problems in this stage are:

- Performance begins to lag due to fatigue and burnout. Try easing off on expectations a bit. Provide breaks from the routine such as an off-site event or time off. Encourage the use of available time off. In smaller ways, break up the routine with short impromptu gatherings. This may be a good time for that unexpected pizza party at that place down the street.

- A major change in the larger environment upsets resources or time lines. If this happens, collect and share accurate information to dispel rumors. Identify how the change will affect the work of the group. Give people a chance to vent. Accept their negative feelings about the change. This provides some catharsis. As a group, reassess the goals and time lines and make adjustments as required.

Why Groups Move Up and Down the Model

Reasons why a group may move, or not move, from one stage to another vary according to the stage. For instance, the transition from Forming to Storming seems to occur when any single member desires it. They can simply say, "I think we should ...." and the group will usually move into the discussions that are part of stage two.

Growing from Storming to Norming requires individuals to stop defending their own views and to risk the possibility of being wrong. They have to stop talking and start listening to each other. Norming-stage activity demands a little humility.

The step from Norming to Performing demands that a member trust him- or herself and other group members. And to trust is to risk a breach of that trust. The transition to the final stage of development usually requires that the team be together for an extended period of time. It can also help if they've "weathered a few storms" together and learned to depend on each other.

Adding a new member, or members, seems to be the most common reason for a group to go backward on the model. This is especially true if the group is in the Norming or Performing stages. The addition of a new member during these stages disrupts the "group personality." The new member hasn't shared the group experiences that led the team through its development. As a result, the group must revert to an earlier phase and assist the new member, or members, to develop along with the group. An enthusiastic new member, one who has a stake in the group's purpose, can proceed through the steps fairly rapidly. An opinionated new member, one with a strong hidden agenda, can slow the process considerably.

One of the most beneficial activities for the group occurs in the first two stages: Development of a shared goal. If the project goal the group develops is clear and motivating, the group will use this as a touchstone in all subsequent stages as a means of focusing group activity. The Storming stage will be resolved when the entire group has reconciled its various hidden agendas and personal needs with the project goal. The Norming stage will focus on implementation — working on achieving that goal. The Performing stage will focus on the group's successes, and the personal and group sense of achievement and worth. If the same team undertakes a new project soon after the first one is completed, they can carry over much of their group development and significantly shorten the "ramp-up" time for the new project.

There are certain clues you can look for that indicate when a group is ready to move (or is moving) from one stage or development to another. In the move from Forming to Storming, the most common trigger is when someone in the group simply asks, "Why are we here?" When the focus shifts from social interactions to task-related interactions, Storming starts.

The ability to listen seems to be the most important trait in helping groups move from Storming to Norming. In some cases, where the group as a whole wants to get into the Norming stage but some members try to stay rooted in Storming, groups have been known to reject those members. On the other hand, this transition can be more or less permanently blocked by a strong member or sub-group.

The transition from Norming to Performing usually requires unanimous agreement among group members. This transition, if it occurs, marks a significant change in group dynamics and it may occur over a period of time.

Overall team cohesiveness seems to depend on how well group members can relate in the same phase at the same time. A group will proceed through the stages only as far as its individual members are willing to grow. Each member must be willing to give up something, usually some degree of individuality or independence, at each step in order to make the move to the next step. To grow from Forming to Storming, for example, each member must give up the comfort of non-threatening social topics and risk the possibility of conflict. By beginning to focus on the "what" and "how" of the task at hand, the likelihood of conflict increases. Moving into the Norming stage requires members to put aside a continued discussion of the group's purpose and commit to a purpose with which they may not totally agree.

Negotiation

Perfectionists make poor negotiators. If you hold out for the perfect deal, you'll likely never close, you'll almost always have to leave something on the table.

Lewis D. Eigen
Executive Vice President,
University Research Corp

Negotiation skills are a necessary part of the toolkit of any successful project leader. At some point, you will negotiate for resources, assistance, expertise, time, almost everything connected with your project. The following is a very brief summary of the main points from the best book on Negotiation I have ever found: *Getting to Yes: Negotiating Agreement Without Giving In*, by Roger Fisher and William Ury, Penguin Books, 1981. For more on the subject get this book. Not only is it a great text on negotiation, its a pretty enjoyable read. And, even though it was published two decades ago, it's still relevant.

Negotiation is a two-way process. It usually involves a significant amount of give-and-take. When difficulties arise, you can try for agreement in several ways. You can give in to the other person — they win, you lose. You can try to smooth over the disagreement — this is trying to make the problem go away. You can try to suppress the points of contention — if you're in a position of sufficient power, this may work. You can try splitting the difference — this is a straight-down-the-middle compromise. You can try arguing — if you're loud enough, you might get your way. You can try persuading — you know, sell, sell, sell. Or you can try to find common ground on which to bargain and negotiate differences.

As a project leader, the difficulty of getting another person or department to adopt your point of view or go along with your requests may be complicated by the fact that you lack the "power of the hierarchy." You may lack formal authority. You may not be the other person's boss. You may not have the right to command or to give orders that others are expected to follow.

One way of getting your way is to provide a sound rationale for your position. This is the power of intellect or expertise. People will generally go along with someone who is perceived as being an expert on the issue under discussion. Showing your expertise involves communicating your rationale with reason and logic. Within a single functional area, this tactic can be useful, but project leaders usually must operate in more than one functional area. It's difficult to have (or to be perceived as having) expertise across many disciplines. You should, however, try to have a working knowledge of a number of functional areas. At the very least, you need to have some fundamental understanding of each area with which you must work. Truly effective project leaders are usually seen by people in other functional areas as knowing something about their discipline and appreciating their point of view.

The problem with trying to rely on logic and reason in managing differences is that reason does not always prevail. Logic, data, and reason do not always point to a clear solution agreeable to everyone. Competing points of view cannot always be resolved by logic. This is particularly true when each is based on a sound rationale. An example might be people from very different technical backgrounds (for example computer programming and marketing, or financial analysis and production) who must arrive at a common course of action. The backgrounds they bring to the discussion are so divergent that satisfaction on common ground may be very difficult.

Facts, Goals, Methods, Values

Most negotiations revolve around one or more of the following issues:

- Facts

- Goals
- Methods
- Values

As you move down this list, the difficulty of reaching an agreement increases until you get to the issue of Values, where disagreements can rarely be resolved.

- Facts are verifiable. They can be examined, tested, and agreed upon from sound evidence. Agreeing about the facts of a situation is not usually very difficult. If everyone agrees with the premise used to develop the facts, agreement should be easy. For example, if everyone agrees that marketing's research shows that the company's market share is indeed lower than it was last year at this time, you have agreement on that fact.

- Goals are a little rougher. If the goal being negotiated is based on facts, the task is much simpler. Getting agreement about a goal usually requires that everyone agree that the goal is supported by the facts, that it is worth achieving, and that everyone commit to it. Using the same example as above, if everyone agrees that market share is down, it is probably not too much of a stretch to gain agreement about a goal to increase market share. The negotiation will probably focus on determining the target increase and the time line.

- The majority of negotiations around projects center on methods — the "how" of the project. For every goal there are likely to be as many ideas about how to reach it as there are people involved. Logic, practicality, difficulty, expense, etc., are all things that have to be considered when seeking agreement about methods. Still sticking with the market share example, several methods might achieve the goal of increasing market share. The company could lower prices. It could increase advertising. It could change marketing strategies to open new markets. It could introduce new products into existing markets. It could...you get the picture.

- Values are generally not negotiable. Our values are so much a part of us that, for the most part, we wouldn't change them even if we could. The good news is, people's personal values don't often come into conflict with a project, but if they do, trying to negotiate an agreement that results in someone changing, or compromising, a personal value will most likely end with no resolution and can have significant negative consequences. Most people don't like having their values questioned. This is why your parents told you to never argue politics or religion. If you encounter a value-based issue, try to find some way around it without having to confront the individual.

    One example of a potential values conflict that could arise on a project is the issue of overtime. If the project is running behind schedule and there is a need to get back on track, one option might be to work two or three Saturdays and a few late evenings. For many, this is not a problem, particularly if they are compensated for the extra time. However, some people simply do not see this as a viable alternative. Their value system places more importance on time with family than time at work. The occasional late evening or partial Saturday is not a problem. However, a series of them begins to raise the specter of conflict with deeply held values that some people are unwilling to compromise. This may be something that cannot be resolved. Your best bet may be to shake hands, agree to disagree, and get on with your life.

Four Tactics for Building Agreement

The old idea of a good bargain was a transaction in which one man got the better of another. The new idea of a good contract is a transaction which is good for both parties.
Louis D. Brandies U.S. Supreme Court Justice

According to Fisher and Ury, there are four tactics that can help build agreements in which all parties participate and where they can feel they've achieved a good resolution.

The first three should be viewed as needing to be done in order. The final point surrounds the other three. These tactics are:

1. Create a common ground
2. Enlarge areas of agreement
3. Gather and use information
4. Focus on issues, not personalities

Create a Common Ground

Forming a strong foundation is the most important step in building any lasting agreement. What do you and the other person already have in common? On what do you already agree? What are you both trying to accomplish? In the case of projects, ideally the project goal should sum up the common ground. This is almost the exact opposite of the way many negotiations start. In far too many instances, the parties come together, stake out opposing positions, and begin to batter their way to the center. This approach is based on identifying that center first and working outward from it to a larger agreement.

You want to focus on what you have in common, not on where you disagree. Pushing people apart at the beginning of a dialogue rarely helps build an atmosphere of cooperation. Agreeing on a common ground highlights the important interdependencies. When my success depends on your success, and vice versa, we are both more likely to work through our differences than when our successes are completely independent.

This is just one more reason why you should work so hard at the beginning of the project — in the pre-work and planning activities. You want to involve all the affected parties in determining the project's goal and creating a work plan and schedule that underscores the critical interdependencies.

Enlarge Areas of Agreement

Once you've agreed on a common starting point, the second step is to build on and expand the common ground you have established. You have to move out of the "selling your idea" or "if I can only convince them" mode. If possible, you should try to find some benefit for the other party if they agree with your proposal. In some cases, this can be as simple as "With your help, the project will get done. Without it, it won't." If the project itself is important to the person or to the company in general, this is often a sufficient benefit all by itself. In other cases, the benefit may need to be more personal or more specific. Many of these benefits can be uncovered by doing a thorough stakeholder analysis up front.

The process of expanding on common ground usually takes some time. You need to allow each party to get their ideas on the table. Too often, participants in a conflict get involved in attacking and defending, and devote almost no time to listening and trying to build an agreement. This agreement-building process is facilitated when we:

- Allow each person to state his or her position without interruption.

- Allow a brief period of time for questions of clarification only.

- Ask "How can we each get what we want?"

When arguing is leading nowhere (which can happen fairly quickly), the skilled negotiator will switch to what are called "statements of possible exchange." For example, "If you would be willing to do X, I would be willing to do Y." This transforms an argument into a discussion and a potential deadlock into a probable settlement.

Gather and Use Information   Working through fundamental issues together helps to create a working foundation for discussion. Some of these issues are:

- Who is involved or concerned with this issue?

- Who can help resolve the conflict?

- Is all the information needed to resolve the conflict available?

If you cannot agree which parties are really involved or concerned with the issue, some important points of view may not be represented in the negotiations. The needs of these people will not be represented in the proposed solutions and you may have the beginnings of another conflict.

The issue of the information needed to resolve the conflict is a critical one. If insufficient or inaccurate information is used to reach an agreement, the agreement is flawed from the outset. Be sure to have all the available information when you are in a negotiation situation. This can be the key to success.

You may find yourself in a conflict over a problem, for example a scheduling conflict that you and the other party can't resolve. When you have actually reached a dead end, don't continue to try to batter an agreement out of someone. It may soon escalate from negotiation to assault. The good news about working on projects inside an organization is that you can usually find someone higher in the organization to make the decision if necessary. (Does the term "project sponsor" ring any bells?) When you are really stuck — when you and the other party simply can't come to an agreement that will resolve the problem — try for an agreement to take it to the next level.

Focus on Issues, Not Personalities   It is absolutely crucial to depersonalize conflict. When someone feels they must defend themselves from personal attack, they typically react with one of the two aspects of what psychologists call the "fight or flight" response:

- They fight back, which only escalates the disagreement and makes finding common ground much more difficult. In a fight, the other person's energies are devoted to getting back at you, not on solving the problem.

- They flee. They may not physically leave the room but they're gone nonetheless. When this happens, you don't get people to commit their energies to problem-solving. Even if they agree on an action, there will be no real commitment to follow through once you're out of sight.

One of the best ways to focus on issues and not on personalities is to be future-focused. "What are we going to do about this?" rather than "Why can't you be more reasonable?" or "Who got us into this mess?" By being future-focused you emphasize building agreement on a future action rather than on blaming each other for past problems. Remember, everyone has 20/20 hindsight. This does not mean you don't want to explore the past for insights into the causes of the problem, but emphasizing the past often leads to one person having to defend his or her actions, or blame and scapegoat someone else. "What are we going to do to ensure that this doesn't happen again?" is a statement of allies against a problem, not against each other.

Negotiation Techniques

Most successful project leaders are effective negotiators. Much has been written about how successful negotiators behave — what they do and what they try to avoid doing as they build agreements between people. Management consultant Clifford Bolster reports in his studies that technically trained managers frequently discover, much to their discomfort, that they rely way too heavily on reasoning and logic in trying to get others to do what they want. He observes, "Negotiation is a process that may be used when logical reasoning has run its course, and represents a critical skill for the technical manager today."

The objective of negotiation is to reach an agreement that satisfies all parties. Satisfaction is an emotional, not a logical, experience. Negotiation is not an optimal, dispassionate problem-solving experience. Analysis and reasoning are not the only skills needed to determine the cause of the problem and to reach the solution that has the best chance of solving the problem.

By effectively managing disagreements through negotiation, you will achieve positive outcomes from the inevitable conflicts which arise in projects. You can get the job done most effectively when you build agreements that energize participants. Conflict, in and of itself, is not a bad thing. People don't usually come into conflict over things they don't care about. Conflict can create some of the energy that is vital to managing projects from inception to completion. It's when conflict is allowed to get out of control, or when it begins to get into the realm of personalities, that it becomes a problem.

Anticipating the sources of conflict and understanding the ebb and flow of conflicts in a project environment will increase your ability to harness this energy. Paradoxically, finding — or, if necessary, creating — areas of agreement is an important starting place for negotiating differences. By effectively managing disagreements through negotiation, you will achieve positive outcomes from the inevitable conflicts which arise in projects. You can get the job done most effectively when you build agreements that energize participants.

Conflict, in and of itself, is not a bad thing. People don't usually come into conflict over things they don't care about. Conflict can create some of the energy that is vital to managing projects from inception to completion. This is particularly true in conflicts over methods — "how we're going to do this." It's when conflict is allowed to get out of control, or when it begins to get into the realm of personalities, that it becomes a problem. Conflict that escalates into a personality battle is one of the most destructive things that can happen to a project team. Remember, project teams don't blow up over technical issues. Teams blow up over interpersonal issues. Anticipating the sources of conflict and understanding the ebb and flow of conflicts in a project environment will increase your ability to harness this energy.

Communication

Communication is not just words, paint on canvas, math symbols or the equations and models of scientists: It is the interrelation of human beings trying to escape lonliness, trying to share experience, trying to implant ideas.

William M. Narsteller
Advertising Execuitve

Of all the skills a project leader needs to be effective, communication is probably the most important. Without good, two-way communication in and around the project, trouble is almost guaranteed.

Most of the material in this section deals with face-to-face, verbal, interpersonal communication between the project leader and project team members and stakeholders in the project community. There is, however, a new wrinkle in the communication matrix in many organizations — telecommunication technology. In the broadest sense, this technology falls into two categories: Voice and text.

The advances that have been made in the last few years and the ones that are still coming at an alarming rate, have, in some cases, greatly complicated life for some in-house project managers. This is particularly true for those of you in larger organizations with more than one physical location. If you compound this by being in a technology company, the picture gets even more complicated.

Here's the deal: Projects work best when the people working on them can have regular face-to-face contact. Unfortunately, the new communication technologies are very pervasive. They're everywhere. And some companies actually seem to believe that e-mail is just as good as a person-to-person meeting. It simply isn't true. E-mail is a wonderful tool. It allows us to communicate with a wide range of people quickly, and if we save the messages, it creates a great documentation trail of the communication. The problem is, it frequently gets over-used. I know of organizations where people who sit next to each other in cubicles use e-mail rather than standing up and talking to each other. This is simply ludicrous.

E-mail is great for things like documenting written status reports, sending out meeting minutes, posting test results, etc. It's not so great for things like discussions (unless you're in a real-time-chat environment), group problem-solving (unless you have plenty of time), and the type of give-and-take you can only get in a conversation.

A stop-gap measure that is sometimes used is the conference call. While this allows the group to talk, it leaves out the visual clues that are so much a part of conversation. Video conferencing, if you have it available, helps but few organizations have it as yet. As greater communication bandwidth becomes available, this may become a more useful tool.

See Chapter 7: *Process Tips for Distributed Projects*, for a discussion of the issues faced by projects being worked on in multiple locations.

Now, back to the discussion of communication technology and projects.

Most of us have played "phone tag" with someone. You call and leave a message; they return your call and leave a message; you return the call and leave a message; they respond to your message; your machine calls their machine; your machines strike up a relationship and elope.

Voice mail, like most of the telecommunication technologies is great if it is used properly. If messages are returned in a timely manner; if enough information is left in the message to allow for a return message that answers the question; if you don't get stuck in a phone-tag loop. Use it if necessary but don't assume that you've really communicated as well as you could if you actually talked to someone.

PROCESS TIP

Use voice mail as an adjunct to face-to-face communication

Voice mail can have an impact on the communication process of a project. The need to pass information among the members of the team on a fairly frequent basis make the use of voice mail almost inevitable. You, as the project leader, are likely to be the initiator of much of this communication and, as such, you should know how to use voice mail effectively. Here are some hints:

- First of all, voice mail should never be used as the only communication channel. It should by use to trigger a person-to-person conversation whenever possible or necessary. Unless your system has the capability of letting you know your message has been heard, understood, and acted on, you need some kind of confirmation response.

- Be brief and specific in your message. Don't ramble. Keep the message as short as possible and still get all the necessary information across.

- If you are asking a question, specify what you need in response and ask that the person contact you (or your voice mail system) with the answer. Attach a time-frame to you request. If you use voice mail a lot, things can fall through the cracks pretty easily. If you thing this might happen, learn to keep notes to yourself that list the messages you've left and with whom. Many personal-calendar or personal contact programs (like Outlook and ACT) have a journal function. This can be a good place to set up a call-reminder list.

- Specify when you will be available for a return call. If you set aside time everyday to work on project-related tasks, this is also a good time to get responses to voice-mail messages that you've left. Whether you do this or not, try to shortcut the "phone tag" problem by telling the person you've left the message with when they can actually talk to you.

- If you are passing on information, be clear and concise.

- When trying to schedule a meeting, give alternative dates and times and ask that the return message specify which alternative will work. Networked calendar programs usually have a meeting-scheduling function that can also be used for this.

Written Communication

In the text category, we have two major technologies:

- Fax
- Electronic Mail (E-Mail)

Fax technology has come a long way from its beginnings. Fax modems are now included in most personal computer systems. The quality of the faxed document has improved significantly from the early days.

Faxing information has become common-place and can be an excellent way to transmit printed (either text or images) material very quickly from one site to another. The fax, however, is not a truly interactive device. Most of its uses center around sending information in one direction for review or instruction. There is little if any personal contact between the parties.

E-mail, on the other hand, has enjoyed an explosion of use in the last few years. Like many technologies before it (including the fax) it has begun to generate its own work. What was once perfectly acceptable to send by "snail mail" (the U.S. Postal Service) now must be transmitted instantaneously by email. The capability to send the same message to a large number of people with the press of a button has added to the general overuse of this technology. Anyone with e-mail will soon find themselves buried in messages, most of which they don't really need. E-mail is an enabling technology. It is not a substitute for a good interpersonal communication process.

The amount of time that can be eaten up by going through one day's accumulated e-mail can be frightening. Many people are so overwhelmed by the load, they simply delete messages that don't appear important without reading them. Others actually read everything that comes through and use up valuable time that could be put to better use.

One use of e-mail that is a real boon to project management is the ability to use it to collect and distribute project status reports, meeting minutes and other project-wide information that needs to be documented. It is also useful for keeping stakeholders (other than team members) updated on progress.

PROCESS TIP
E-mail is NOT the answer to all communication situations
If you must use e-mail to communicate about your project, follow some of these basic rules to increase its effectiveness:

- E-mail is not a substitute for personal communication. Use e-mail only when it is the best choice for the communication. If a phone call would really be better, make the call. Even better, talk to someone face-to-face.

- Clearly identify the subject of the message in the header. This can be the thing that gets your message read when others are being summarily deleted.

- Send e-mail only to those people who need to see the message. Don't use the "Send to Complete List" function for everything.

- Keep the message short and to the point.

- If a response is required, be specific about what you need and when you need it.

- For crying out loud, use the spell checker! E-mail has become a haven for badly written, massively misspelled text. Don't contribute to the problem.

Interpersonal Communication

Have you sometimes wondered why it seems so difficult to communicate with some people? And why at other times you immediately hit it off with someone you've just met? In those instances, there seems to be a basis of understanding that amounts to more than could be explained by a common background or related professions.

Or perhaps you've been surprised by an abrupt breakdown in understanding when talking to a friend or business associate. You may have spent several minutes presenting what you see as relevant information — background material, pertinent facts, logical opinions, various options, etc. Your friend and associate has been growing progressively more restless. Then you decide to tell him how it feels, and suddenly you have instant communication.

What accounts for this change? And why do we seem to relate better with some people than with others?

The Four Basic Communication Styles

Eloquence is the power to translate a truth into language perfectly intelligible to the person to whom you speak.
Ralph Waldo Emerson
1803-1882
American Essayist and Poet

The secret was unlocked by Carl Jung, a Swiss psychoanalyst, in a monumental work, Psychological Types, originally written in the 1920's but not translated in its entirety and published in the U.S. until 1974. Jung's work is part of the basis of one of the most popular personality assessment instruments around, the Meyers-Briggs Personality Type Indicator.

What really accounts for personality differences, Jung said, is that every individual develops a preference for one of four major behavioral functions:

- Intuiting: Speculating, imagining, envisioning, daydreaming, creating, innovating.

- Thinking: Rationally deducting, analyzing, ordering facts, identifying and weighing options, reflecting.

- Feeling: Empathizing, perceiving, associating, remembering, relating.

- Sensing: Acting — doing, relying on sensory data, combating — competing, striving for results, living in the here and now.

Behavior patterns, Jung claimed, are reflected by infants during their first days of life. Study young children, he said, truly observe them and you will discover that they process experience on different primary channels. Jung contended that children in elementary school could be validly classified as Intuitors, Thinkers, Feelers, and Sensors.

The Intuitor child sits alone, apparently daydreaming. In reality, the child is forming global concepts, integrating experience in a constant quest to determine the "why" of things. Knowing something because the teacher says it's true is not sufficient. They must discover why a thing is true. In the absence of such discovery, they will summarily reject the premise.

The Thinker child prides himself or herself on being correct. They demonstrate a structured and systematic approach to learning. They gather facts, not ideas. Their concern is to systematize, to collect and infer, but not to dream. Their approach is information-centered.

The Feeler child responds to mood, their own as well as the emotions of others. They learn through their emotions. They are empathetic and sentimental. They demonstrate keen interpersonal radar. Whether or not they engage in an activity with true commitment depends upon its perceived meaning in terms of past experience, not future possibilities or book-learned facts. Their touchstone of reality is meaningful memories.

The Sensor child is the doer, the fast mover, the restless jack-in-the-box, the learner who must grab the rock or the doll in their own hands to know its reality; the child who is sent to the principal's office today and who emerges as the head of a dot-com start-up tomorrow. They dissipate anxiety through action, they know by doing — not by imagining, thinking, or feeling.

So what does all this have to do with an adult in today's workplace? Most of us are really only larger versions of the children we once were. We carry over to adult life most of the basic habits and practices of our early years. According to Jung's theories, the following can be considered true and valid:

- First of all, everyone of us uses a blend of the four behavioral styles. No one is a walking "pure style" or cardboard creature.

- Despite using a blend or "style-mix," most people rely mainly on a primary or dominant style or styles.

- An individual's weaknesses, or areas of key behavioral or communication difficulty, often represent an over-extension of their strengths. What we do well, pushed too far, becomes a weakness.

- An individual's style is reflected in their behavior and is therefore observable and identifiable.

Jung's theories have been translated into action terms, making the theory "see-able" and "do-able." If people do use these four main styles to process information (receive) and to broadcast information (send), then it follows that one of the primary functions of these styles is to serve as communication channels.

No style should ever be considered good or bad. No one style is more "right" or "wrong" than another. The communicating styles we have developed over the years have little to do with intellectual abilities, aptitudes, performance, or concerns with mental health or illness. You use four main channels of communication; so do I. So does every manager and every subordinate, every salesman and every customer, every husband and every wife, every teacher and every student.

If you and I are communicating in an everyday mode, say discussing a project-related issue, we should be engaged in adult-to-adult communication. In Transactional Analysis, this is called a parallel transaction. Calling this a "parallel transaction" assumes that we are both sending and receiving on the same channel. But, it's not necessarily so.

Why? Well, if you are a primary Sensor (action-oriented and immediate in your thinking), you want to know immediately what I am proposing — what's the bottom line of what I'm suggesting? If I'm a primary Thinker (analytical and detail-oriented), I may want you to know all the facts and insist on giving you a long, detailed rundown on my fact-finding and historical review of the situation. See any potential communication disconnect? We are not really communicating in parallel.

When and How to Use the Various Styles

How well we communicate is determined not by how well we say things but by how well we are understood.

Andrew S. Grove
Former CEO, Intel Corp.

It's very difficult to have a successful communication if I'm trying to talk to you on one channel and you're receiving on another. When you add stress to the equation, the whole thing gets even more complicated. Many of us undergo a sort of Jekel-and-Hyde personality shift under stress. For some people, their primary style simply becomes stronger — a moderate Intuitor (big-picture thinker, good at integrating lots of seemingly unrelated concepts) may, under stress, become so involved in the "big picture" that they loose sight of the immediate need for decisions and action. The normally fast-moving, hard-charging Sensor may become, under stress, a conservative, cautious, weighing Thinker.

Individuals can learn to read their own communicating styles more accurately, and to read and assess the styles of others with whom they work on a daily basis. What follows is an overview of the four primary styles. Think of this as the "Readers' Digest" version. It is not intended to be a definitive examination of the styles nor is it intended as a "gospel-like" guide to interpersonal communication. Most of us will recognize either ourselves or people we know in these descriptions. That actually is the beauty of this — behavior is an indicator of style preference. Once we are aware of it, we can use the information to help bridge communication gaps and develop our ability to communicate with a wide range of people who process information in very different ways.

Notes on the Four Communication Styles

So, who are these people? How do you spot them in a group? How does all this relate to project management?

Let's take the last question first. Projects are completed by people. Without the active participation of people working on your project, it won't get done. As a project leader, you need to be able to communicate effectively with all the people connected with, or impacted by, your project. The following notes should help you to identify the primary styles of most of the people with whom you will interact. And knowing that, you should be able to more effectively communicate with them.

One special note: One of the things that Jung discovered in his research was that, for most of us, our communication weaknesses are frequently over-extensions of the strengths of our primary style. These will be identified in the notes below. It's very important to have as good a mix of styles as possible on a project team. Teams that have over-representation of one style tend to be more likely to exhibit the weaknesses of that style.

The Intuitor   The Intuitor is the big-picture thinker of the group. Intuitors deal very well with abstract concepts and theories. They tend to be quite intuitive and can often make surprising connections between seemingly unconnected ideas, concepts, or facts. Intuitors are very good at linking the various parts into a single whole. Their time-orientation is toward the future.

On projects, Intuitors tend to be the keeper of the vision. They tend to understand the long-range implications of the work being done and can help keep the team focused on the goal. Their ability to deal with large complex concepts makes them very valuable in planning.

The Intuitor's weakness can be an over-extension of the very thing that makes them what they are: When they get too deeply into the conceptual and abstract, they can simply disconnect from reality. They can drift off, thinking lofty thoughts and not getting anything of practical value done.

A project team made up primarily of Intuitors may develop some wonderful concepts and plans but, without some help from the other styles, is unlikely to actually get anything of a practical nature done.

> **PROCESS TIP**
> **Communicating with an Intuitor**
> When communicating with and Intuitor, keep these things in mind: Allow enough time. Start with an overview and explain where you want to go with your suggestion. Show that your ideas are innovative, unique, original, unusual, creative, etc. Conceptualize your ideas and tie them into overall concepts. Show the impact on the future.

The Thinker   Where the Intuitor is the big-picture person, the Thinker is into the details. Thinkers tend to like structure and order. They like facts, backed up with analysis and logic. They tend to be somewhat formal in their dealings with others. They do not cope well with "cloudy, blue-sky pictures." Thinkers do not usually make hasty decisions. They think things through very thoroughly and weigh all the options before deciding on a course of action. Their logic is a source of pride. They are meticulous and organized. Their time-orientation is all three: Past, present, and future, but always from a fact-based point of view.

On projects, Thinkers are the keepers of the details and records. They focus on the small things that go into the overall work. They are aware of the necessity for good records and careful planning.

Once again, their greatest potential weakness is an over-extension of their strength. Taken too far, their love of details can be seen as nit-picking. If allowed to get out of hand, their need for comprehensive plans and careful analysis can be seen as the "paralysis of analysis" that keeps the planning going long after the time has come to get the work started.

As with any of the styles, a team made up predominantly of Thinkers will tend to accentuate their potential weakness — too much detail. Thinker dominated teams can have a real problem getting the actual work started. They do, however, usually have excellent documentation of what they haven't done.

PROCESS TIP
Communicating with a Thinker
When communicating with a Thinker, keep these things in mind: Gather your facts and line up your sources. Get organized. Provide the Thinker with enough facts that they will come to the same conclusion you did. Have some alternatives. Organize your presentation — use a systematic progression. Use the scientific method. Be prompt. Be factual and objective, avoid emotion. Be precise and exact, avoid ambiguity.

The Feeler   Feelers tend more toward the interpersonal aspects of life and less toward its mundane side. Feelers are usually very people-oriented. They tend toward informality and they base much of their work life on relationships. Their interpersonal skills are naturally quite good and they usually use them to good advantage when dealing with others. They are empathic by nature and can usually "read" the emotional state of a group very accurately. Because their time-orientation is the past, Feelers are a bit more likely to be into nostalgia and memorabilia.

On projects, Feelers can help hold the group together. Their natural abilities with people make them invaluable in dealing with the emotional ups and downs of most projects. They can also contribute relevant past experiences and a good sense of the human impacts of the project work.

The Feeler's potential weakness lies in carrying their natural affinity for people to extremes. They are so good at "seeing the other person's point of view" that they may not be able to stand up for, or support, an unfavorable position. Decisions with negative human impacts can be very difficult for a Feeler.

A team full of Feelers is likely to deteriorate into one giant group-hug. So much time could be spent making sure everyone is "ok with this" that "this" never actually gets started, much less completed. Feelers need the balance of the other styles to provide the impetus to take action.

PROCESS TIP
Communicating with a Feeler
When communicating with a Feeler, keep these things in mind:
Be informal, make time for some small-talk. Allow enough

> time to make a personal connection. You can meet with them over lunch or in an informal atmosphere. Personalize you presentation, and show its impact on people. Capitalize on tradition and past practices.

The Sensor   The Sensor is the "doer" of the group. Sensors are action-oriented, hard working, and can handle a lot of work. The saying, "If you want a job done, give it to a busy person," seems made to describe the Sensor. They deal with the world through all of their senses and they tend to take large bites. Their time-orientation is the here and now. They usually have a high energy level that is often coupled with a high need to achieve. Sensors don't usually relax very well. They may seem to expend as much energy "relaxing" as most people spend working.

On projects, Sensors are the driving energy to get things done. Give them the task and then get out of the way. They usually require little supervision once they are started. Sensors provide momentum and a sense of accomplishment to the project team. Sensors do not make the best planners but they can contribute excellent information about the work to be done.

The Sensor's potential weakness is the very thing that makes them so valuable: their energy level. If allowed to get away from them, their energy can roll right over slower, less driven team members. Their need for action can lead them to be short-sighted and poor (or incomplete) planners. They can sometimes be perceived as being rude when actually they were so focused on what they were doing they didn't see the person they ran over.

A project team full of Sensors will definitely get things done. But they may not be the right things. For some Sensors activity implies progress, but, in reality, it doesn't. It just implies activity. Without some guidance and a little control, Sensors can easily go off on exciting tangents that aren't part of the project plan.

> **PROCESS TIP**
> **Communicating with a Sensor**
> When communicating with a Sensor, keep these things in mind: Be direct and to the point. Show the results first. Be brief. "I'll only take a minute of your time." Focus on the immediate payoff. Use pictures, charts, models, and visual aids that will impact the senses. The more tangible, the better. Show the Sensor the "one best option."

It is important to restate that no one is a cookie-cutter version of any of these styles. Everyone exhibits some of the characteristics of all of them. An individual with a strong dominant style may exhibit behaviors closer to those described for that style. Someone with a balance of styles (no strong dominant) will be much harder to pin down. The good news is, a balanced style individual is easy to communicate with in almost any style.

> **PROCESS TIP**
> **Look for a balance of styles on your project teams**
> A little balance is a good thing. It should be obvious from the previous descriptions that a balanced project team stands a much greater chance at success than one that is too heavily weighted toward one style or another. The good news is that no one is really this one-dimensional. Everybody is a mix of all the styles, and most people have a pretty good internal balance among them. However, if you notice that your team is beginning to exhibit the weaknesses of a particular style, look for ways to bring them back into balance.
>
> You may need to call on one of your less dominant traits to fill in the missing characteristics. This isn't really all that hard but it can require some conscious actions on your part and a little concentration.

Style-Flexing

If you accept these concepts and their relationship to increased personal awareness, it's time to look at the idea of style-flexing. Jung indicated that individuals rarely outgrow or discard their primary styles. In other words, a person's communicating style tends to be quite stable through time. What we can do, however, is learn to "flex" our communication styles to better match with those of the person with whom we are trying to communicate. Style-flexing means adjusting your communication style to better match the style preferences of your audience. This means being able to communicate with another individual on their primary channel rather than trying to broadcast to everyone in the same style.

It would be difficult, if not impossible, to style-flex continuously over a 24-hour period. That is, if you're primarily a Thinker, it would be unrealistic to expect you to be able to communicate effectively in the Feeler style for an entire day. But most communications are much shorter than a full day. How long is an average workplace interaction? Fifteen minutes? How about an average meeting — an hour? How long is a typical manager-subordinate peformance review session — an hour or two? Most people can, with practice, learn to style-flex very effectively for limited periods of time.

And style-flexing is, in itself, not the only key. Sometimes just asking a person the "right question" can thaw a difficult communication.

- To an Intuitor: "How do you feel about the basic concept underlying this proposal?"
- To a Thinker: "Based on your own analysis, how would you evaluate the relevance of the facts I've presented?"
- To a Feeler: "I've given this a lot of consideration but I'd like to know how you feel we're tracking."
- To a Sensor: "I hope I haven't bored you; what's your reaction to the main point here?"

If you take the time to practice style-flexing you should see a noticeable improvement in your communication effectiveness. Contrary to the way it may appear on the surface, this isn't being "phony" or "artificial." It's being practical and attempting to communicate in the most effective way possible with a wide range of people.

The Role of Listening in Effective Communication

Talking is only half (or maybe only a third) of interpersonal communication. The rest is listening. Effective listening is more than just hearing — it's understanding what you are hearing. Developing effective listening skills is critical. Without them, no matter what your intelligence, your ability to understand and retain what you hear will be low. Effective listening is active listening — consciously paying attention and actively processing what you are hearing. There are specific things that you can do to increase your listening skills. Most of these are fairly common-sense points but they're worth reviewing.

- Limit your own talking. You can't talk and listen effectively at the same time.

- Be interested and show it. You must convey a genuine concern and a lively curiosity. This will encourage others to speak freely so you can better understand their needs, wants, and viewpoints. Most of this is demonstrated through the silent tongue of body language. Your posture, the position of your head, whether your eyes are focused on the speaker or wandering around the room, all are clues to whether you're actually interested in what's being said.

- Tune in to the other person. Are you giving your full attention or is your mind wandering? Concentrate on shutting out outside distractions.

- Think like the other person. They have problems, needs, and wants that are important. You'll understand and retain what they're saying better if you try to understand their point of view.

- Ask questions. If you don't understand something, or feel you may have missed a point, clear it up now before it embarrasses you later. Most people are more than willing to restate something if it will help the listener understand it better.

- Hold your fire. Do you jump to conclusions without hearing others out? Plan your response only after you are certain you have a complete picture of their point of view. Pre-judgments are dangerous. A pause, even a long pause, doesn't always mean they've finished saying everything they want to say. Wait until you're sure.

- Listen for ideas, not just words. You want to get the whole picture, not just isolated bits and pieces. If any ideas seem unclear, ask questions for clarification.

- Use interjections. An occasional "yes", "I see", or "is that so", shows them you're still there. Just don't overdo it. You don't need to interject a sound every fifth word.

- Turn off your own worries. This isn't always easy, but personal fears, worries, and problems not connected with the person speaking form a kind of "static" that can blank out the person's message.

- If appropriate, prepare in advance. Remarks and questions prepared in advance, when possible, free your mind for listening.

- React to ideas, not to the person. Don't allow your irritation at things people may say, or their manner of saying it distract you.

- Notice non-verbal language. A shrug, smile, gesture, facial expressions, and other body movements often speak louder than words.

- Don't jump ahead. Avoid making assumptions about what the other person will say. Don't mentally (or worse yet, verbally) complete their sentences for them.

- Take notes. It shows you're paying attention and it will help you remember important points.

- Get feedback. Make certain you're really listening by asking questions to confirm with the speaker what you understood.

Communication Skills Self-Assessments on the Web

There are two communication skills self-assessments you can take via the World Wide Web at www.ProjectManagementTools.com. The first is a Communication Styles Assessment that will return a short report of your communication strengths and weaknesses. There is also a short Listening Skills Self-Assessment. Both are on the web site.

Project Planning

4

Introduction

Project planning is the most critical single activity on any project. Without a well-thought-out plan, your project is in trouble before you ever start to work on it. There are numerous ways to plan a project. The tools and techniques you use to do your planning are much less important than the process of planning itself.

The project plan has multiple uses. First and foremost, the project plan is your primary tool for managing the project. Tracking activity is impossible if you don't know what is supposed to be happening. Judging the quality of work is guess-work without some criteria for making that judgement. Maintaining the schedule can't be done if you don't know what that schedule is. Problem-solving can't even be started unless you can determine whether you have a problem. The project plan is your road map for the project journey. The finished project plan is the source of all the management tools necessary to track and control the project.

In addition to this very personal reason for developing a comprehensive project plan, there are other uses for the plan documents:

- It can become a self-management tool for project team members. A good, comprehensive plan can show people what they need to focus on; what other activities are related to the actions they're engaged in; how their work outputs will integrate with other outputs; etc.

- It can be a very effective communication tool. It can be used to explain the complexity of the undertaking; justify resource requests; support changing the deadline; etc.

- Good plans can serve as templates for future, similar projects.

Meeting these additional requirements may involve creating a project plan that includes more detail than you, personally, need to track and manage the project. But, the focus of your planning should be on developing a plan that will meet all of your needs first, and additional needs thereafter.

The Process of Planning is the Important Thing

The plan is nothing; planning is everything.
Dwight D. Eisenhower
1890-1969
34th President of the
United States

If you are a "just do it" kind of person, planning may be a strain. But, it is impossible to overemphasize how important it is. In developing a project plan you are trying to identify and document:

- The actual work that needs to be done.

- The appropriate sequence of that work.

- Which tasks can be done in parallel, which must be done sequentially, and which can overlap.

- When the individual tasks should start and be finished.

- Who should be doing what, when.

- Where and when significant decisions or approvals will be needed and who the decision-makers are.

- Where problems are likely to occur, what impact they might have on the project, and what to do about either preventing or mitigating them.

- Which tasks need to be watched more closely than others.

- What deliverables are being created along the way and how to know if they're any good.

- Which tasks need greater detail in the plan than others.

- When and how the final deliverable of the project will be handed off to the customer.

At the beginning of a project, all of this is, to some extent, unknown. What is known is usually not in sufficient detail or depth to be of much use in the day-to-day management of the project. Figuring all of this out is the purpose of project planning.

Project planning, at least at the beginning, is usually a sloppy, chaotic, stop-and-back-up-and-try-it-again kind of process. There is usually some confusion about the work to be done. There will likely be conflicting ideas about how complex or simple it will be. You'll find different opinions about what things need to precede other things, what things can't even be started until other things are finished and what things are otherwise interdependent. There will be questions about who needs to do what, when. Disagreement about what constitutes a major task versus a sub-task or minor task is likely. You and the team will probably experience multiple paranoid fantasies about what is likely to go wrong and what can be done to prevent it. A highly rigid planning process will only make determining all of this (and everything else you need to know before you get deeply into your projects) more difficult.

In most cases, good project plans are the result of a repetitive process — planning that is done in "layers." The "layers" are created in successive passes through the plan. In the first several passes, flexibility is the key. If you try to finalize pieces of the plan too early, you'll find that you have forgotten pieces; others are out of their correct order; details are missing; etc. Project plans are almost never "set in stone." At best, they're set in semi-firm Jell-O®. The chances that some part of the plan will need to be changed as the project progresses are almost 100%. In fact, including "plan review" points as part of the plan is a good way to make sure that the plan continues to reflect the realities of the developing project.

PROCESS TIP
Try to assemble some members of the project team to
help with the planning

Project planning is best done by at least some members of
the project team as a group activity. It can be done by a single person, but the process presented here is intended for,
and usually results in a better end product when done by, a
group. This is really a case of several heads being better than
one. Multiple perspectives on the project will give you a
much better chance of creating a comprehensive project plan
that takes into account all of the aspects of the project.

This doesn't need to be a huge group. At the very least,
try to have one other person involved in the planning. Two
or three additional people (with information and expertise
related to the project) are even better. Remember, most projects will involve issues and tasks with which you are not
totally familiar. You will likely need input from others
whose expertise is different from yours. This will go a long
way toward developing a plan that actually reflects the
needs of the project.

Project management software is just that — project MANAGEMENT software. It is not designed as project planning software. In most cases, it isn't
appropriate (or even particularly usable) for the planning activity. Most project management software programs assume that you know what needs to be
done, how long it will take, who should work on it, etc., before you sit down
to enter your project into the software. The flexibility needed at the beginning
just isn't part of the package.

There is one other handicap that comes with software — you're limited to
viewing what you can fit into a single computer screen. For most projects, this
will not be anywhere near the total project. Being able to view the total project — beginning to end — is very useful in helping to spot inconsistencies and
potential problem spots.

Now, having said that, it is important to note that many of these programs
are very useful for tracking the project once it is planned. There are, however,
some important conditions that need to be met for these programs to be useful.

• First and foremost, in order to effectively track project activity, someone
must take the responsibility for maintaining the data. The main thing that
is tracked in these programs is schedule — tracking which activities are on
time, which are ahead of schedule, and which are falling behind. In order
to track this, you will need an effective means of collecting accurate schedule information.

   ○ **Caution:** Watch out for "percent complete" reporting. This is a common technique for collecting schedule progress. In this process, proj-

ect team members are asked to report the percentage of a task that has been completed during a reporting period. Unfortunately, this rarely results in a report of the percentage of the work that has been completed. It usually results in a report of the amount of scheduled time that has elapsed. For example, if a task was scheduled to take two weeks the report after the first week of work would likely be that 50% of the task is complete. Now, it is true that 50% of the scheduled time has elapsed, but that's not what you need to know. You need to know how much of the work has been completed. Only 10% of the work may have been done.

- If you are using a project management software package, try to keep the information as current as possible. This may require blocking out a period of time everyday to do this. Given how complex most of these programs are, using them everyday is probably a good idea. It will cut down on the time it takes to remember how to use it each time.

- One of the features most of the major software packages share is the ability to save a "baseline" plan. This is the version of the plan that you've decided is "as good as it's going to get" at this point. Saving the baseline is extremely important if you really want to understand how the project — as it played out — deviated from the original plan. When you use the baselining feature, all of the subsequent activity is tracked against this reference point. This can show where things started to go wrong — where the schedule began to slip (or, in some cases, where you picked up some time by finishing activities early). The hitch is, most of the programs will allow you to "re-save" the baseline. Basically this means that you can cheat and reset your measurement point throughout the project. If you use the baseline feature, realize that it will show, very clearly, how, where, and when the project went off track. It will also provide invaluable information for analyzing and understanding the lessons that can be learned from knowing this.

  In the latest version of the most popular packages, there is a feature that allows you to save multiple baselines for analysis purposes. This feature still captures the original baseline but also allows you to save subsequent baselines (for example, at the end of each project phase) for more detailed analysis.

- One feature that can be very helpful is ability to "manage" a common pool of resources who are working on multiple projects. These features allow you to list all the resources available for project work and to track how each person is scheduled across multiple projects. It can help with the problem of over-booking. Again, however, this feature is only as good as the data that is being used.

- Project management software can be very useful if you need it. That's the key. If you really need the functions and features of these programs, use them. If you don't, be careful that you don't end up trying to kill flies with a sledgehammer.

PROCESS TIP
A note on planning software (if you can find it)

As of the publication of this book, there were very few project planning software programs out there. One of the best is Project KickStart from Experience In Software. Information on this program is available at www.projectkickstart.com.

Personally, I prefer planning with a group of real, live people rather than alone, but in some situations, it just isn't possible or practical. So, having an alternative planning process is a very good idea. The features of planning programs (many of which are not specifically designed for projects) vary widely. Here are some of the features to consider if you want to try one.

- Look for one that is "prompt-driven" — one that "asks" questions to help you through the thought processes of planning a project. This feature makes the software more an assistant than a recording tool.

- Look for one that allows you to approach your project from different angles. For example, look for a program that will allow you to begin with either identifying tasks or goals. Or maybe identifying obstacles that need to be overcome. Or even starting with the resources you have available. This feature allows you to plan according to the information you have available. If you have it all, great, but if you don't, this feature can help point out the places where you need more information, decisions, input, etc.

- Look for planning software that also produces some of the basic tracking tools such as a Gantt chart (schedule chart), resource report, and one or two others that you find useful. This feature might make it possible to use the output of this program to manage simple projects without having to go to the larger, usually more complicated, project management packages.

- Finally, look for a planning package that is compatible with whatever project management software you want to use. Ideally, the planning program should be able to create an export file that is compatible with your project management software. The last thing you need to do is create your plan in one package and then have to reenter all the data into another program. This is an almost guaranteed way to introduce errors.

Project Planning in Layers

A thousand words are worth a picture.
Anonymous

Let's assume that you're taking the advice about planning with a group of people rather than alone in isolation. As a preliminary, before asking the team to start planning the project, it's a good idea to provide some sort of framework. If you try to begin the process without any kind of starting point most people will have trouble getting going. They need something to start from.

One of the simplest frameworks is identifying the major sections of the project. These are usually called project phases.

PROCESS TIP
A simple set of tools for project planning

Here is yet another use for self-stick notes. They provide a quick, flexible, inexpensive planning tool that is perfect for dealing with the sloppy, chaotic, confusing mess that is the project planning process. In addition, a major advantage of Post-It® Notes over computer programs is the ability to see the whole project at once. With the technique described here, you can create a version of your project plan that you can step back from and view in its entirety.

Materials needed:

- Post-It® Notes or other self-stick, removable note pads (recommend 3"x 5", 3" x 3", and 1fi" x 2" sizes)

- Some type of background sheet. 30"- or 36"-wide rolls of paper in approximately 50-foot lengths are available in many office supply stores.

- Masking tape (to hang the paper on the wall).

- Marking pens.

- Brightly colored adhesive dots (fi" or larger diameter). Two colors are recommended, usually red and blue.

Each of the three sizes of Post-It® Notes has its specific use in this process:

- The 3" x 5" size is used to record the tasks of the project.

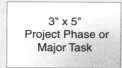

3" x 5"
Project Phase or
Major Task

- The 3" x 3" size has three uses.

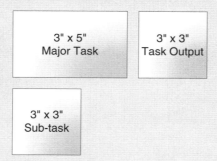

3" x 5"
Major Task

3" x 3"
Task Output

3" x 3"
Sub-task

- Placed on the plan as a square, it is used to record sub-tasks or the outputs or deliverables of major tasks or groups of tasks.

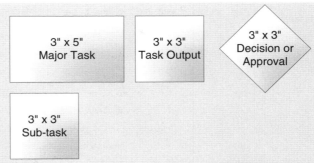

- Placed on the plan as a diamond, it indicates a decision or approval point. The diamond shape is used to illustrate that there are three possible outcomes to every decision:

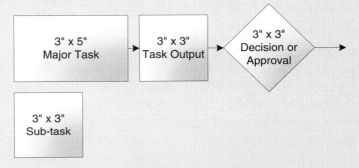

- Approval to proceed (the process arrow goes from the right hand point to the next task).

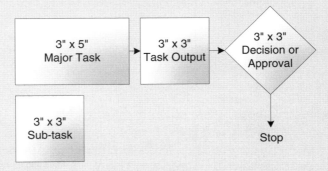

- Approval denied (the process arrow goes out the bottom point indicating "stop").

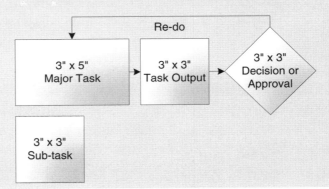

○   Approval granted contingent upon some aspect of the work being re-done and re-submitted for approval (the process arrow goes out the top point and loops back to the task that must be re-done).

- The 1-1/2″ x 2″ size is used to record additional information such as individuals working on a particular task (resources), schedule information, or notes.

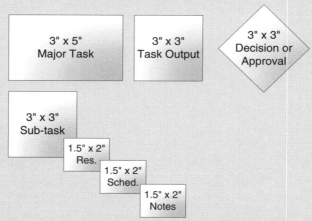

As each step of the planning process is described, check the Process Tips for that section to see how to apply this technique.

The Process Tip for project phases is: Providing these large building blocks (Phases) gives the team a context in which to think about the tasks that need to be done to complete the project. Record these phases on the 3″ x 5″ Post-It® Notes and space them along the top of the planning sheet.

Project Phases

There are a couple of ways to look at the idea of project Phases. On one hand, there is the process approach, which I will call the PMI® model. In this case, every project is seen as having the same set of Phases regardless of the content of the project. The most common version of this is the Phase-set commonly used by PMI®, the Project Management Institute. This is the professional organization for project managers. PMI® certification (PMP®, Project Management Professional) is recognized world-wide and a valuable professional certification. In this model, all projects have these four Phases:

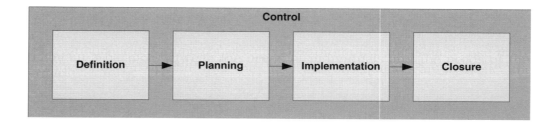

- Definition — In this phase the project is defined (big surprise). This encompasses the activities as described in Chapters 1 and 2, this phase ends with formal approval to begin planning the project.

- Planning — This phase includes all of the planning activities in this chapter: Defining major tasks and their sub-tasks; organizing the sequence of work; assigning responsibilities for the work; scheduling; identification of the Critical Path; and contingency planning.

- Implementation — This phase covers all of the actual work on the project output and includes completing the tasks of the project; tracking activity to the plan; delivering the final output; and any project-related follow-up.

- Closure — The Closure Phase of the PMI® model includes finalizing the project; archiving project documentation; and post-project evaluation.

As a model of the total process, this is a good one. It is, however, pretty generic and doesn't go into much detail about the unique characteristics of most projects.

Another Way to Look at Project Phases

Another way to look at project Phases is to define phases that are unique to each project. Using this approach, the first two phases of the PMI model fall into the categories of pre-work and planning. The actual phases of the project define the work to be done to get the project (already defined and planned) completed. You can think of each phase as being a sort of mini-project since most project phases will end with some kind of deliverable and a decision whether or not to proceed to the next phase.

For most projects, these phases are very easy to define. In a lot of ways, they are sub-projects. For example, a product development project might have phases like:

- Research market feasibility
- Design the product
- Prototype the product
- Test market prototype product
- Prepare product for production
- Implement production

  A process development project might have phases like:

- Research and document process requirements
- Design initial process flow
- Test and refine process
- Implement new process and train users

  A software development project might have phases like:

- Specify functional and design requirements
- Prepare and test design
- Prototype "look and feel" samples for user approval
- Code software

- Integrate software elements, test and debug
- Install software, train users, and debug (again)

Notice how many of the project phases shown above, if strung together with commas, would look a lot like the opening sentences of a good project goal statement? The opening sentence of your project goal is a good place to check when you're trying to name your phases. This is also a good test for the project goal: Does the goal state the major activities (the phases) that will be completed in the course of the project. The phase-level is an appropriate level of task detail for most project goals.

Identify Tasks in Each Phase

Once project phases have been identified, the next step is to break each phase into the tasks needed to accomplish it. Remember to try to stay at a fairly high level in terms of detail at this stage. Don't try to identify the small, individual work activities — shoot for the larger groups of activities that can be further sub-divided.

PROCESS TIP

Brainstorm major tasks in each Phase

Have the team brainstorm tasks that need to be done for each phase. Try for the larger pieces of the project first. It is also helpful to ask people to try to think in terms of verb/noun phrases. Combining an action verb with a noun describes both the work that needs to be done and the output of that work, better than the noun alone. For example:

- Prepare survey
- Conduct survey
- Write functional specifications
- Build prototype
- Input data
- Regression-test software

As tasks are suggested, write them on the large (3" x 5") Post-It® Notes and stick them under the appropriate phase. At this stage, don't worry about the order of the tasks. This is the first pass at the plan and you should be more concerned with capturing the larger scale tasks under all the phases.

At this time, it is also a good idea to identify as many major decision or approval points as you can. You should probably concentrate on those decisions that are made, or approvals that are given by people outside the project team. These usually involve either management or the project's customer. Most project phases end with a decision or approval to proceed or not. This decision is made based on the work (and the work output) of the phase.

Other decisions and approvals will happen throughout the project, but the ones you need to focus on in the plan are the ones that are out of the direct control of the project team. Identify these, and the others (which are usually made by team members) will be much easier to track.

Remember, a decision is recorded on the 3" x 3" Post-it® Note placed on the planning sheet as a diamond.

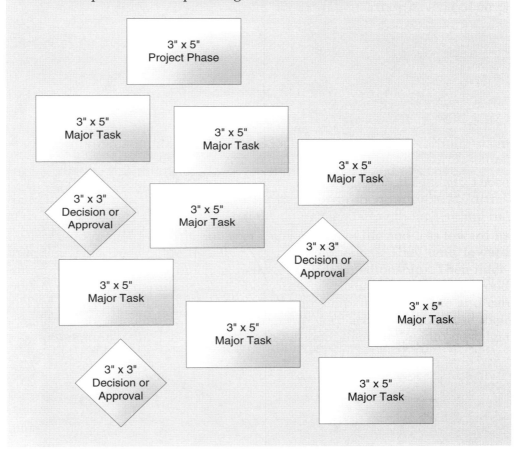

Organize Tasks at a High Level   When the group seems to be running down, stop for a while and try to organize the tasks. This is the first pass at imposing order on the project. Don't be overly rigid. Simply try to put the tasks in a logical order under each Phase.

PROCESS TIP
Establish the basic relationships among the tasks
For the most part, there are three basic relationships that tasks have with each other:

- Finish-to-start
- Start-to-start
- Finish-to-finish

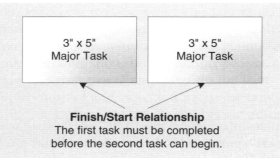

Finish/Start Relationship
The first task must be completed
before the second task can begin.

- Finish-to-start: One task must be completed before the next task can begin. This is also sometimes termed a predecessor-successor relationship.

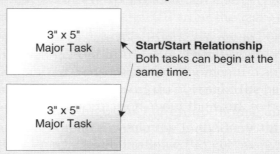

Start/Start Relationship
Both tasks can begin at the
same time.

- Start-to-start: Both tasks can be started at the same time because there is no dependency between their outputs. Sometimes, these are termed parallel tasks.

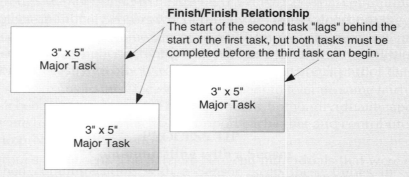

Finish/Finish Relationship
The start of the second task "lags" behind the
start of the first task, but both tasks must be
completed before the third task can begin.

- Finish-to-finish: In this case, the two tasks can start at different times but both must be completed in order for succeeding tasks to begin. This is the situation that creates "slack" or "lag time" in project tasks. If two tasks share a finish-to-finish relationship and one of them will take longer to complete than the other, the shorter task has more time available than needed. This is "slack" (looseness) in the schedule, or the task "lags" behind its partner task.

The trick with organizing the project the first time is to stay away from focusing on scheduling it at the same time. You're not ready to schedule this thing yet. Focus on the relationships among the tasks, not on how long one will take, or much worse, how much time you have to get them done. You can worry about all of that a couple of steps further on.

Some helpful questions to ask during this process are:

- What needs to be done first?

- Once we've done that, what can we, or what should we, do next? (This one gets asked over and over again in this process.)

- Is there anything that can be done at the same time? (Things that are not dependent on each other in any way: task activities, people involved, etc.)

- Is there anything that can overlap this task? (This sometimes means that some part of a task needs to be completed before something else can begin, but not all of the preceding task must be complete.)

PROCESS TIP
Sequence tasks in the order in which they will be done

Sequencing project tasks is critical. Everything you will do from here on out in planning is dependent on the basic organization of the work. This is called the Work Breakdown Structure (WBS) of the project.

Organize the project on the planning sheet. Remember that time runs left to right along the sheet.

Place tasks horizontally, left to right, across the planning sheet if the tasks follow one another. This is the "finish-start" relationship.

Place tasks vertically down the sheet for tasks that can be done in parallel. These tasks do not have to finish together. In

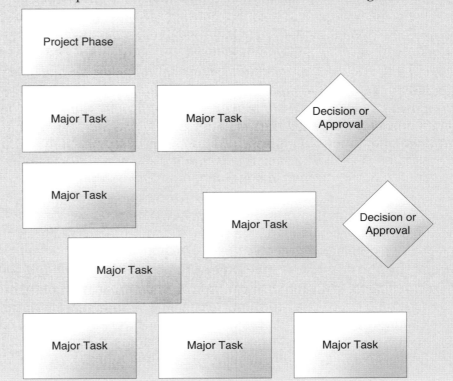

fact, one task may be significantly longer than another. The basis of the "start-start" relationship is the beginning point for the tasks.

When you have the "slack" or "lag" relationship, offset the trailing task under the leading task. This is the "finish-finish" relationship. In this case, it is the completion of the tasks that must be aligned.

At this stage your plan is a work in progress. Remember to leave some space between tasks (both vertically and horizontally) for additions and details. While doing this, it is likely that other tasks will be suggested as the holes in the plan become more obvious. Write them on Post-It® Notes and stick them in the appropriate places on the plan.

You may want to try more than one sequence for the project. This is one advantage of the Post-It® Note technique. It is very easy to move the pieces of the developing plan into new configurations. In fact, most project plans have to be significantly rearranged at least once and frequently several times as information is developed and new or different tasks are identified.

Add Detail

The next step in the process is to identify those tasks that need further detail in order to be manageable. This is a judgement call on your part. What you need from the plan is sufficient detail so that you can effectively track and control the project. To do this, you need to know what questions to ask about the work being done. You also need to know how to determine whether the answers you're getting make sense. This is yet another place to drive home the point about building a project plan in the first place — the plan is your primary project-tracking tool. As such, it needs to contain sufficient information for you to be able to track the work being done — even if you don't know all that much about the work someone is doing. Here's the criteria for determining how much detail is enough.

- If you are comfortable that you understand the work involved in a task at this higher level, don't go into more detail about it. For example, if "prepare survey" means all of the following to you: Drafting multiple versions of each question; testing all questions to determine which ones actually yield the information you're looking for; building more than one version of the survey instrument to see if the format, type size, layout, (or script for phone interviews) etc., work the way you want them to; you don't need to detail out and organize the sub-tasks.

- If, on the other hand, you aren't comfortable with your understanding of the work involved — after all, you're an engineer, not a market researcher — get the additional details on the task. Also, be sure to record how you can determine whether or not progress is being made and how to judge the quality of the work output.

This will probably yield a plan in which some tasks are only identified at the highest level, while others have two, three, or even four additional layers of detail. Make it as detailed as you need.

> **NOTE:** This approach ignores the additional uses for the project plan. Things like team-member self-management, communication with a larger audience, or future-project template, and focuses on your own selfish needs as the project leader. If you need to use the plan for some of these additional purposes, it may require more detail than you, personally, need.

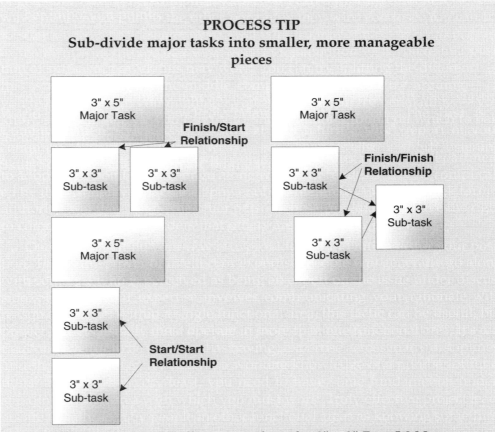

PROCESS TIP
Sub-divide major tasks into smaller, more manageable pieces

Detail tasks are usually captured on the 3" x 3" Post-It® Notes. In a way, each major task that is sub-divided becomes a tiny project inside the phase inside the overall project. The same rules of organization apply at the sub-task level as they do at the higher level: Left to right for sub-tasks that follow each other, top to bottom for sub-tasks that are done in parallel; offset for tasks that have slack or lag relationships.

If you need to further sub-divide some of these sub-tasks, you can either keep using the 3" x 3" notes or drop down to the smaller 1fi" x 2" size. However, be sure you're actually going down to a level of detail that is really necessary. You need to know that the two pieces need to be connected. You don't need to know how many times to turn the screwdriver to tighten the screw.

Connect People to the Tasks

When you are satisfied that you have sufficient details on the tasks, it's time to start connecting people to them. Somebody has to do each task in the project. These things don't do themselves.

There are several relationships a person can have to a task.

- They can be responsible for seeing to it that the task gets done. This may mean they need to do all the work themselves, or it can mean that they are the one person out of several working on the task that you will contact to find out how it's going. They need to schedule time and produce some kind of work output. This person is Accountable for the task.

- They may be a worker on the task — not the person responsible for it but a contributor to its completion. This person also needs to schedule time and produce some sort of work output. This person is a Participant in the task.

- They may have information that is important to the successful completion of the task, but will not otherwise participate in its completion. This person does not have to schedule time or produce a work output other than providing the information when requested. This person provides Input to the task.

- They may need to be informed about the task in some way such as being told when the task is approaching completion so they can gear up to do the next task in line. (This relationship is internal to the project.) Or, they may be a manager or other stakeholder in the project who needs to be kept informed of progress. (This relationship is external to the project.) This person needs to Review the work output of the task.

- They may need to approve the work output of the task or of an accumulation of work output on the project. This person must provide a Sign-off for the work.

These relationships can be captured by the acronym "PARIS."

- P = Participant: Provides work output for the task but is not Accountable for it.

- A = Accountable: Responsible for ensuring that the work of the task is completed correctly and on time.

- R = Review Required: Needs to review the work and provide feedback but does not have approval responsibility or authority.

- I = Input Required: Has information necessary to the successful completion of the task.

- S = Sign-off Required: Must approve work output in order for the project to proceed.

The Responsibility Matrix

Leadership appears to be the art of getting others to want to do something you are convinced should be done.
Vance Packard
Journalist

The Responsibility Matrix is an excellent tool for graphically displaying the relationships between the people working on, or stakeholders in, the project and the tasks to be completed.

This tool can be expanded to include not only the project team members but also important stakeholders in the project. The use of the PARIS code can further refine this tool and expand its application to include managing information. Tasks are listed down the left side of the matrix and individuals involved in, or stakeholders in, the project are listed across the top. At the intersection of a person and a task, the person's level of involvement in that task is indicated by one of the letters from the PARIS code.

PROCESS TIP
Connect people to the tasks

Responsibility Matrix

List the appropriate project information.

The PARIS Code is included as a reminder of what the letters mean.

If you are using Task Identification Numbers, enter them in the first column.

List the Tasks of the project in the second column.

List Team Members and other Stakeholders (managers, customers, your sponsor, etc.) across the top.

You can enter Task Start and Task End dates here.

Link each person to the appropriate Tasks using the PARIS code.

Project: Date:
Project Leader:
Project Sponsor:

Team Members and Stakeholders

The PARIS Code:
P = Participant
A = Accountable
R = Review Required
I = Input Required
S = Sign-off Required

ID   Tasks   Task Start Task End

As much as possible, resource assignment should be on a volunteer basis. Most people are much more likely to follow through on tasks they've volunteered for than those that have been assigned to them. This is particularly true of tasks that are assigned by a peer without their input. The people in the planning session should be people who will be working on the project. They are the ones who will be doing the tasks. Ask them to volunteer for those that are appropriate.

Capture individual names and involvement codes on 1fi" x 2" Post-It® Notes and attach them to the tasks or sub-tasks.

Starting at this point in the planning process it is best to do these assignments from the bottom up. Begin at the sub-task level. Assign the resources necessary to complete the detailed work and, from that group, select the person best suited to be given the responsibility (Accountable) for the whole task group.

At this first pass through resource assignment, you're mainly looking for two levels of involvement:

- The "A's" — the people who will be responsible for seeing to it that the tasks are completed (the people you will be asking about progress on the tasks); and,

- The "P's" — anyone who must provide work for the tasks to be completed.

If you can identify the "Review," "Input," and "Sign-off" relationships for any of the tasks, by all means include them. However, as a general rule, these relationships become more clear as the plan gets closer to finalization. And nothing says you can't go back and add more information as the plan develops.

In many cases, the person responsible will be the person who also does all the work. Therefore, you will have tasks with only one name connected to them. In other cases, particularly at the higher levels of the project, one person will be designated as responsible for a large task that will be sub-divided and worked on by several other people. You need to be able to identify all of them, even though your primary contact about the task will be through the person Accountable.

The more complex a project is the more important this organizational hierarchy becomes. In fact, it is not uncommon to have multiple Responsibility Matrices at descending levels of detail on very large or complex projects. However, even in simple projects, the relationship between people and tasks is an important part of the plan and your ability to track and manage the activity.

PROCESS TIP
One "A" and ONLY one "A" for every task

Have one, and only one, "A" for any single task. For sub-divided tasks, each sub-task should have an individual designated as accountable. If the person accountable for the major task is also responsible for all of the sub-tasks, you don't need to indicate the same person over and over. The convention of this is that the "A" applies downward and to the right until you indicate another "A." If a task looks like it requires more than one person to be accountable, sub-divide the task.

Shared responsibility rarely works under the best of conditions. In one case, one of the people sharing the responsibility ends up taking on all the responsibility. In another case, neither person takes the responsibility and the task founders. In a project environment, the time pressure is usually so extreme that the normal discussion-to-consensus approach that shared responsibility implies is simply impractical.

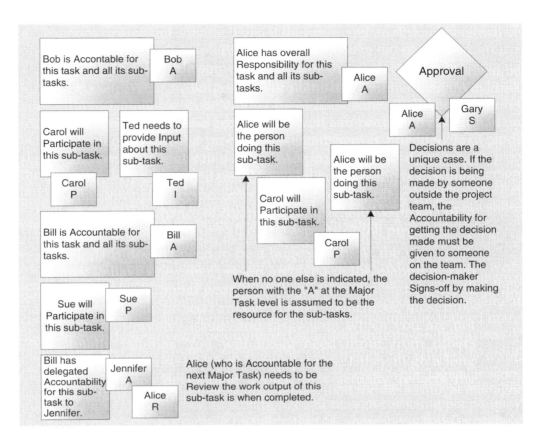

Review the Work Load

Once you've gotten people assigned to the various tasks, take a careful look at the plan. If you see the same name over and over, you may have a problem with over-allocation of one person's time. Look for "underloads" as well as overloads. Do you have someone who is only working on one or two tasks? Can they take over or assist with others? What skills do they have that might be useful on some other part of the project. (Refer to the Skills and Influence Matrix you did during the Pre-Work.)

Schedule the Work

Now that you've identified phases, major tasks and sub-tasks, and identified the people who'll be doing the work, you are in a position to begin scheduling the project — developing estimates of how long tasks will take to complete. It is strongly recommended that you do this by going to the people who will be doing the work. Project scheduling is one of the most difficult activities in the planning process. This is exacerbated by the fact that most in-house project leaders don't have any real authority to schedule other people's time, nor do they have any control over it.

You need input from your team members about the time they have available and the other demands on their time that will, most probably, cause conflicts with the project schedule. You can simply ask for their best-guess estimate of when they can deliver each of their tasks. This will give you a reasonable estimate of the time the project will take.

There is a real temptation to try to fit the project into the established time frame — to make it fit the deadline by saying, "We only have this much time available so that's how long it will take." Bad idea. In this first run at the project schedule, avoid trying to fit the project into the deadline. Strive for realistic estimates from the team about how long tasks are really going to take. Remind people to take their existing and potential work loads into consideration when they are giving you their estimates. You will end up with a much better idea of what is involved with your project if you do this.

The final calculation will frequently show that the project will run significantly over the established deadline. Now what? How will you know where to try to cut time out in order to pull it back into line? Here's a technique that can help. Ask team members to give you their best guess about each task in two ways:

* Task time (work time). This is the actual work time required to complete the task. How many hours (days) of actual hands-on work are involved in doing the work? If your organization charges time back to the projects that are done, this is the estimate of the time that would be charged against your project. If your organization doesn't charge time back, the principle is still the same. This is an estimate of the actual effort required to complete the task.

* Duration. This is the time it will take to get the Task time to do the work — to actually deliver the work output. Given all the other things that the team member has to do — other projects, standing commitments to their "real" job, meetings, etc. — how long will it be from the time the task is started until the finished work can be delivered?

Hopefully, it is obvious that Duration — not Task time — is your scheduling estimate. Task time is collected for other reasons.

Duration will almost always be greater than Task time. Given the work load most people have, a range of between 4-to-1 and 8-or-10-to-1 is not unrealistic. Every business is different. In some businesses, a ratio of 15-to-1 would not cause a reaction. In others, anything over 6-to-1 would cause eyebrows to raise. Whatever is appropriate for your organization is the range you should use as your gauge for whether an estimate is out of line or not.

One way to think about the issue of Task Time versus Duration is to consider how long it would take you to accomplish four hours worth of new work — of a standard priority (nothing special, just work it in; no, you can't move other work out of the way to get this done). I you can get it done in two days, that's a ratio of 4-to-1. If it would take you three days to get it done, that's a ratio of 6-to-1. Four days, 8-to-1. By the end of the week (by far the most common response) yields a ratio of 10-to-1.

There is one situation in which Task time can be greater than Duration. It is when you have multiple people working on the same task. For example, on a software application development project, you might have eight programmers working on writing code. Each of them has committed 80 hours (two person-weeks) of Task time to the effort. They can each devote 25 percent of their available time over a Duration of eight weeks to your project. This gives us a ratio of 4-to-1. Assuming that all eight programmers are working on the project during the same eight-week period, you could achieve 16 weeks of Task time in a Duration of only eight weeks.

PROCESS TIP
Capture estimates for both Task Time and Duration
Record time estimates on the small (1fi" x 2") Post-It® Notes and stick them to the appropriate tasks. Choose a time increment and stick with it throughout the plan. If you start with hours, stick with hours for everything. This makes the Critical Path calculations (coming up) easier.

There are a couple of ways you can easily capture both estimates and make them easy to interpret:

* Separate Task time and Duration by a slash mark, i.e., 4/16 (4 hours Task time in 16 hours Duration).

* Indicate Task time with a "T" and Duration with a "D," i.e., 4 T, 16 D.

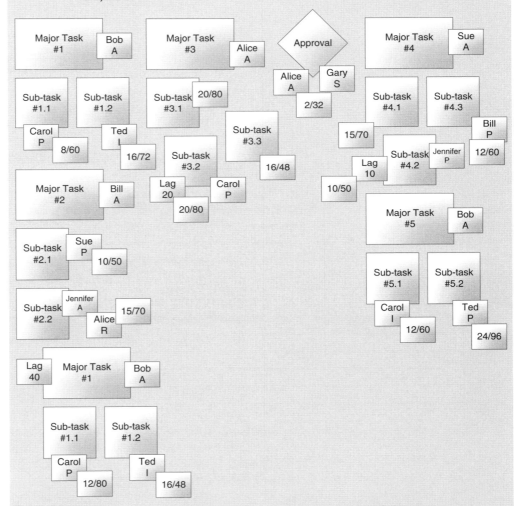

There is a practical reason for wanting both of these estimates even if your organization doesn't do charge backs (the usual reason for getting Task-time estimates). Let's assume you need to shorten the overall time required for your project. (I know, this seems like a far-fetched idea but, hey, it happens.) For some strange reason, your first run at the schedule shows that the project will still be going on seven weeks after the project deadline. Now, we need to look at where you can carve some time out of the thing.

As an example, let's say you have two parallel tasks (start-to-start relationship, both starting at the same time). Let's also assume that both tasks have the same Task time, say 4 hours, but they have very different Durations. Let's say the first task has a Duration of 16 hours and the second task has a Duration of 40 hours.

Which task has the most room to gain significant time? Obviously, the second task has much more room to spare, at least on the surface of it. For some reason, it's going to require a full week to complete this 4-hour task. Even though there may be any number of good reasons for this task being estimated at such a long Duration, the likelihood of being able to pull several hours, or even several days, out of that Duration is pretty good. What it will require is that the project task be elevated in priority — it needs to be allowed to take precedence over some other tasks that the team member needs to accomplish. This may require some negotiation with the team member and his or her manager, but the impact on the overall timeline of the project is probably worth the effort.

Another option would be to add resources to the long-duration task, thereby getting the work done sooner.

Be cautious in going after long durations as the only way to shorten a project timeline. If only works when there really is some way to raise the priority of the project task. This may not be possible or practical.

Scheduling a project is an exercise in guess-work at best. It is based on attempts to predict conditions that will exist in the future. Unfortunately, things change — sometimes radically — between the time a project schedule is first created and the point in time when the work is actually done. Even the best systems in the world can't always account for the unexpected. Base your schedule estimates on the best information you can muster but realize that they are still estimates — not facts. Be aware of the fact that you will most likely need to revise them throughout the project. The illustration on the next page shows and explains the Duration estimates for various tasks.

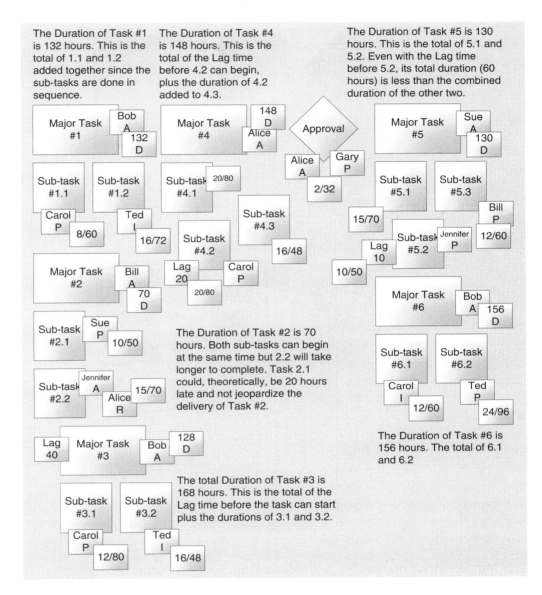

The Duration of Task #1 is 132 hours. This is the total of 1.1 and 1.2 added together since the sub-tasks are done in sequence.

The Duration of Task #4 is 148 hours. This is the total of the Lag time before 4.2 can begin, plus the duration of 4.2 added to 4.3.

The Duration of Task #5 is 130 hours. This is the total of 5.1 and 5.2. Even with the Lag time before 5.2, its total duration (60 hours) is less than the combined duration of the other two.

The Duration of Task #2 is 70 hours. Both sub-tasks can begin at the same time but 2.2 will take longer to complete. Task 2.1 could, theoretically, be 20 hours late and not jeopardize the delivery of Task #2.

The Duration of Task #6 is 156 hours. The total of 6.1 and 6.2.

The total Duration of Task #3 is 168 hours. This is the total of the Lag time before the task can start plus the durations of 3.1 and 3.2.

You need to know both Task time and Duration in order to make good decisions about where time can be salvaged. There's more on this subject in the next section.

PROCESS TIP

Schedule from the bottom up

You will achieve a more comprehensive overall schedule estimate if you schedule from the bottom up. That is to say, if you have sub-tasks, get estimates at that level rather than at the major task level. When the sub-tasks are scheduled, it's fairly easy to determine the overall estimate for the larger task.

However, the reverse is not always true. You may have an estimate for a major task that is quite long. Knowing how that estimate was pieced together from the estimates for all of the sub-tasks involved can be very helpful in adjusting the schedule. This also ties into the discussion that follows on the Critical Path.

Estimating Predictable "Loops" in the Schedule

There is one other situation that needs attention in this discussion about project scheduling. That is the issue of looping activities in a project. Loops occur when work is actually planned to go through an activity more than once. The most common example of this is a testing activity. It is rare for tests to result in a "pass" in just one loop. Just ask anyone who has ever worked on a software project. Tests are included in the project specifically to ensure that the work output meets all the requirements — they're there to give an opportunity to fix problems before passing the work along.

The problem is that we usually can't predict just how many times the work will need to go through the testing loop before it finally passes. So, how do you schedule these things? There is no foolproof way. The best advice may be to think carefully about both the current situation and past experiences with similar situations. In the past, how many times has similar work had to go through the loop before passing? What does that tell us about this case? Is there anything in the current project that makes us believe the situation will be substantially different?

There are a couple of ways to address the actual schedule estimate for a looping activity. The simplest is to make a good guess at how long it will take to go through the loop once, and then multiply that by the number of times you anticipate having to go through it. Frankly, this will usually give a slightly inflated answer. This brings us the second alternative; calculate the time through the loop the first time and then apply a percentage reduction to each successive round. For example, if the first time through looks like it will take 8 hours, it may be reasonable to assume that subsequent rounds will find fewer problems and therefore require less time. If we apply a 25% reduction factor to this, it gives the following estimates for successive rounds:

- First time: 8 hours
- Second time: 6 hours
- Third time: 4.5 hours
- Fourth time: 3.4 hours

If we assume four trips around this loop, the first calculation (four times through at 8 hours each) would give an estimate of 32 hours. Using the reduction factor, the estimate is 21.9 hours.

A word of advice: Whenever possible, schedule for slightly more time than you think you'll need. These things almost never go completely according to plan.

The Gantt Chart

The most common format for displaying schedule information is the Gantt Chart. At its most basic, a Gantt Chart is a simple horizontal bar chart with the tasks listed down the left and the project timeline across the top. This is a common output of most project management software programs. There are also smaller computer programs that produce only Gantt Charts. Bars are drawn

The 90/90 Rule of Project Schedules: The first 90% of the task takes 90% of the time available, and the last 10% takes the other 90% of the time.

Arthur Block
Writer and Humorist

from the scheduled start to the scheduled completion of each task. As work is completed, the bars showing scheduled task durations are filled in to show progress. Most Gantt Chart programs will allow you to show the following:

- Percent complete
- Early start
- Late start
- Early completion
- Late completion

This example also shows Summary Tasks. A Summary Task is a large group of related tasks. It can be as large as a complete project phase or as small as a single, but complex, task. Most of the software available allows you to display different levels of detail on the schedule. For broad-scope reviews, simply displaying the Summary Tasks is often sufficient. For more in-depth management and tracking, the more detailed levels of task scheduling are important.

Most Gantt Chart programs or functions will let you set the time increments that are appropriate for your projects (hours, days, weeks, months). This example has months as the "macro" increment and weeks as the "micro" increment.

Most Gantt Chart programs (or the Gantt Chart functions in larger programs) automatically number tasks in the ID column. In most cases, this is the identifier the program uses to track tasks.

Tasks are listed in the second column. Notice the outline format. The Major Tasks from our examples are shown in bold to indicate the status as "Summary Tasks" and the sub-tasks are indented under them.

Start and finish dates are listed in the third and fourth columns.

The program will usually calculate the task duration in the fifth column.

Bars are drawn from the start date to the end date.

Summary tasks look different than other tasks in most programs.

ID	Task Name	Start	End	Duration	Oct 2000				Nov 2000			Dec 2000		
					10/1	10/8	10/15	10/22	10/29	11/5	11/12	11/19	11/26	12/3	12/10	12/17
1	**Task 1**	**9/29/00**	**10/24/00**	**18d**												
2	Task 1.1	9/29/00	10/11/2000	9d												
3	Task 1.2	10/11/2000	10/24/2000	10d												
4	**Task 2**	**9/29/00**	**10/16/00**	**12d**												
5	Task 2.1	9/29/2000	10/16/2000	12d												
6	Task 2.2	9/29/00	10/11/2000	9d												
7	**Task 3**	**10/4/00**	**10/26/00**	**17d**												
8	Task 3.1	10/4/2000	10/18/2000	11d												
9	Task 3.2	10/18/2000	10/26/2000	7d												
10	**Task 4**	**10/26/00**	**11/21/00**	**19d**												
11	Task 4.1	10/26/2000	11/9/2000	11d												
12	Task 4.2	10/30/2000	11/13/2000	11d												
13	Task 4.3	11/13/2000	11/21/2000	7d												
14	Approval	11/21/2000	11/27/2000	5d												
15	**Task 5**	**11/27/00**	**12/14/00**	**14d**												
16	Task 5.1	11/27/2000	12/5/2000	7d												
17	Task 5.2	12/5/2000	12/14/2000	8d												
18	**Task 6**	**11/27/00**	**12/22/00**	**20d**												
19	Task 6.1	11/27/2000	12/6/2000	8d												
20	Task 6.2	12/6/2000	12/22/2000	13d												

Find the Critical Path

There is a concept in project planning that is very important for the next step in planning. It is the idea of the Critical Path that runs through every project. In fact, there's a whole project management methodology based on it called, oddly enough, Critical Path Method or CPM. In a very simplified definition, the Critical Path of a project is the longest series of tasks and activities (in terms of time) that must be done in sequence.

In every project, there is some series of tasks that must be done one after the other. In most cases, this is because work on each successive task is dependent on the output of the work on the previous task. But, just to confuse things a bit, it is also possible to have tasks that need to be done in sequence based on who needs to do the work. For example, a critical resource — the only person in the company with the necessary skills — is needed on five different tasks. If more resources were available, some of these tasks could be done in parallel. However, since we only have the one person, guess what, he or she can't work on five things at once. Things have to be strung out and that impacts the overall project schedule.

The above example is uncommon but possible. In a more normal situation, by this point in the planning process, your plan may have several lines of tasks running through it — tasks that can be done in parallel. You need to determine which of these parallel lines will require the greatest amount of time to complete. This is your Critical Path. Tasks in parallel lines that require less time are not on the Critical Path. These tasks can be completed late (as long as their completion time doesn't exceed the time on the Critical Path) and have no appreciable effect on the overall time required for the project. A delay on the Critical Path delays the delivery at the end of the project.

For example, let's say you have a series of three tasks in sequence with durations of 24 hours, 10 hours, and 16 hours; and, you have a series of tasks in parallel with them with durations of 16 hours, 8 hours, and 12 hours.

The first string of tasks will take 50 hours to complete. The second string of tasks will take 36 hours to complete. If both sets of tasks need to be completed before the project can proceed to the next set of activities, the first set is on the Critical Path. The second set of tasks can be as much as 14 hours late and still not affect the start of the next set of activities. If, on the other hand, the first set is delayed by even one hour, the whole project could potentially be delayed by one hour.

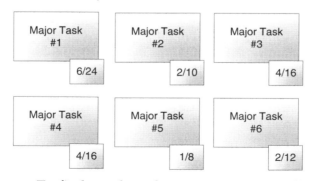

This string of tasks is on the Critical Path. It has an overall duration of 50 hours. A delay of even one hour has the potential to move the project deadline.

This string of tasks has an overall duration of 36 hours. There are 14 hours of "slack" in this string - the last of these tasks can be 14 hours late before it will impact the deadline.

To find out how long your project will take after this first pass at the schedule, simply add together the Durations of all the tasks along the Critical Path. This will tell you how much time you need to remove from the Critical Path in order to come in under the deadline. And, in most projects, you will have to remove time.

PROCESS TIP
Make the Critical Path obvious on your developing plan
You can identify the Critical Path tasks by numbering them in sequence on the task-description Notes (yet another use for the 1-1/2" X 2" size) or by using the blue adhesive dots (remember the list of supplies from early in this chapter?). If you use the dots, it makes it easy to visually follow the Critical Path through the project — just connect the dots.

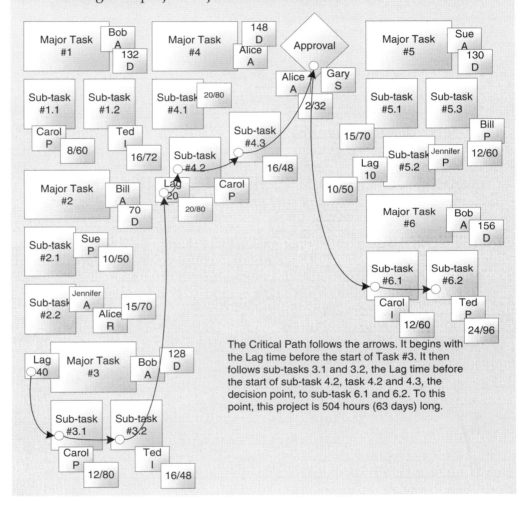

The Critical Path follows the arrows. It begins with the Lag time before the start of Task #3. It then follows sub-tasks 3.1 and 3.2, the Lag time before the start of sub-task 4.2, task 4.2 and 4.3, the decision point, to sub-task 6.1 and 6.2. To this point, this project is 504 hours (63 days) long.

Now comes the task of adjusting the schedule. There are several things you can look for:

- First of all, look for those tasks with large discrepancies between Task-time and Duration. Take them one at a time and see what adjustments can be made.

- Check to see if you can adjust the order in which tasks are completed. Try rearranging the project in a different order. See if rearranging them will yield a shorter timeline.

- Look for tasks along the Critical Path that don't really have to be there. Look for tasks that can actually be done in parallel with the Critical Path.

- Look for ways to overlap tasks. Is it possible to begin a task with only partial output from the preceding task?

- Look for tasks that could be completed faster with additional resources. Just keep in mind that throwing bodies at the problem will sometimes just make it worse. Adding people isn't always the answer.

PROCESS TIP

Negotiations about shortening the Critical Path

When you find the need to negotiate to shorten a duration, look for things you can do, or that you can facilitate, that will help free up the time needed. Facilitation can be as simple as working with a team member to help them rearrange their schedule to fit the project work in ahead of some other, less high priority work. Or it can mean working with a team member's manager to actually get some work off-loaded from them onto someone else so the project can get done. However it works out, remember that in most cases you will be the supplicant — you're the one asking for the favor — arrogance doesn't usually work too well in these situations. Go into it in the spirit of compromise. You might be amazed at how cooperative people can be when given the chance. Remember, your project may be the most important thing on your agenda at the moment, but it may not rank all that high on other people's agendas.

This is one of those places where good pre-work can really pay off. If you did a pretty comprehensive stakeholder analysis up front, you should know (or, at least have a good idea) what benefits your stakeholders are looking for from your project. And your team members' managers are stakeholders, too. If you can tie cooperation on the scheduling issue to achieving the expected benefit, it builds a powerful case. This isn't foolproof but it can go a long way toward helping resolve scheduling conflicts.

Contingency Plan

It is a bad plan that admits no modification.
Publilius Syrus
1st Century B.C.
Latin Writer

Murphy is alive and well and lurking around waiting to prove that, "if something can go wrong, it will." You can't really prevent him from messing with your project but you can reduce the likelihood that he'll show up as often as he might like. And you can develop plans for dealing with him when he does show up.

Look over your plan as it is now. By this time you should have a pretty comprehensive plan developed — a plan that has most of the work outlined, resources assigned, and schedule developed. Take a careful look at it. Think about how it will actually play out. You should be able to spot a number of points in the project where "something can go wrong."

Potential problem points come in a wide array of sizes, shapes, and levels of severity. They may be connected to critical interfaces between activities:

- If activity A and activity B are not completed at the same time, a schedule slip is likely.
- If the vendor doesn't make the delivery schedule, everything will slide.

They can be work-output-dependent:

- If the solution we think will work, doesn't, we'll have a real problem.
- If the research tells us something we haven't anticipated, the rest of the plan may be wrong.

They could be resource-related:

- If Bill can't learn how to do this in time, we're in trouble.
- If Sue gets pulled off our project to work on that other project, we don't have a replacement identified.

They can even be decision-related:

- If Mr. Smith doesn't review this and give us a decision in the time-frame we've set, everything is delayed.
- If they ask us to re-work some part of this, the whole project will fall behind schedule.

As a general rule, there are certain points in most projects that should always be examined for potential trouble. If you don't look at anything else, evaluate the potential for problems at these points:

- Any point where two or more activities converge or where their outputs have to be combined. These integration points always have the potential to be a problem. If the activities aren't on schedule or if the pieces don't fit, you have a problem.
- Any activity which is effectively out of the direct control of you or the project team. This includes the obvious things like work being done by outside vendors or other areas of your own company. It also includes decisions and approvals being made by managers not directly involved with the project.

It should be obvious that one of the first places to look for potential problems is along the Critical Path of the project. However, don't ignore the secondary and other paths. Sometimes this is where the real problems can occur. You really should look at everything in the project plan and ask these questions:

- What could go wrong here? (Remember Risk Assessment from Chapter 2: *Project Pre-Work*? Same idea.)
- On the Probability Scale, rate how likely it is to go wrong.

Probability Rating

	Very Low 1	Low 3	Moderate 5	High 7	Very High 9
Probability of Occurrence	Very unlikely to occur (less than 10% chance)	Possible but still unlikely to occur (10%-25% chance)	25%-50% chance of occurance	50%-75% chance of occurance	Greater than 75% chance of occurance

- On the Impact Scale, if it does go wrong, that how bad it will be. Remember that rating impact requires that you look at the impact on each of the three major constraints of time, resources, and output.

Impact Rating

Impact on Constraint	Very Low .5	Low 1	Moderate 2	High 4	Very High 8
Cost or Resources	Insignificant cost increase or impact on resource utilization	Less than a 5% cost increase or 5% change in resource utilization	5%-10% cost increase or 5%-10% change in resource utilization	10%-20% cost increase or 10%-20% change in resource utilization	Greater than 20% cost increase or 20% increase in resource utilization
Schedule	Insignificant schedule impact	Less than 5% slipage in schedule	Overall project schedule slipage of 5%-10%	Overall project schedule slipage of 10%-20%	Overall project schedule slipage greater than 20%
Output Quality or Performance	Impact on quality or performance barely noticeable	Only very demanding applications are affected	The change in quality or performance requires customer approval	The reduction in quality or performance is unacceptable to the customer	Project deliverable is effectively unusable

Once again, we come to a case of making judgements and decisions based on inadequate or incomplete information. So, what else is new? Use the Probability/Impact Calculator to identify those tasks that require Contingency Plans.

Probability/Impact Matrix

Probability	Risk Score = Probability X Impact				
9	4.5	9	18	36	72
7	3.5	7	14	28	56
5	2.5	5	10	20	40
3	1.5	3	6	12	24
1	.5	1	2	4	8
	.5	1	2	4	8
			Impact		

Contingency Plan Risk

☐ Contingency plan probably not required   ▨ Contingency plan should be considered   ■ Contingency plan required

Contingency planning is not just "disaster-recovery planning." It is also "disaster-prevention planning." In fact, the first thing you should do when you have identified a potential problem point in a project is to look for ways, in the project plan itself, to mitigate either the anticipated probability or impact, or both. Preventing the problem is always better than recovering from it.

Look for ways to build preventative steps into the plan. Going back to the examples of potential problems, let's look at some preventative measures that could be taken.

For problems connected to critical interfaces between activities:

- If activity A and activity B are not completed at the same time, a schedule slip is likely.
  - ○ Could you ensure that the two activities are completed on schedule by monitoring them more closely? How about having supplementary resources available to pick up the slack if one starts to slip? Is there some activity that could be added to the project before these tasks get started that would help ensure that the tasks get done on time?
- If the vendor doesn't make the delivery schedule, everything will slide.
  - ○ Would assigning someone to monitor the vendor's progress help? Have you checked out this vendor's historical performance on delivery? Could you set up an alternate vendor, just in case?

For problems that are work-output-dependent:

- If the solution we think will work, doesn't, we'll have a real problem.
  - ○ Is there any way to pre-test the solution? Should you maybe develop an alternative solution along side the preferred option?
- If the research tells us something we haven't anticipated, the rest of the plan may be wrong.
  - ○ Could you build different plans for the project based on various potential outcomes of the research? Is there some way to get preliminary results from the research before it is completed so that adjustments can be made before the final results are delivered?

For problems that are resource-related:

- If Joe can't learn how to do this in time, we're in trouble.
  - ○ Is Joe the right person for the job? What can be done to increase Joe's chances of learning the necessary skills? Should you be training two people instead of just one?
- If Sue gets pulled off our project to work on that other project, we don't have a replacement identified.
  - ○ Can you identify an alternative person to replace Sue if needed? Can you monitor the "other project" to see if Sue's involvement in it is becoming more likely? Can you work with Sue's manager to ensure that she stays on your project?

For problems that are decision-related:

- If Mr. Smith doesn't review this and give us a decision in the time-frame we've set, everything is delayed.
  - ○ Can you pre-warn Mr. Smith that the information is coming and stress the need for a timely decision? Should you maybe check Mr. Smith's calendar to see what might interfere with him being able to focus on the issue when it gets to him? Can you get Mr. Smith to designate an alternate decision-maker in case he's not available?
- If they ask us to re-work some part of this, the whole project will fall behind schedule.
  - ○ What can be done to lessen the likelihood that the re-work will be requested? Can you schedule more frequent reviews of the work in

progress? Can you add some additional quality checks? If the re-work still looks likely, can you actually schedule time for it into the project?

If, after all of the preventative actions are included, you still think the potential problem deserves attention, build an actual contingency plan. Most contingency plans never have to be implemented but, when it does become necessary to use one, it is awfully nice to have it available.

There are three major components to a good contingency plan:

1. A description of the "trigger event" — how will you know you need to go to "plan B."

2. A statement of what to do if the "trigger event" happens — "plan B."

3. A list of who to tell that you're now on "plan B."

The "Trigger Event" This is the description of the situation that will tell you that you have a problem. It should be as clear and concise as possible. It should also describe an observable set of conditions. For example:

*   Delivery of raw material delayed. ("I went to the receiving dock and the stuff wasn't there.")

*   Expected outcome not achieved. ("Well, that didn't turn out like we expected it to.")

*   Decision not made on time. ("He was tied up in meetings off-site for three days.")

The "trigger event" is your signal to implement the contingency plan. Describe the conditions of the situation you anticipate, and when and if they occur, go to "plan B." Don't wait and hope things will get better. They usually won't. They usually get worse.

What To Do This is the description of the specific actions to be taken as a result of the "trigger event" happening. This can be as simple as "contact the alternative vendor," or as complex as a completely re-planned project from this point forward.

Most of the time, the contingency actions fall somewhere in between these two extremes. The important thing is to have a documented plan ready for dealing with the situation. You can think of this as a mini-project-plan that can be "pasted over" a piece of the existing plan in case of an emergency. The level of detail is a judgement call on your part. It should contain sufficient detail to allow you or a team member to track and monitor the work and the effects of that work.

Who To Tell This is a very important part of the contingency planning process. Every contingency plan should have a list of the people who need to be notified that the project is now on "plan B." Obviously, this list should include the members of the project team. It should also include any managers who have an interest in the project. If the problem is going to affect either the timing or the content of the final deliverable, the customer should also be included.

PROCESS TIP
Contingency Planning is great group game

If there was ever a place for a lot of heads working on an issue, this is it. Contingency planning benefits significantly from taking multiple approaches to the problem from multiple angles. Be sure that the contingency planning effort is given enough time. This is one activity you don't want to shortchange. If you've developed your plan on the wall, walk through the whole thing — beginning to end — with the planning team and anybody else you can include. (This is a good place to involve others who will work on the project but who were not part of the whole planning effort — "fresh eyes" can frequently spot things that those familiar with the situation might miss.)

As you step through the plan, ask the questions:

- What could go wrong?
- How likely is to go wrong?
- If it goes wrong, how bad will it be?

Try for a consensus about the ratings of both probability and impact. If someone in the group is way off from what everyone else is rating a task (say, everyone else is rating it Low/Low and one person is rating it Medium/High) — probe to find out why. If the issue seems to need further investigation, do it.

One thing to try to avoid is making final decisions in the middle of identifying potential problems. Plan to go through the plan twice: Once to identify potential problems that need attention, and again to develop the responses to those problems — either through changing the current project plan or by developing contingency plans.

When you identify a spot where you believe you need to look for a way to mitigate the problem through planning, or where you think a contingency plan is needed, mark it with a red dot. (Remember the other colored dots recommended in the planning materials?)

When you've been through the plan completely, go back and address each "red dot" issue, one at a time. Develop and document your plans. Leave the dots in place as indicators that the issue has been dealt with.

SPECIAL NOTE: If you rearrange the sequence of activities to deal with the problem, remember to re-examine your Critical Path. If you've changed the sequence, added resources, or in some other way altered the original plan, you have probably changed the schedule as well. Review the overall schedule, and the Critical Path in particular, in light of the new layout and adjust it as necessary.

Use this as a thinking guide

Fill in the appropriate project information.

Describe the "Trigger Event." Include enough detail to ensure it will be spotted if it happens.

Rate the Probability and Impact.

Describe anything that can be done in the plan to mitigate either the probability or impact.

Describe your specific Contingency Plan actions. If necessary, include a reference to where additional detail can be found.

List everyone who needs to be told that the project is now on "Plan B." Check them off and date when they were notified.

Contingency Planning Form

Project:	Date:
Project Leader:	
Project Sponsor:	

Description of the "Trigger Event"

_____
_____
_____

Probability	Impact	Planning Actions
☐ Very High	☐ Very High	_____
☐ High	☐ High	_____
☐ Moderate	☐ Moderate	_____
☐ Low	☐ Low	_____
☐ Very Low	☐ Very Low	_____

Contingency Plan

_____
_____
_____
_____

Notification List   Notified Date

_____ ☐ _____
_____ ☐ _____
_____ ☐ _____

Major contingency plans should be discussed with the project team during or after the planning activity. This is a "comfort" issue as much as an informational one. It is nice to know that someone has thought about what could go wrong and has made some plans, just in case. This discussion can also result in additional issues that may need to be addressed by contingency plans.

Discussing contingency plans with managers, sponsors, and customers is also a good idea. At the very least, you are making them aware of the potential risks faced by the project, and demonstrating your managerial capabilities by having anticipated and planned for them.

Finalize This Version of the Plan

When the group is satisfied that the plan that has been developed through this process represents a realistic view of the work to be done, the people who will do it, and the time it will take to get it done, adjourn the session and prepare the plan for review and approval.

PROCESS TIP
A variation on the Post-It® Note Process
As a variation on the Post-It® Note process, you can use Post-It® Notes of different colors to signify different things. For example, you can use one color for all the activities that need to be done by one department and different colors for activities involving other departments. This makes it easy, particularly

on large cross-functional projects, to keep the various interactions among departments clear.

You can use the same idea to show the Critical Path of the project. Simply change all the task notes along the Critical Path to a different color. This is useful when using the wall-size plan as a tool for communicating with the larger organization.

Project Budgets

Under budgetary pressure (arbitrary or not) it is remarkable how many options one discovers one can live without.

J.R. Schlesinger
U.S. Secretary of Defense

Depending on the level of control you have over the resources dedicated to your project, you may need to develop a budget.

Of all of the items that can be budgeted, labor is the most common. Budgeting labor involves identifying the probable time each team member will need to spend on their portion of the project work and determining the cost of that time. This is another reason to capture Task-time in your schedule estimates. Task-time is what is usually charged to the project.

The hourly rates used for budgeting in most organizations include not only the salary of the employee but also a group of expenses sometimes called the "burden." These expenses include the employee's portion of the company benefit package such as health insurance, vacation, and sick time. They may also include a pro-rated overhead expense, or fixed overhead allocation, which amounts to the portion of the overall expenses of operating the business. Your payroll or accounting department is probably the best place to look for these figures.

Once you know how the company accounts for each employee, you can begin to develop a budget that accounts for the labor costs of everyone working on the project. Start by identifying how many hours each team member is expected to devote to the project. Remember, this is Task-time not Duration. It is sometimes useful to do this in smaller portions, such as individual project phases or significant groups of tasks, rather than for the total project. This is particularly true if the project is to be long (over six months), or if certain team members will only be involved in certain phases or portions of the work.

PROCESS TIP
Project budgeting is not a mystery

Project budgeting is not really a mysterious activity. For the most part, like so much of project planning, it's an exercise in guesswork. You are attempting to predict the future. Since that is the case, you should, whenever possible, give yourself some flexibility. Most project budgets are calculated to include a contingency or "padding" factor. This is usually a percentage of the original calculation added as a "just in case" cushion. Most of the time, it is limited to 10% to 15% of the total budget. Your organization may have a formula for calculating budget contingencies. If so, use it. If not, consider adding a contingency amount to any budget estimate you create.

Budgeting labor is a fairly straightforward process. Simply multiply a team member's labor rate (the number used to determine the total cost for that employee including wages and any additional costs) by the number of hours that person is expected to work on the project.

PROCESS TIP
Budgeting labor

This budget form is a simple example of an aid for labor budgeting. Note that there is a column for Contingency funds included in this form. This may or may not be something you wish to show as part of your calculation. If you choose not to calculate a contingency for the total project, you should calculate, and include, contingency funds in the estimates for each project phase. If you download this form from the www.projectmanagementtools.com web site, the calculation functionality is built into the form.

Project Budget Worksheet - Labor

Project:		Date:	
Project Leader:			
Project Sponsor:			

Team Member	Rate	Hours per Project Phase or Task Group						Total
Totals								

Fill in the appropriate project information.

List team members down the left.

Indicate each person's charge rate.

Estimate how many hours each person will spend in each project phase.

Total both horizontally and vertically.

Budgeting other items, such as machine time, production capacity, services, etc., follows the same essential process as budgeting labor. Once you know the cost of the item to be used, you can develop a budget to track it. In this case, the cost figures are usually figured on a "rate-per-unit" basis. For example, machine time may be calculated at "X" dollars per hour; materials may be calculated at "X" dollars per piece (dozen, foot, pound, ounce, etc.).

PROCESS TIP
Budgeting non-labor items

Here's a form for calculating non-labor items. Note that this form also has a "Contingency" column. To use this one, list the items to be budgeted down the left, indicate the rate per unit and how many units are budgeted for each project phase. If you download this form from the www.projectmanagementtools.com web site, the calculation functionality is built into the form.

Project Budget Worksheet - Non-Labor

Project:		Date:	
Project Leader:			
Project Sponsor:			

Item	Cost/ Unit	Units per Project Phase or Task Group								Total
Totals										

Fill in the appropriate project information.

List items to be purchased or charged to the project down the left.

Indicate the charge rate (the per-unit cost) for each item.

Estimate how many items will be needed in each project phase.

Total both horizontally and vertically.

The Project Budget Checklist in Appendix A: *Project Planning and Management Checklists*, outlines the most common elements of a project budget. Each organization has its own process and format for budgets, and the best assistance you can get in developing yours will come from your organization's accounting department. Ask for information and assistance from the people who do this for a living.

> **Special Note:** Most of the integrated project management software programs on the market have functions that simplify the development and tracking of these various "budget" items. If you need to track one or more of these, look for a program that has the features you need.

Other Plan Elements

In addition to the major pieces of the project plan already discussed, there are some other pieces that can be included that focus on specific aspects of the project, like test plans, integration plans, and transfer plans.

Test Plans In many projects, there will be a necessity to test and verify some of the work that has been done. This is very common in software development projects but can also be part of many other types of projects. Test plans can be developed that detail exactly how work output will be tested, what tools will be used to conduct the tests, how results will be validated and verified, etc.

Test plans are sometimes developed outside the general project planning effort. They are usually developed by the people who will be doing the testing. They should include all the information necessary to conduct and evaluate the test.

One important thing to keep in mind about tests is that they are rarely only done once. Most test activities result in work being re-done and sent back through the test — sometimes several times — before the work finally passes the test and the project proceeds. This is a major consideration in project scheduling. (See the discussion under the heading, Schedule the Work earlier in this chapter.)

Test plans should be fully documented and included as part of the overall project plan package.

Integration Plans

If at first you don't succeed, use a larger hammer.
Anonymous

At some point in almost every project, various pieces must be brought together and made to fit. In most projects, this occurs several times. Knowing where these points are (based on the project flow chart and the project schedule), and what must happen when the deliverables are brought together, is the basis of your integration plan. Any tests required to verify that things are working as expected should be included as part of the integration plan.

Depending on the complexity of the activities at each integration point, your plans can be as simple as notes about what should happen. For more complex integrations, it may be advisable to develop more comprehensive plans. These can include a flow chart and schedule for the activity, a responsibility matrix (if enough people are involved), contingency plans, etc.

Every integration is a potential trouble spot. Therefore, integration points may need contingency plans in case something goes wrong. If the integration doesn't work as it should, delays are likely, some tasks may need to be re-done, additional resources may be required, etc. Think about the integrations that will be needed for your project and plan and document them carefully.

Transfer Plans

Our one major goal is to create satisfied customers. Hence, all systems, objectives, training, and measurements are designed to improve customer satisfaction.
John A. Young
Former President & CEO
Hewlett-Packard

This is usually the final piece of the overall project plan package. It is the detailed plan for how you will get rid of the project's output when you're through. It is important to develop the basic elements of this plan early in the project even though it is likely that some of the details will change as you approach the actual transfer of project output.

For some projects, transfer is a very straightforward hand-off of the output. You simply give the finished product to the customer, thank them for their business and walk away. (Oh, if only it were that simple!) In other cases, particularly in projects to develop and implement processes, transfer and implementation can be fairly involved. In these cases, there is usually some disruption in the work flow of the customer. The old process needs to be phased out as the new process is phased in. This situation deserves some careful planning. You want the transfer to be as painless as possible and this usually requires some careful coordination between the project team and the customer.

The transfer plan should be developed in close cooperation with the project's customer. It should outline, in appropriate detail:

- The various pieces of the final package of project output to be transferred — what will be delivered at the end of the project.

- How the transfer will be coordinated — who will be involved, who will make decisions, etc.

- Who will be responsible for what parts of the transfer — which parts are the responsibility of the project team and which parts are the responsibility of the customer.

- When the transfer will occur, how long it should take, and how disruptions in the customer's work, if any, will be handled.

- Details of any on-going support that might be needed once the output is transferred. This should include any requirements for documentation or training that will be needed. If there is a need for specific documentation or training, development of these outputs should be included as part of the project plan, just like any other tasks.

Once the transfer plan is developed, you should monitor the project with an eye to the agreed-upon output. It is very common for the ultimate deliverable to change from the beginning of a project to its final handoff to the customer. Any significant changes should be communicated to the customer immediately.

Even barring significant changes to the output, it is a good idea to schedule a review of the transfer plan somewhere about the middle of the project and again close to the actual point of transfer. These reviews should be included in the project plan as tasks.

Other Planning Issues

In addition to everything else, there are still some things to consider while you're doing your planning. Three issues in particular deserve some discussion: Monitoring plans; management reporting issues; and team meetings and status reporting.

Monitoring Plans

If you can't measure it, you can't manage it.
Anonymous

You've probably detailed a lot of activity that must be done in order to complete the project. You should take the time to develop a plan for monitoring the critical activities — those things, usually along the Critical Path, that must be completed.

There is a danger in trying to monitor too much of the detail of a project. The result is, more often than not, that some of the major activities are allowed to get off track. Focusing too narrowly is at least as dangerous as focusing too broadly.

Most monitoring plans are simply notes to yourself of those things you should be watching. Keep these notes on your personal calendar, in your project notebook or even on your copy of one or more of the plan documents. You should have included reviews of work in progress in your overall project plans, but these "formal" reviews are not enough to really monitor all the work being done. Here are some tips about which things to monitor:

- Watch every activity along the Critical Path.

- Monitor activities leading to points where contingency plans have been developed or are likely to be implemented. Watch those activities that you've tried to "plan your way around" very carefully, since these are points where you may need to step in rather quickly, if your current plans don't work as expected.

- Monitor integration points carefully. These are the points where the outputs from two or more activities come together. If the integrations don't work, you may be facing a serious delay in the project.

- Watch test activities and results. Even if you've planned on doing a test three or four times, it may turn out that you need to do it six or seven times to achieve a pass. This will probably affect the overall project schedule.

Talk with team members frequently and handle problems as they arise — don't hope they will go away by themselves — they won't. They will just escalate into full-scale crises.

Remember, you have a team of "experts" in the various activities of the project. Delegate some of the monitoring responsibilities to appropriate team members. Use their expertise to help with the monitoring process.

Management Reporting

Big Brother is watching you.
George Orwell
1903-1950
English Author

On almost every project, you will periodically report your progress to someone. Most likely this will be to some level of management and other stakeholders in your project.

Setting out a plan for doing this, and a schedule which details specific reviews and presentations, will make your life much easier. Trying to "just keep everyone up to date" in an informal manner is both slip-shod and prone to error. The chances are very great that you'll miss someone or some important piece of information.

Management presentations in the middle of the project can take advantage of the roll-up features of many of the project management software programs (being able to "roll up" tasks and schedules into summary detail). Most managers don't need to know all the details of the work to be done. They need an overview of the project. Be aware of the "need-to-know" level of your audience and prepare a presentation that delivers what they need. Be prepared to go into additional detail if requested.

This plan may be as simple as a schedule of staff meetings where you will give a short update on the project. It may include a format for written reports and "official" management presentations and a schedule of updates and "walk-throughs" for various managers and departments.

However you decide to maintain communication with the people interested in the progress of your project, detailing the activity in a plan will help you ensure that this critical communication is maintained. Remember to schedule these reviews on the Flow Chart, the Schedule, and the Responsibility Matrix as project tasks.

> **PROCESS TIP**
> **Use the Responsibility Matrix to identify your presentation audience**
> Consider using the Responsibility Matrix as a tool to identify when and to whom reports should be provided. Including managers, customers, and other stakeholders on the Matrix can be very helpful. Use the "R" (Review Required), the "I" (Input Required), or the "S" (Sign-off Required) codes to indicate the points where they need to be involved in the project. This can be very helpful in planning and tracking this activity.

Team Meetings and Status Reporting

You people [his subordinates] are telling me what you think I want to know. I want to know what is actually happening.

Creighton Abrams
1914-1974
Commander, American Forces, Vietnam

Formal project team meetings are, unfortunately, rare on most projects in most organizations. This is an inconvenience but it is not, necessarily, a major problem. If you are paying attention to your project, you'll be in fairly constant contact with most of the project team.

If you can hold project team meetings, schedule them regularly if possible. A project team meeting is the time and place at which the various team members can update each other. Try to pick a day and time that can be fairly consistent throughout the project. This makes it easier for people to plan for the meeting.

These meetings provide an opportunity for recognizing successes and for dealing with problems before they become disasters. They are also an excellent tool for developing and maintaining the "sense of team" that is very helpful in promoting project success.

There are some important things to keep in mind about these meetings:

- Always have an agenda for the meeting. Distribute it the day before the meeting if possible. A sample agenda format is included in Appendix B: *Project Planning and Management Forms*.

- These meetings should be "project" meetings. The agenda should focus on project-wide issues — things of concern and interest to all team members. No one likes to sit through a meeting where two or three people debate and solve technical issues of no interest to the team as a whole. Keep the meeting focused on broad project issues and handle the individual or small group problems outside the meeting.

- Schedule the meeting for a specific length of time (usually one to two hours) and adjourn it when that time has come. If all the agenda items have been covered before the scheduled end-time of the meeting, adjourn early. There's no rule that says, just because you scheduled it for an hour and got done in forty minutes, you have to keep going until the hour is up. On the flip side, if the agenda is too long, identify the items that will be held over to the next meeting. If an emergency meeting is necessary to deal with some pressing issue, schedule it. Just don't let this meeting run over its scheduled time.

- Always take minutes and distribute them within 24-hours of the end of the meeting. (This is a great use for e-mail. You can even include other stakeholders in the distribution.) A sample meeting minutes form is included in Chapter 7: *Checklists and Form Masters*.

- Use the meeting as a forum for "cheerleading" and recognizing the successes of team members of the team as a whole.

- A regular part of each meeting should be a status report from each team member. There is a caution on this one: Even if you get a verbal status report from everyone, you still need to have a written status report from every team member. Meeting minutes and notes are usually not enough information to effectively track project activity. The written status report should provide additional detail. This is discussed in more detail in Chapter 5: *Project Implementation*.

Deliverables at This Point

The deliverable at this point is the project plan. Whether it is a formal management presentation of the plan, with all the "bells and whistles" or a simple review with the project team, finalizing the plan is a major milestone on any project.

If a formal management presentation is required, give it careful thought. Consider your audience and what they really need to know in order to understand and support your project.

If the plan is presented in a management presentation, it is an opportunity to draw attention to significant issues about the project. You should be sure to include the following that are appropriate in your presentation:

- A walk-through of the complete project plan with emphasis on any of the following that are of concern:
  - Major "unknowns" in the project. This can include such things as not knowing what the results of research will show, or the direction they will require you to take the project. It could be not having enough information about a new technology at this point to make a decision about using it. It could be not knowing the cost of some portion of the project. Or it could be any number of other issues that are not clearly enough defined to make solid decisions.
  - Tight schedule points where deadlines might be missed.
  - Resource concerns such as limitations, skill levels, availability, etc.
- An explanation of the reporting mechanisms and the frequency with which you will be keeping others informed of progress on the project.
- Any special concerns you might have regarding the project.

PROCESS TIP

Use the Post-It® Note plan as a focus for your presentation

This presentation is a great place to show off your Post-It® Note plan. If you are concerned that your audience may not understand the complexity of what you are about to undertake, you can use the wall chart, created in your planning, as a visual aid. These "rough" plans can be very impressive. Describing the Post-It® Note Process and demonstrating how the project unfolded in planning shows thoroughness. It also lends credibility to your having considered the project from a variety of angles before settling on a final plan.

Alternate Plan Styles

There are a number of ways to graphically display the project plan. What you have developed in the planning process is essentially a flow chart of the project. Taking this information and displaying it in a more presentable graphic form makes it very usable as both a communication and negotiation tool.

The examples on the following pages are all variations of the same information displayed in different formats. These examples are presented here to demonstrate the variety of ways of developing and displaying project plan information.

Work Breakdown Structure (WBS) Alpha-Numeric Format

Work Breakdown Structure is a task list for the project in outline form. Most of the project management software packages on the market require a WBS outline as one of the primary inputs for the program.

Constructing a Work Breakdown Structure outline is simply a matter of taking the tasks captured in the planning process and organizing them as a written outline. Major tasks form the first level, sub-tasks form the subsequent levels of the outline.

There are two basic outline formats that can be used: Alpha-numeric and decimal. The alpha-numeric version looks like this:

I. Building plans completed
II. Build offices
   A. Frame walls
   B. Install plumbing
      1. Plumbing rough work
      2. Finish connections
      3. Install fixtures
   C. Install drywall
   D. Install systems
      1. Install heating and cooling system
         a. Install controls
         b. Install connections
      2. Install heating and cooling ventilation system
      3. Install fire-suppression sprinkler system
      4. Install electrical and communication lines
      5. Install phones
      6. Install computers
         a. Complete network connections
         b. Test network and systems
   E. Paint walls
   F. Install ceiling tiles
      1. Install gridwork
      2. Install ceiling tiles
   G. Lay carpet and tile
   H. Install moldings and complete finish-work
   I. Clean-up
   J. Furniture delivered
      1. Set up desks and chair groupings
      2. Set up file cabinet groupings
      3. Set up remaining furnishings
   K. Final clean-up
   L. Office construction complete/final acceptance

Work Breakdown Structure (WBS) Decimal Format

The decimal version looks like this:

1. Building plans completed
2. Build offices
   2.1. Frame walls
   2.2. Install plumbing
      2.2.1. Plumbing rough work
      2.2.2. Finish connections
      2.2.3. Install fixtures
   2.3. Install drywall
   2.4. Install systems
      2.4.1. Install heating and cooling system
         2.4.1.1. Install controls
         2.4.1.2. Install connections
      2.4.2. Install heating and cooling ventilation system
      2.4.3. Install fire-suppression sprinkler system
      2.4.4. Install electrical and communication lines
      2.4.5. Install phones
      2.4.6. Install computers
         2.4.6.1. Complete network connections
         2.4.6.2. Test network and systems
   2.5. Paint walls
   2.6. Install ceiling tiles
      2.6.1. Install gridwork
      2.6.2. Install ceiling tiles
   2.7. Lay carpet and tile
   2.8. Install moldings and complete finish-work
   2.9. Clean-up
   2.10. Furniture delivered
      2.10.1. Set up desks and chair groupings
      2.10.2. Set up file cabinet groupings
      2.10.3. Set up remaining furnishings
   2.11. Final clean-up
   2.12. Office construction complete/final acceptance

There are a number of ways to graphically display the project plan. What you developed in the planning process is essentially a flow chart of the project. Taking this information and displaying it in a more presentable graphic form makes it very usable as both a communication and negotiation tool.

The following examples are all variations on the basic flow chart and contain most of the information displayed in different formats. Programs such as Visio® and ABC Flowcharter® are ideal tools for converting the wall-sized plan to a more portable version. Most of the more popular word processors like Microsoft® Word® and Corel® WordPerfect® contain enough graphic functions to do the job but they take a bit more effort.

Standard Flowchart

A standard flow chart shows tasks, sub-tasks, decision points, the flow of work, and dependencies between tasks. One advantage of this chart style is the ability to show what happens as a decision point if the decision is "no" or if a portion of the work leading to the decision must be redone. This style also parallels the planning process as described here.

Enhanced Flowchart

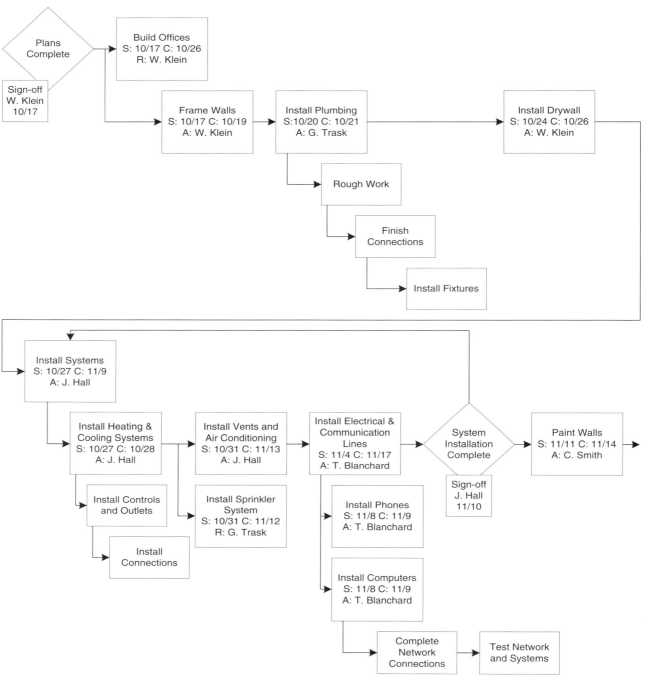

In this version of a flow chart, the standard information has been enhanced by the addition of the starting (S:) and completion (C:) dates for tasks and the names of those Accountable (A:) for each task. This combines some of the information from the schedule and the Responsibility Matrix into a flow chart.

In this example, there is an assumption that the sub-tasks fall under the responsibility of the person identified as accountable for the high-level tasks of which they are a part. If this is not true, or if schedule detail is needed at the sub-task level, it can be added.

Flowchart Over a Time Grid

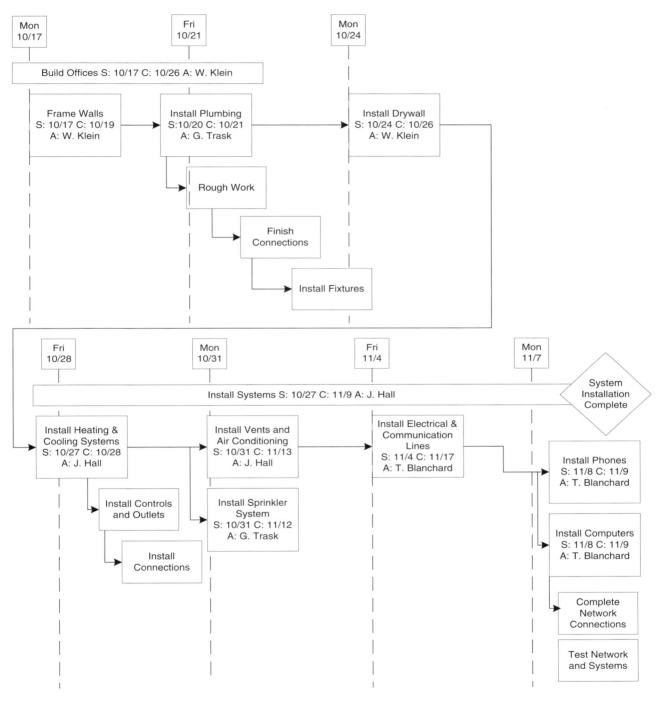

It is possible to lay a flow chart over a time grid and thereby create a combined flow chart and schedule. Usually, the left side of each task box is placed to correspond to the scheduled starting date for that task. Decisions are frequently displayed above the tasks they impact. Summary tasks, such as the "Build Offices" and "Install Systems" groups of tasks, are shown as bars corresponding to the duration of the complete set of tasks that make them up.

PERT (Program Review and Evaluation Technique) Chart

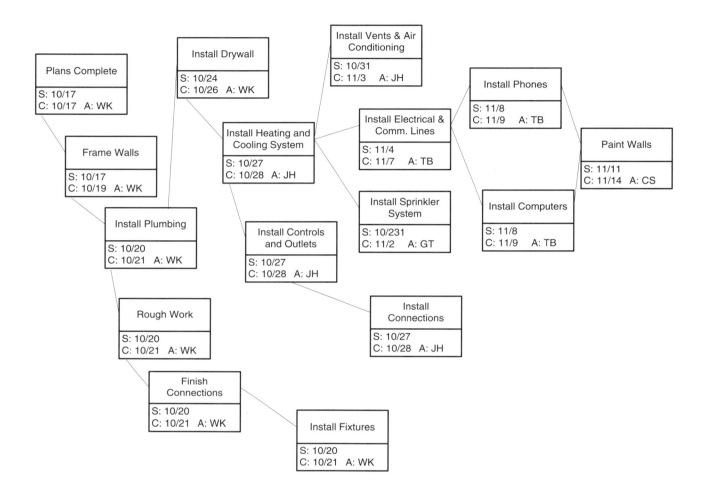

A PERT chart is essentially a network diagram showing the relationships among tasks. As of this writing, most automated PERT-charting programs will not allow you to indicate and reverse directional flow of work (such as would occur in a decision to rework or a testing loop). The built-in assumption is that all work moves forward. Most PERT programs do, however, require the inclusion of starting and completion dates and many also provide for assignment of tasks to individuals.

Timeline Chart

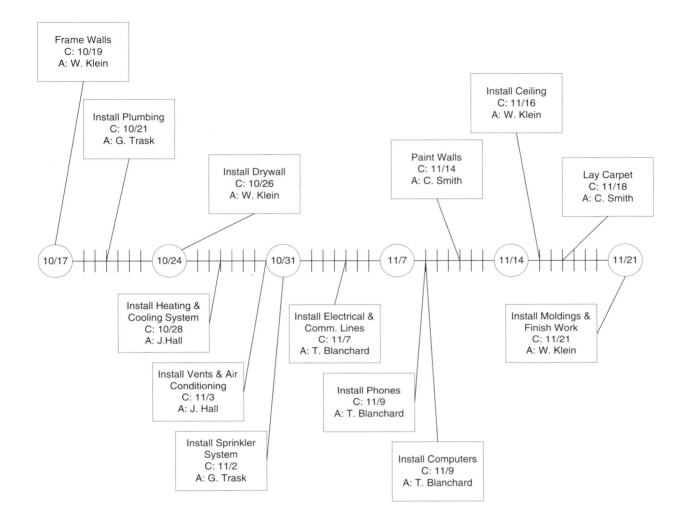

This chart style uses a central timeline as the base. A convenient time interval is used as a reference (in this case, the dates are all Mondays) and appropriate time interval marks are placed between the reference points (in this case, days). Tasks are shown in the boxes. The boxes are connected to the timeline as the starting date of each task. Completion dates and accountabilities are listed in the boxes.

This chart style can be very useful for building a very quick schedule for a project. However, it does not lend itself to very complex or very long-duration projects.

Issues by Project Type

Process Projects

- Developing a complete analysis of the potential impacts of the proposed process. It is important that the project leader and the project team clearly understand the full implications and impacts of the proposed process. This information can only be obtained by working directly with the people who will use the process and those who support both them and the process.

- Determining the internal and external support needed to develop and implement the proposed process. Internal support personnel should be actively involved in the planning process. Depending on the complexity of the proposed process, there may need to be involvement from outside vendors of services and equipment. If needed, information regarding external vendors should be gathered at this stage.

- Identifying pre-process and post-process impacts and how to deal with them. This is part of the development of an overall understanding of the proposed process. It is usually a good idea to develop a "process map" showing the capabilities and limitations of the various process steps and how they inter-relate.

- Identifying critical points in the development process where user (Alpha) tests might be needed. The more complex the process, the more useful incremental tests become. Alpha tests are designed to demonstrate and verify pieces of the process in order to insure that the project is still "on track." Alpha tests should also show whether the various elements being developed meet customer requirements and expectations.

Product/Service Projects

- Defining the exact specifications of the product/service. When developing a product or service for sale to external customers, it is important to establish the parameters early in the development process. This sets the boundaries of the development process and can save significant time and money by eliminating certain options before development begins.

- Defining the specific market niche to be addressed. As global competition increases, niche marketing becomes more and more important. One size no longer fits all. Defining the needs and expectations of a specific niche helps focus development activity.

- Identifying internal and external support needed to develop the product/service. Most product or service development projects require extensive support inside the organization and some support from outside. Identifying support needs early allows planning to include them.

- Identifying potential trouble spots in the organization's systems which could impact customer delivery. The world outside the company is usually far more complex and unpredictable than the world inside. Any number of factors could impact delivery of the product or service. Identifying potential trouble spots allows realistic contingency planning.

- Identifying production requirements and ensuring that they can be met. After the product is developed, it must be manufactured. After a service is developed, it must be delivered. Identifying these needs during planning will build most of the elements of the transfer plan.

- Identifying critical points in the development process where customer (Alpha) tests or input might be needed or desirable. Small-scale, incremental tests are always a good idea. They provide information needed for minor (or major) course corrections. Alpha tests are generally tests of "pieces" of the finished product during which potential customers are asked for their input about the direction of development. Usually these tests are arranged and managed by Marketing but some members of the development team should be included.

- Identifying points in development where customer reactions to the product are needed (Beta or Market Tests). Beta tests are generally tests of final prototypes (all the functions of the product or service are in place) and are used to develop information for final fine-tuning before production begins. Beta tests are also generally arranged and managed by Marketing and should include some members of the development team.

Software Projects
- Defining the exact specifications of the software (functionality, user interface, platform requirements, media for distribution, etc.). As with any project, software projects need clear parameters within which to operate. Given the speed and scope of development in computer software, it is perhaps more important to establish boundaries in this type of project than in most others. Necessary performance is the key — don't add bells and whistles that don't directly affect the application of the software to the problem being addressed.

- Defining the process needs to be addressed for the customer. This is the means by which the limits of performance can be set. What does the customer need the software to do? How will it be used? What other programs will need to integrate with it? Etc.

- Identifying internal and external support needed to develop the software. Support for software development projects usually involves a number of functions other than writing code. There is documentation to be developed, packaging to be designed, reproduction and distribution to be completed, after-sale (or after-installation) support to be established, updates to be scheduled, etc. Externally, there are retail sales to be developed, distribution channels to be established, demonstrations to be scheduled, etc. You need to know these requirements in order to effectively plan the development and transfer plans.

- Identifying when Alpha (limited functionality) and Beta (full functionality) tests are needed. Alpha and Beta tests are very important in software development projects. Software development seems to deviate from customer needs far more easily than other types of projects and, therefore, the "course-correcting" that can be achieved through incremental testing is more necessary.

- Setting limits on "raw" research. This is an outgrowth of the speed and complexity of computer development. Most new applications require some degree of "pure" research — research which simply looks at what is possible given the current state of the art. However, this research should be focused on finding information that will aid in developing a product that will meet customer needs, not on finding out how much functionality can be crammed into the program.

- Establishing the integration requirements (with other software, with various operating systems, etc.). This is also part of the process of bounding the development process. What other programs will need to integrate with the developing program? What systems will be supported? Etc.

5

Project Implementation

Introduction

The activities of daily project management are essentially cyclic in nature. They follow a pattern of: Monitoring and measuring, with problem-solving when things aren't going according to plan, and periodic reporting.

But first, the project has to get underway.

In this chapter, you will look at:

- Getting the project started — Project Kickoff.
- The cycle of project management including: Monitoring and measuring work output, status reporting, task management, people leadership, information management, project documentation, change control, and problem-solving.
- Some tips on keeping things moving once you've gotten them started.

Project Kickoff

> Management's job is to see the company not as it is...but as it can become.
> **John W. Teets**
> Chairman, Greyhound Corporation

In a perfect world, projects would not really start until the planning has been completed. But in case you haven't noticed, we don't live in a perfect world. However, in the interest of providing a view of what "should" happen, we're going to pretend that "plan complete" signals the actual beginning of project implementation. From the following discussions, pull those ideas, tools, and techniques that you can realistically implement in your particular situation. Ok, here comes the fantasy.

Once the planning is completed, it is time to launch the project. This should be marked with some sort of event. The larger the project, the larger the event. The smaller the project the less grandiose the event but there should still be something that marks the actual beginning of project work.

The opening event of a project should be appropriate for the project. For a really significant project such as the development of a new product or a radically new piece of software, a fairly significant opening event is appropriate. This can entail an off-site meeting at which the project team plans and then works through a simulation of the project, spotting potential trouble spots and developing a sense of teamwork. It could include a formal announcement to the organization that the project is underway, and a "pep talk" about its impact if successful.

Smaller-scale projects can be launched with a simple meeting of the project team. This can be done over coffee or can be a scheduled meeting with a full agenda.

The point to having an opening event is to signal the start of the project. This is usually more for the team than for the organization. It marks the beginning of some concentrated work for the team and a little recognition of that fact. It is also recommended that there be a closing event for the project. This is discussed in Chapter 6: *Project Closure*. These two events bracket the project, providing a clear beginning and a clear ending.

An Agenda for the Kickoff

Regardless of the size of the project or the kickoff event, there are a couple of things that should be covered:

- A review of the plan and schedule.
- A review of the "ground rules" for the project.

As discussed in Chapter 2: *Project Pre-work*, and in Chapter 4: *Project Planning*, most of the key players on the project hopefully have been involved in the development and review of the project plan. There are, however, additional players on most projects. These are the support personnel and additional team members who will play possibly limited, but nonetheless critical, roles in the project. The project kickoff is an appropriate point to involve everyone in a review of the project.

Review the Plans and Schedule

At the very least, you should review the project plan and the project schedule. This review should include:

- A step-by-step walk-through of the plan and the schedule with particular attention to the critical path.
- A discussion of the major milestones or deliverables throughout the project.
- A walk-through of the major contingency plans.

Be prepared to answer questions or provide additional information. This is the team's chance to voice concerns and expectations about the project. Allow for this.

PROCESS TIP
Your wall-chart is a good tool for "walking through"
the project plan
This is another good use for the wall-chart plan. The walk-through can be just that — the team literally walks along the project as each section is discussed. It is also a good idea to provide a smaller copy of the plan to each team member. A really good software tool for this is Visio®, but any decent graphics program or the drawing function in programs like Microsoft®

Word can be used to create a printable version of the plan. Programs like Microsoft® Project, Premavera®, Project KickStart®, and Milestones, Etc.® can produce printable versions of the schedule in the form of a Gantt Chart.

Set the Ground Rules

Funny thing about most people, they'll usually try to either live up to or down to the expectations that are set for them. In reviewing the "ground rules" you should make your expectations clear. People will generally do what you want them to if they know what it is. Some of the issues you should consider including in this part of the meeting are:

- Communication issues.
- Expectations about participation in project work and project meetings.
- How conflicts will be resolved and how problems will be solved.
- Expectations about status reporting.
- How you will keep the team updated.

Let's look at each of these issues in a bit more detail.

Communication Issues

You need constant, clear, honest communication about project activity. You have no hope of maintaining even a semblance of control over your project if you don't know what's going on. This is more than just timely status reports. This is conversations about the project, mini-meetings in the halls, quick verification phone calls, short documentation e-mails, and all the other little things people do to keep each other informed. Information is the life blood of any project and the more you know, the better able you will be to deal with the unexpected. And, you can always expect the unexpected.

PROCESS TIP
Make it easy for people to communicate
It is important to provide all the mechanisms necessary for good communication as part of the project environment. Make sure you have at least a couple of alternative communication tools available for team members. For example, if you have the capability, you can set up a project bulletin board on the company's computer network where people can post project-related information. You can set up a "red folder" notification system. This is an actual file folder, usually a very noticeable color (like bright red) that is used to alert the recipient that what is inside needs to be handled immediately. You can hold "stand-up meetings" at the beginning of the day. These meetings are just what they sound like — no chairs, everybody stands and sets the day's agenda, then goes and does it. Stand-up meetings should never be more than five or ten minutes long; they should always be tightly focused; and they should be documented in brief notes. This one is a great way to deal with

immediate problems and small shifts in project focus on a daily basis.

Expectations About Participation in Project Work and Project Meetings

You need to set expectations about participation in the work of the project as well as in project meetings and reviews. Obviously, you expect that people will do the work they are responsible for. Also, most projects require some level of collaboration among team members. Anything you can do to foster this collaborative work will only enhance project performance.

In addition, if you have the luxury of holding regular project-team meetings, you should emphasize that these meetings are not really optional — they are required. Setting the meetings at the same time each week is helpful in getting people to attend. Making sure the meetings are productive is helpful in keeping them coming back.

Management or customer reviews are another issue that may need to have some expectations set about participation. In particular, if you expect the team or some of its members to participate in these reviews, you should set out your expectations for that participation and you should detail how you will support and be involved in them.

How Conflicts Will be Resolved and How Problems Will be Solved

Set some parameters around how conflicts will be resolved and how problems will be solved. This may seem like borrowing trouble. It isn't. Conflict will happen. If not directly within the project then between the project and the organization. It's almost impossible to avoid some degree of conflict on a project.

Look back over the discussion of Facts, Goals, Methods, and Values in the Negotiation section of Chapter 3: *People Skills for Project Leaders*. Most of the conflicts within the project will likely center around "Methods" issues — the "how to do it" of the work. This is energizing, stimulating, creative conflict. And, as long as it stays focused on Methods and doesn't deteriorate into personalities, this type of conflict can be very good for a project.

The type of conflict that needs management (usually, immediate management) is the kind that centers around personalities. This conflict must be dealt with as soon as it becomes apparent. It is also important to note that this kind of conflict can be disguised as Methods conflict. You need to keep an eye out for tensions between team members and deal with them as soon as they show up. If you are truly uncomfortable with this type of intervention, find a friend in your company's Human Resources department who knows how to work with this. In all the years I have worked with projects and project teams I have never seen a project team blow up over a technical issue. I have seen projects blow up over technical issues, but project teams blow up over interpersonal issues.

The most common form of conflict between the project and the organization is around priorities — who gets the resources and when they get them.

Fact of life: In a conflict between the needs of the organization and the needs of a project, in most cases the organization wins. The best thing you can do is to try to anticipate these conflicts and develop strategies to deal with them. Have a pre-project conversation with key managers about the project. Discuss where you see potential conflicts over resources and get their input about how to either prevent the conflict or deal with it when it happens. This type of preventative planning goes a long way toward preventing priority conflicts from derailing projects.

> **PROCESS TIP**
> **Discuss potential resource conflicts up front during stakeholder analysis**
> The identification and discussion of potential resource conflicts can be easily woven into your stakeholder analysis during project pre-work. As the Needs and Wants of the project are being negotiated and agreed-upon, the discussion about possible priority problems can be included as part of the negotiation. You will be able to circumvent many problems by addressing them early.

Expectations About Status Reporting Tell team members what you expect from them in the way of status reports, when you expect them, and what you will do with the information. Of all of the communication issues, this is the big one. Simply talking about project status is not the same thing as getting good, documented status reports. It's so important that there is a whole section in this chapter devoted to it.

How You Will Keep the Team Updated Let the team know up front how you will keep them updated on progress and issues of project-wide concern. This is the flip side of the team providing information to you. You need to complete the information loop and get project information back to the team and to other parts of the organization.

Information to the team becomes even more important when you do not have the luxury of regular team meetings. When your primary source of project information is a written status report, it is important to remember that the rest of the team probably needs to see some of that information as well. The good news is that, with today's computer technology and e-mail, it's a fairly easy task to "cut and paste" pieces of individual status reports into one project status report. You can then send it to the team and anyone else who needs to see it. The bad news is, you have to do it and do it regularly. This is not something that can be put off. The "time value" of information drops quickly as time passes. Make this a regular part of your project leadership tasks. There's more on this in the Status Reporting section below.

Laying out these expectations up front, and getting agreement about them, will save massive headaches later in the project.

There is another element that can, and usually should, be included in the kickoff: Cheerleading. A little "motivational" talk about the importance of the project to the organization (or some part of it), and a reminder of the importance of success to each team member, is always in order. Don't try to turn a simple project into the moon landing, but try to find encouraging and "inspirational" words for whatever project you work on.

The Cycle of Project Management

Once the project is under way, your job as a project manager is one of monitoring, measuring, problem-solving, and reporting. This cycle begins on the first day of the project and continues right up to, and sometimes even after, the handoff at the end.

Monitoring and Measuring

> Information gathering is the basis of all other management work, which is why I spend so much of my day doing it.
>
> **Andrew S. Grove**
> Former CEO, Intel Corp.

The monitoring and measuring activities are constant and totally intertwined. Whatever you monitor, you also measure. This is the point behind the project plan. The plan shows you what to monitor and how to measure it.

The project leader's job on this issue is truly one of management — of ensuring that what needs to be done gets done on time, within budget, and meeting performance standards.

Due to the lack of true managerial authority being granted to most project leaders within organizations, much of this "management" must be done through the use of influence that is not backed up by hierarchical power. This doesn't make the situation impossible, just more interesting. Your ability to negotiate, convince, compromise, and get people to perform will be tested throughout the rest of the project.

Having a committed team, strong support from the project's sponsor, customer, and management, and a good set of project plans are the keys to successfully carrying out your project. If you encounter situations you cannot resolve, ask for help — either from your sponsor, team members, the project's customer, management, or others within the organization. Remember, your job is to get the project done, not to do it all yourself. You may need to learn to delegate. If so, do it. It's almost as good as cloning yourself. Learn to use and depend on the expertise of team members. Delegate responsibility and authority for problem-solving when the person with the problem is the appropriate person to solve it. Delegate responsibility and authority for decision-making when appropriate. Just remember to close the information loop — you can't afford to have problems out there that may or may not have been solved. You need to know. You can't afford to have decisions out there that may or may not have been made. You need to know.

PROCESS TIP
Model the behavior you want to see regarding problems

This one actually works in two directions. When you need to ask for help, don't present a problem without also offering your ideas about how the problem could be solved. Doing this shows that you have thought about the situation and are actually asking for confirmation that your solution is the right one. You're likely to find that, more often than not, your proposed solution will be the correct one. If you really don't know how to solve the problem, try offering a couple of alternatives and look for feedback about which one to try or how to adapt an alternative into a solution. Oddly enough, doing this will get you a reputation for solving problems rather than simply dumping them on someone else.

> Now, for the other direction: When team members come to you with a problem, you should always ask for their ideas about how to solve it. If you get a reputation for always asking for suggestions, people will get in the habit of thinking things through before bringing them to you. This can get a lot of problems solved by other people. More on this in the section on Task Tracking and Management later in this chapter.

Monitoring and measuring (managing) the tasks of the project involves implementing and then tracking the plan you've developed. Your plan should allow you to:

- Track activities by individual, by time, and by budget (if applicable). This is the main activity in project monitoring — making sure that what is supposed to be getting done is getting done.

- Spot problems early. While usually focused on schedule issues, you should also be able to spot potential quality and other output problems as they are developing, instead of after they've impacted the project. Not only are you looking for the trigger events that signal the need to implement a contingency plan, you're also looking for those unexpected glitches that you didn't anticipate.

> **PROCESS TIP**
> **Pay particular attention to test and validation activities**
> One particularly valuable activity to watch that helps track progress and anticipate problems is any test or validation tasks in the project. These are the points at which unexpected problems are most likely to occur. Careful monitoring of these activities can frequently head off big delays and other problems.

- Make course corrections quickly. If you're lucky (and thorough) your contingency plans will anticipate about 80% of the things that could go wrong. Good contingency plans will allow you to make the necessary adjustments in the tasks, schedule, and resources to deal with problems. The other 20%, under most circumstances, will be solvable with some quick action on your part. The key here is to take the actions necessary as soon as the problem becomes apparent.

- Gather the information necessary to make valid decisions. Everything you see and hear in the process of monitoring and measuring your project's progress is data for decision-making. You will need to make decisions virtually every day on your projects. Most of them will be small, simple choices that are well within your authority. It's those other decisions you need to watch out for — the major ones that are outside your authority. These usually involve significant changes to one or more other major project constraints of time, resources, or output. Knowing where to go to get these decisions made is one of the reasons you went to all the trouble of doing all that stakeholder analysis and identification of sponsors and customers. Now is when they become really useful.

Major point: Your job is not to make every decision related to the project. Your job is to get the decisions made.

Your main focus in daily activity should be to coordinate activity. Don't fall into the trap of trying to complete the whole project by yourself. This is one of the most dangerous traps for inexperienced project leaders — trying to "do" too much of the actual work on the project. Yes, as a participant in the project, you have task responsibilities like any other team member. But, you also have the added responsibility of overseeing the entire activity. You need to periodically swim up out of the mud at the bottom of the pool (where all the action is) into the clearer water at the top and survey what's going on with the whole thing. This dual focus may be a new skill you need to develop. If so, work on it as hard as you work on your other project-related skills.

PROCESS TIP
Develop a routine for monitoring your projects
Here are a couple of ideas to help you develop a routine for monitoring the project.

Try setting aside a block of time — preferably at the same time — every day that is devoted strictly to project monitoring. This can be a half hour every morning when you make phone calls to, or meet with, team members; update status; work on getting problems solved; etc. The key is to make it a routine — something that you do every day.

Another way to monitor regularly is to hold that "start-of-the-day stand-up meeting" described in this chapter. Scheduling a ten-minute meeting every day can be a great way to get a quick overview of project status. A variation of this is the "coffee-break meeting." In this one, everyone meets in the lunchroom for a coffee break and combines the daily update with a nice caffeine rush.

Status Reports

Information may be accumulated in files, but it must be retrieved to be of use in decision-making
Kenneth J. Arrow
Nobel Laureate in
Economics

Obviously, an integral part of monitoring and measuring is some form of regular, documented status reporting from team members. You could rely on your ability to contact everyone on the project team on a regular basis and depend on your memory and some notes to always ask the right questions — this is not recommended.

If you can hold regular team meetings, this is an ideal forum for getting these updates. However, even if you have team meetings — where everyone gives a verbal update on their activities — you still need to have something in writing. You need a document trail of the progress of your project. This is one of the absolutely essential pieces of project documentation.

It is also important that status reporting be done on a regular basis. Frankly, a weekly schedule is probably the best. If your project has a long lead time and lots of extra time, you could let this slip to bi-weekly — again, not recommended. Tasks left to themselves for any extended period of time have a disturbing tendency to get off track. If you let a task proceed for more than two weeks without checking on it, the chances that it is drifting off track are better than 50/50 (sometimes much better). Status reporting is not that hard and it should be done weekly. You can stimulate and simplify the process for your team by providing them with a fill-in-the-blanks format for activity.

Status Report

Project:	Date:
Project Leader:	Reported by:
Project Sponsor:	Interval Since Last Report:

Activities/Accomplishments	Since your last Status Report, what have you accomplished on your project work?
Challenges/Discoveries	In working on the project, what problems did you encounter and what discoveries did you make?
Actions Taken on Challenges/Discoveries	What did you do about these problems or discoveries - actions taken, results achieved, people informed, etc.?
Planned Activities	What are you planning to accomplish prior to your next scheduled Status Report?

Fill in the appropriate project information. Note the "Reported by" and "Interval Since Last Report" lines.

This is the area for reporting progress on project work.

This area is for documenting problems or opportunities encountered.

Here is where the actions taken on the problems or opportunities should be explained.

This is the forecast for the next period of project work.

Status reporting is an excellent application for e-mail technology. It is not a replacement for face-to-face meetings with team members, but it is a good way to collect the written version of the report. If you use e-mail to collect team-member status reports, compiling and summarizing the main points from your team and adding your own status update is an excellent way to create an overall project status report. This can then be sent to management, customers, and other stakeholders.

Whatever process you use, the key is consistency and regularity. Status reporting should become a process that is part of every project you do. It is your primary source of information for decision-making, problem-solving, tracking, and controlling your projects.

Task Tracking and Management

The management of tasks also involves people, information, and problem solving. As the project leader you should be the focus of project activity. You will probably be the one who gets asked to "fix it" when things aren't going right. You will probably be the one asked to make decisions, settle disputes, find resources, answer questions, etc. In order to do all of these things successfully, you must be aware of what is going on, in all aspects of the project, at all times.

> The reason a lot of people do not recognize opportunity is because it usually goes around wearing coveralls and looking like hard work.
> **Thomas A. Edison**
> 1847-1931
> American Inventor

There are several specific things you can do that will help you maintain a good overview of project activity:

- Be accessible. Don't lock yourself away from team members. The old MBWA concept (Management By Walking Around) applies. Get out and wander around in your projects. Talk with team members whenever you see them. Hold quick, casual, "how's-it-going" meetings. Make it clear, by your actions and your words, that you are available to anyone anytime regarding the project.

PROCESS TIP
Dedicate time to project activity daily

If you use the idea of daily, dedicated project time described earlier in this chapter, make it an open-door activity. Let the team know that, during this time, you are available to everyone to deal with project-related issues. This may require that you actually defer other issues that come up during this "dedicated" time. This is not as hard as it might sound. Simply learn to say, "I'm focused on my project right now. Can I ask you to come back (call back, etc.) after 9:30? I'll be free to focus on your problem at that time." This can take practice but it's a habit worth developing.

• Ask questions. The normal, reflexive response to, "How's it going?" is, "Fine." Sometimes that's true. But, usually it's useless. "Fine" doesn't tell you anything. You need specifics. You need information. You need data. You need to ask specific questions designed to give you the information you need to make decisions. You should be aware of what each individual or group should be doing. Asking specific questions will frequently uncover small problems that have the potential to become large crises. This is another reason for having a good, comprehensive project plan. The plan tells you what should be happening. Use the plan as a starting point for almost every discussion with team members. Ask questions that require information in response.

• Update the project plan and schedule daily. If it is possible to hold a "stand-up, work-of-the-day" meeting each morning, this is the perfect time to update the posted plan and schedule. If the daily meeting is not possible, wander around the project team early in the day and gather the information needed to update the information. Doing this will not only keep you informed but will also encourage team members to work on having progress to report.

PROCESS TIP
Post the project plan and schedule

If you can post a copy of the project plan and schedule, in some conspicuous place, it makes a great rallying point for the team and an excellent place to hold those stand-up meetings. If you can't post it, be sure that everyone on the team has a copy and that their copies are updated when any significant changes occur. It is a good idea to reissue the plan documents every couple of weeks simply to reflect the current status to the project in relation to the plan. The frequency of this depends on the pace and progress of the project. Obviously, if nothing much has happened over the last couple of weeks, you probably don't need to reissue the plan. If, on the other hand, changes are happening pretty fast, you may need to reissue the plan every two or three days.

- Deal with problems immediately. If you uncover a problem (or a potential problem), deal with it. If you can solve the problem on the spot, do it. If the problem requires the participation of others, take, or assign, the responsibility of getting the required people together as soon as possible. If you assign this responsibility to someone else, make arrangements on the spot to be informed of the results of the meeting. Be specific about what information you need.

Problem-Solving
Don't duck the most difficult problems. That just insures that the hardest part will be left when you're most tired. Get the big one done — it's downhill from then on.
Norman Vincent Peals
Clergyman and Author

Keep in mind that you don't have to personally solve every problem that comes up. If you try to, you won't get much else done. You have a team of people who are quite capable of solving most of the problems they encounter. Let them.

On those occasions when your personal involvement is needed, most of the time it will be in the form of guidance, facilitation, decision-making, or direction-setting. The rest of the time it will be a need for your technical expertise. Whenever possible, guide team members toward finding a solution rather than "fixing it for them."

PROCESS TIP
Don't go around randomly adopting other people's monkeys

When someone comes to you with a project-related problem, they have "a monkey on their back" and they would very much like to have you adopt the monkey. Don't do it! Monkeys are obnoxious, noisy, smelly little creatures that get into everything and mess up the place. When someone comes to you with a monkey on their back, you want them to leave with the monkey. You'll have enough monkeys of your own to deal with. You don't need to unnecessarily adopt other people's monkeys.

Your first response when someone wearing a monkey comes through the door should be something to the effect of, "What do you think we should do about this?" Encourage team members to always bring possible solutions along with their problems. You will find, over time, that most people who are bringing you a problem are either asking for permission to implement a solution they have already developed, or for a decision about which of a list of possible solutions they should try first. Do not fall into the trap of trying to solve every problem personally. You won't be able to house and feed all those monkeys. And, people will quickly learn that if they don't want to deal with the monkey, all they have to do is give it to you.

In Appendix A of this book there is a problem-solving process model. Appendix B contains several problem-solving tools which can be very helpful in dealing with the major problems that can surface during a project. The caution about using this process is that it is very data-intensive and time-consuming. It should be reserved for problems that do not have readily apparent solutions. These tools are also available for download from the www.projectmanagementtools.com web site.

- Implement contingency plans as necessary. The chances are very good that you will have to implement one or more of your contingency plans before the project is completed. If this becomes necessary, be sure to inform everyone on the team that the direction has changed. Tell management about the situation and detail what you are doing (and are going to do) about it. You should also tell your customers about it if the implementation of the contingency plan is going to cause a change in either the content or timing of the final deliverable. Otherwise, you probably don't need to tell the customer about every shift in direction. Be sure that everyone understands the trade-offs that will result from the change in direction. Change the posted project plan and the schedule to reflect the new situation and be sure that team members' individual plans and schedules are also updated.

- Never miss an opportunity to recognize success, effort, or good work. Saying "good job," "nice work," or "thank you" takes virtually no time and the payback in performance is usually totally out of proportion to the effort. These simple phrases are some of the most powerful in the English language when it comes to encouraging people to perform well.

PROCESS TIP
Never miss an opportunity to recognize someone's success

It would be difficult to emphasize the importance and effectiveness of this point too much. If you want to get a reputation as someone who is good to work with on projects (or in any other aspect of your life), do this. The astounding thing about this is how effective it actually is. It doesn't speak all that well for how most of us feel we're treated at work when simply thanking someone for a job well done brings such a profoundly positive reaction.

However, remember, you can't fake sincerity. If you don't mean it, don't say it. But, if someone really has done an exceptional job on something, recognize them for it. The reactions are usually very positive and the benefits multiply over time.

Leading the Team

Human beings are compounded of cognition and emotion and do not function well when treated as though they were merely cogs in motion.... The task of the administrator must be accomplished less by coercion and discipline, and more and more by persuasion.... Management of the future must look more to leadership and less to authority as the primary means of coordination.

Luther H. Gulick
President and Chairman,
National Institute of
Public Administration

Maintaining the project team as a team includes dealing with conflicts and problems between team members and between the team and other functional areas. It also includes ensuring that individual issues do not prevent progress on the project; these are also part of your responsibilities as project leader.

Project teams, even those that are ad hoc in nature, generally work well. It seems that the opportunity to do something new and different energizes people and helps create the sense of shared responsibility and cooperation that is the hallmark of a good team.

However, even the best of teams have times when things don't work as well as they could. Team problems must be dealt with as soon as they are discovered or they will begin to affect the work-output of the team members. In some organizations, interpersonal issues are not openly addressed. They are suppressed in favor of "professionalism" and "focusing on the task." Emotion is viewed as "unprofessional" and not acknowledged. We may be professionals but we are also people. We have emotions and they can get banged up. Ignoring the emotional component of people only makes the problem worse.

Frequently, the more technically-oriented a project team, the greater the tendency to suppress people issues in favor of task issues. This is a very dangerous tendency. People are unique individuals, with individual wants and needs. They are not machines designed to perform tasks. The problems that destroy project teams are almost never technical in nature. Technical problems can destroy projects but teams are a different matter entirely. The things that destroy project teams are usually emotionally based. Managing these issues is a significant part of your job. Refer to Chapter 3: *People Skills for Project Leaders*, for more information on some of these issues.

PROCESS TIP
Distributed projects and virtual teams have special issues

Many projects are now being done by "distributed" or "virtual" teams — people spread all over the place, sometimes even internationally. This can be both good and bad when it comes to dealing with team issues. On the plus side, most of the daily interactions between team members will tend to be by e-mail or phone. This both limits the time they spend in contact, and allows them to remain "one step removed" from each other. On the minus side, this is not a situation that is really conducive to developing a "team" in the true sense of the word.

Most of the problems that will emerge in distributed-team environments will be a result of poor or misunderstood communication. Monitor how communication is working among team members. If a lot of e-mail is being used, ask to be copied on it and periodically check it for clarity and "tone." Abrupt-sounding e-mails can be just as irritating as an abrupt conversation — sometimes they can be even worse since, unlike speech, e-mail just sits there staring at you. If you notice a problem developing, step in with some coaching on how to "soften the tone" or "clarify what's being asked."

Distributed teams also need more attention when it comes to encouraging collaboration. Being in several locations, in different time zones, or different countries doesn't really lend itself to a high level of interaction on a regular basis. You can address this to some degree by scheduling conference calls or setting up "chat" sessions on your internal network or even on the World Wide Web. If you do this, you need to involve everyone on the team. This doesn't solve the problem, but it does encourage people to think of themselves as part of an undertaking larger than just their tasks.

Chapter 7: *Process Tips for Distributed Teams and Projects* contains several more tips for dealing with the issue of projects done in a distributed environment.

Managing Information and Documentation

Effective management always means asking the right question.
Robert Heller
Editor

You will succeed or fail based on the quality of information you have, and pass on, about your project. Information is the life-blood of a project. The very nature of most projects makes them information-intensive.

Different projects require different levels of on-going documentation. Whatever documentation you have decided is necessary for your project should be updated on a regular basis — daily if possible, never less than weekly.

You need to know just about everything that is going on all the time. You also need to maintain the "document trail" for the project by keeping pertinent information organized and available. In some organizations, project documentation is routinely kept in a project log — an actual, physical, bound book. In most, however, project information is kept in computer files. Always back up your files! And, if you are keeping information on a computer, also maintain a file for various pieces of information that are not on the system such as hand-written notes (you know, the ones on the napkin), drawings, etc. Try to keep your project documentation organized and current. There are several pieces to good project documentation. Some of them are essential and others are just a good idea. The essential ones are:

- Project plans and schedules. Not only should you keep the original plans you developed, you should also keep the updates and corrections that happen along the way. This is one of the pieces of project history that is very useful in evaluating a project.

- Status reports. These are the daily historical trail through the project from beginning to end. There is no more complete record of what happened on a project than a good set of status reports.

- Change control documents. This one will be discussed in more detail later in this chapter. For now, just remember that documenting the changes that will almost inevitably impact your project is at least as important as the original planning.

- Post-project evaluation. This one will be covered in the next chapter. However, you should never consider your projects over until you've done some sort of evaluation of the whole thing — process and results.

- Team members need to know about activities that will affect their tasks, how their work will integrate with the work of others, when things need to be done, where to find necessary information or assistance, how to solve problems, etc. Sounds like a communication issue, doesn't it? It is. Treat it as such. A high level of on-going communication, using all the techniques discussed so far, is essential to successful projects.

- Management needs to be kept informed about progress, problems, successes, needs, etc. Not to the level that the team needs to be informed, but still enough to be an issue that you need to be aware of and deal with. Using the Responsibility Matrix or some other tool that lets you schedule management reviews as part of the planning process is an excellent way to get a head start on this one. Remember, however, things don't always go according to plan. You need to be prepared to deal with management (your sponsor or other management) whenever an issue falls outside your authority or control.

- The customers of the project need to be informed about progress, changes in the basic design, timing of incremental tests they'll be involved in, issues around the delivery of the project output, etc. In most cases, the customer is at the lower end of the need-to-know scale. For most projects, the customer's main concern is with the final deliverable. Anything that changes the content or timing of that needs to be communicated. Excessive communication about progress, other than that progress is being made as expected, is usually of a lower priority than most other project communications. This is not a hard and fast rule. Every project and every project customer is different. Keep your customers informed as appropriate.

The majority of the responsibility for keeping information clean, current, and moving rests with you as the project leader. However, you can delegate pieces of it to appropriate team members. Just remember to keep yourself in the loop.

Getting the Information You Need

The best way to get information is to ask for it. Your requests for information-should be specific and should include a time-frame for getting the information to you. Don't be reluctant to ask for what you need.

Gathering information on an on-going basis is necessary for successful project tracking and control. Much of the information you need can be gathered through individual contact with team members. Walk around and talk to people. Ask questions. Send e-mail inquiries. Make phone calls. Regular project-team meetings and a good system for regular status reports should supplement the information you get from individual contact with team members.

Most of the information that circulates around a project can be divided into one or more of three basic categories. Information directed toward or needed by:

- Team members
- Management
- Customers

Team Member Information

An individual without information cannot take responsibility; an individual who is given information cannot help but take responsibility.

Jan Carlson
CEO, Scandinavian Airline System

The project team has the highest level of need-to-know, next to you as the project leader. Daily contact with members of the project team is an opportunity for information to flow both ways — from them to you and from you to them. These "meetings" need not be formal. On the contrary, they should be quick, to the point, and focused on the issues at hand. Most of the time (unless a major problem comes up) these information-passing encounters will take less than five minutes.

When it is either necessary or desirable to get some information in writing, ask that it be kept as brief as possible while still giving all the pertinent details. Keep written information in an organized file that will allow you to find it again if needed.

Management Information

This report, by its very length, defends itself against the risk of being read.

Winston Churchill
1874-1965
British Prime Minister

At some point during the life of most projects, you'll need to make some sort of presentation to management. This may be a simple one-on-one meeting at which you go over the status of project activity. Or it could be a full-blown "event" with overheads or computer-slide-shows, demonstrations, handouts, presentations by team members — the whole nine yards.

There are some important points to consider when preparing for a management presentation:

- Most managers are not interested in the details. This is by no means universally true, but for the most part, managers usually want information in summary form with additional detail available if requested. They need the information necessary to make decisions. They do not need to know all the "nitty-gritty" details of the project. Keep it simple and straightforward. Use a "bullet-point" format for written information. Provide an overview of the issues with only as much detail as is required for a good understanding of the overall situation. If detailed information is needed, provide it in a separate document attached to the summary

- Never present a problem without a possible solution attached. You have been granted some degree of management authority by being made a project leader. Along with that comes a similar degree of management responsibility. A large part of that responsibility centers around problem-solving. You may not be in a position to solve a problem completely. That may be why you are making a management presentation (to ask for additional resources, assistance, etc.). But, you should have some idea of how the problem can be solved. You should be asking for assistance or permission to implement your proposed solution. This is the flip side of the advice given previously about problem-solving for team members. This may be your monkey to deal with.

- Include your plans for the next steps. Bringing management up to date is only half the job. You also need to let them know what you are going to do next. At the end of a presentation, summarize the steps to be taken next and tell them when you will be updating them again.

Management presentations don't have to be monumental events. Organize your information and deliver it in a clear, concise format. Be prepared to answer questions, and in some cases, justify some of the decisions you've made or actions you've taken. Bring whatever back-up materials you think you might need.

Customer Information

Getting information about project activity to the project's customers (or their representatives) is also important. The thing to keep in mind is that decisions about what to tell the customer and when to tell them should be conscious, not accidental. If your customers are internal to the organization, including them on the routing of meeting minutes or status reports is a viable way of keeping them informed. The question is, will that provide more information than they really need? Will being informed of every little bump in the project make them nervous, or will they understand that not every minor glitch is a disaster?

Including key internal customers in management presentations is also a good way to keep them informed. In fact, this may be the best alternative. Most of the issues you bring up at a management presentation will deal with the major constraints around the project and these are the things that your customers need to know.

Involving internal customers in the periodic tests and evaluations of parts of the project is also an excellent way to keep them informed. And it has the added benefit, on some projects, of heading off some of the changes that may be requested later on. This one is really a judgement call on your part, and the choices depend heavily on the type of project being done. Projects to develop new work processes for a customer usually need heavier involvement. Projects to solve a one-time problem may not.

If your project's customers are outside the organization, you need the involvement of someone who can represent the customer's interests and concerns on, or be available as a resource to, the team. For instance, a new-product-development project may have a team member from Marketing on the team. Part of their responsibilities on the project could include involving potential customers in market tests, focus groups, alpha and beta tests, etc. The important thing to keep in mind here is that, even though the ultimate customer is outside the organization, there are probably several customers inside the organization who will need to handle the project output before it leaves the building.

Change Control

Calling this activity "change control" is probably misleading. It implies that you can stop it. Usually, you can't. Changes occur on almost every project. Sometimes they are minor and don't have much impact. At other times, they are so major they require re-thinking the entire project — changing the constraints, getting new resources and moving the deadline.

Most project changes fall somewhere between these two extremes. The issue here is to have in place a system to document the changes made to the project. For this purpose, some form of change control documentation is a good idea.

PROCESS TIP
Experiment until you have a reliable way of tracking changes to your projects
At least for a few projects, try keeping track of every change that happens. Projects don't usually get behind in big blocks.

They get behind a little at a time through changes that, on the surface, don't seem to be all that significant. It's only when the cumulative effect of all those little "tweeks" to the project get added together that you find you're three weeks behind schedule.

Tracking changes to a project can be a tedious, time-consuming job. It's also a very important one. A comprehensive file of documented changes can go a long way toward helping explain how you got where you ended up on a project.

The following form is an example of a Change Control Document that can be used as a model. Using this form, you can document requested changes as part of your on-going project documentation. It can serve as a part of the history of how the project evolved. It is also good documentation of the decisions and actions taken regarding alterations to the project plan and the project's output.

Fill in the appropriate project information. Note the "Change Requested by" and "Request Received by" lines. These will help track the information about each change.

As much as possible, capture the request in the requester's own words. Try to not editorialize.

Rate "Priority" based on how important the requester thinks making the change is.

Rate "Impact" based on your evaluation of the impact making the change will have on the constraints of time, resources, and output and describe the impact.

Check the appropriate decision. Explain "On Hold" and "Modified" decisions.

Sign the form or get the change authorized by someone with the appropriate authority.

Record the date of the decision and the date action was taken.

List and date when you've notified the appropriate people.

Project Change Control Document

Project:	Date:
Project Leader:	Change Requested by:
Project Sponsor:	Request Received by:

Description of the Requested Change

Priority   Impact   Description of the Impact
☐ High   ☐ High
☐ Medium ☐ Medium
☐ Low   ☐ Low

Decision: ☐ Proceed ☐ Put on Hold ☐ Modify ☐ Do Not Change
If put on Hold or Modified, explain:

Change Authorized by: _____ Date of Decision: _____ Date of Action: _____
Notification List   Notified Date

If you use this form as a pattern for a Change Control process of your own, there is one piece of it that you should definitely include — the "Change Authorized by" line. If you have the authority to make the change, sign the form and take the responsibility. If, on the other hand, you don't have that authority, you still have the responsibility for getting the decision made. Use the form as a way of communicating the impact of making the change. In particular, look at changes to the three primary constraints of time, resources, and output. Any change that impacts one or more of these should definitely be documented and authorized.

Keeping It All Moving Ahead

It's kind of like herding cats or pushing on a rope.

Anonymous

The activities of daily project management are continuous and cyclic. You will go through the routine of monitoring and measuring over and over. Periodically, you need to problem-solve. And, also periodically, you need to report on progress to somebody. It is this constant contact with the project and the project team that keeps you informed and on track.

There is a concept that applies to most projects as they are implemented. It is the idea of "momentum." Most project activity starts out rather slow and sporadic. As the project begins to develop, the pace picks up. The energy level of the participants increases and the work gets done faster. As the project nears completion, the level of activity in almost every area will intensify. Last-minute decisions will have to be made about functions and capabilities. Integration problems will have to be solved. Plans for the transfer of project results will have to be finalized.

By paying attention to how your projects "move" through time, you can learn to utilize the "momentum" that builds in your projects to focus activity and keep things on track. Unfortunately, this is not a skill that can be easily taught. The best you can do is watch your projects and identify those times when the pace seems to "ratchet up" a notch. Look for the reasons for the increased activity. Look for ways to intentionally increase the pace at critical points in the project. Over time, you will get a sense of when and how to "nudge" project activity along. Believe it or not, there are also times when you may want to intentionally slow the pace down a bit. Watch your projects for the things that seem to "drop an anchor" on an activity. Save up a few of these for use when things seem to be more "sound and fury" and less actual accomplishment.

PROCESS TIP
Basic activities to keep things moving

You should probably carry out all of the following activities, to some degree, on virtually every project. As a project nears completion, activity usually becomes more intense. These are actions you can take to help keep things under control:

- Be available. Spend time with the team.

- Be calm. Even if you're feeling stressed, try not to let it affect how you interact with others. They will be looking to you to set an example.

- Be prepared to make tough decisions. Chances are you will be called upon to make one or more decisions about what to include and what to leave out of the final package. You need to be ready to make these decisions and ready to justify your decisions to management and to your customers. Or, if you're not the appropriate person to make the decision, you need to know who to go to to get the decision made.

- Be positive and encouraging. Your team will be looking to you for reassurance that "this is all going to work out alright." Being positive and encouraging does not mean you ignore the problems or gloss over their significance. It does mean that you help the team maintain a "can do" attitude.

- Communicate, communicate, communicate. Communicate with everyone who needs to be informed about how things are going. Keep information flowing in every direction.

- Keep the relationships you need to get the work done in good condition. Thank people for their assistance. Recognize both successes and "good trys" that didn't work. Offer assistance but don't take over someone else's tasks.

- Document what you do. The best way to learn from an experience is to be able to go back over it and look at what went right and what went wrong. Keep a simple log of activities related to the project either on paper or on your computer. The things you most want to capture are notes about:
  - What worked
  - What didn't work
  - How problems were discovered
  - How problems were solved
  - Key discoveries made in the course of the project

Issues by Project Type

There are some special concerns that surface depending on the type of project being undertaken. These are issues the project leader should watch carefully during this period.

Process Projects

- Obtaining commitment from all parties to support the project. This issue centers around the need for realistic commitments of time, personnel, and other resources needed to complete the project. Pay particular attention to the need for higher levels of support as the project nears transfer.

- Development-team orientation. Be sure to stress that the final output of the project must smoothly integrate with existing operations and that these operations are to be actively involved in the development process.

- Development-team reporting relationships. Clarify who reports to whom about what. It is more likely that individuals will be faced with the "split-loyalty" issue on this type of project than on others. Clarifying these relationships early will avoid problems later.

- On-going verification of activities with customers. Since your customers are inside the organization, this should be an easy process. It is particularly important to maintain close communication with your customers regarding any changes to the original plan, schedule, or specifications of the project.

- System impacts further defined. As the project progresses, the interaction of the proposed process on other processes should be reexamined and the impacts redefined if necessary.

- System changes made incrementally. In almost every process change, it is possible to "evolve" the new process in stages which can be carefully monitored and adjusted as needed.

- High level of interaction with the ultimate recipient. The final customer should be involved closely in key activities and decisions throughout the project. Since the customer is internal, this should not present significant problems.

- Frequent, small-scale tests of the pieces of the final process. Most processes are composed of several operations working in sequence or in parallel. Testing the process incrementally as each step is developed can prevent delays and misdirected development.

- Constant monitoring of changes in peripheral processes. This is particularly important if the project is part of a larger program of improvement or change. If supporting or dependent processes are being altered concurrently, it is very important to monitor changes in those processes to determine their impact on the project.

Product/Service Projects

- Obtaining commitment from all parties to support the project (can include key customers, key distributors, etc.). Product or service development projects tend to impact a significant portion of an organization (particularly as they near transfer). They also have impacts outside the organization that need to be considered. If, for example, market tests are to be conducted, now is the time for Marketing and some members of the project team to begin to develop the plans for implementing those tests.

- Development-team orientation (should include Marketing representation). The project team should be clearly grounded in the customer need that is to be addressed by the project. The involvement of Marketing in the project should be clearly defined.

- Development-team reporting relationships. Clarify who reports to whom about what. Stress the need for constant focus on the customer need being addressed and the processes which will support that focus.

- On-going verification of project activities with customers. In most cases, this interaction will be with a representative of the customer group. It is important that there be some direct contact with potential buyers of the product or service during the project.

- Prototype (Alpha) tests completed. As the product is developed to the point where a customer can be asked if the overall direction of development is correct (functionality present but not necessarily in final form), an Alpha test should be conducted.

- Production (Beta) test completed. As the product nears final form (functionality complete and most of the features operational), a Beta test should be conducted. This will frequently take the form of a small market test.

- User documentation completed and verified. Packaging, labels, instructions, etc., need to be prepared and any legal requirements met.

- Production systems prepared. The operations that will produce the product must be tested and capabilities verified.

- Distribution systems prepared. The means of getting the product or service into the hands of the consumer must be tested and capabilities verified.

- Customer support systems prepared. The methods of supporting the consumer in the use of the product or service, warranty and service systems, etc., must be readied and verified.

- Market introduction plans finalized. Announcements, press releases, advertising, "grand openings," etc., must be planned and readied.

- Customer feedback system prepared. The means of gathering information and determining acceptance of the product or service must be implemented.

Software Projects

- Obtaining commitment from all parties to support the project (can include key customers/users, platform suppliers, etc.). Software development projects usually require a high level of coordination between the software developers and support functions such as documentation development. Commitments and agreements need to be obtained from all interacting parties about their individual requirements.

- Development-team orientation (should include either a key user or a marketing representative with a clear understanding of the user's process needs). Once again, the need for focus on the process needs of the ultimate user should be strongly reinforced, as should the limitations around the functionality to be included.

- Development-team reporting relationships. Clarify who reports to whom about what. Stress the need for constant focus on the customer need being addressed and the processes that will support that focus.

- On-going verification of activities with customers. User needs are frequent and must be continuously redefined and tested against the direction of development.

- Prototype (Alpha) tests completed. Most software is built as separate functions which operate under a common controlling system. It is usually possible to test individual or small groups of related functions before the complete program is assembled. This can help insure that the necessary features are being developed and included. These tests are usually conducted at the developer's site.

- Regression testing and debugging. As various pieces of the final package are completed they should be integrated and tested for interaction (regression tests). Debugging the software should be done carefully. A new test of the integration should be run after each bug is corrected to insure that no new problems have been introduced.

- Production (Beta) tests completed. Once the final integration has been completed and all regression tests have been run, Beta tests of the program, in a typical user's environment, should be conducted to verify that functionality and features meet user needs.

- User documentation completed and verified. Since the instructions for installing and using the program will likely be developed in parallel with the software, final documentation should be verified against the final functionality and features of the software.

- Production system prepared. The means of transferring the software from the development system to the user system (disk, magnetic tape, CD, etc.) should be readied and tested for accuracy.

6

Project Closure

Introduction

Once the project plan has been executed, project activities completed (as far as the plan is concerned), and the project deliverables are ready for the transfer, it is time to get ready for the actual hand-off to the customer.

This is yet another negotiation piece in the life of the project. Negotiations at this stage are between the project leader (and possibly the core team) and:

- The project sponsor
- The project's customer
- Any support personnel who will be maintaining the project output

If the transfer plan (created as part of the project plan package) has been updated regularly, if the customer has been involved (either in-person or through a representative), if management has been in formed of project activity, and if the support groups have been involved as necessary, this process is simply a matter of formalizing the agreement that the output is ready to hand-off.

However, that's a lot of "ifs." The chances are fairly good that one or more of these parties needs to be brought up to date on things before the actual transfer. Depending on the project, there are some issues that should be considered during this process:

- Whether there is project-specific documentation and/or training needed
- The timing of the actual handoff
- The hand-off process
- Whether there is a need for on-going support and how that will be handled

The decisions made about all of these issues and the actions and responsibilities for carrying them out should be documented in the final version of the transfer plan.

Documentation and Training

Through training your employees you can have a greater degree of confidence that the work will progress through a pattern that you designed.

William F. Cone
Manager of Professional Development, Hughes Aircraft

Some documentation of the project's output is needed for virtually every project. This can be as simple as a written description of the characteristics of the project output — what does it do — or it can be as complex as an operating manual containing detailed instructions about how to use the project output.

Whatever the documentation needed, it should be written in the customer's language and terms. Keep in mind the people who will be using the project output and document it in terms that they can understand and use.

The output of many projects, particularly process-development projects, requires some degree of training to be carried out during the implementation process in order to fully meet the customer's needs. This training should be fully developed as a part of the project deliverables. Training can be conducted by project-team members (as in the case of many internal process projects and some software projects), or it can involve training by others (as in the case of product or service projects requiring outside-customer training by customer support personnel, or even by a third-party training vendor). These projects usually require participation by members of the project team in training the trainers.

As with project documentation, training materials can be simple or complex. They should also be written in customer terms and should provide sufficient information for the customer to effectively use the project results.

Negotiations around these issues should focus on whether the documentation and training meet the needs of the customer and management. Adjustments may be necessary.

PROCESS TIP
Get documentation and training development started early

It is very important to identify the need for customer documentation and/or training early in the project planning process. Documentation and training materials don't "just happen." There can be extensive tasks involved in developing them and these tasks need to be integrated into the overall project.

One important thing to keep in mind is that the project output does not need to be complete before documentation and training materials can begin to be developed. Involve the people creating your documentation and training programs early on in the project. They can begin to outline their materials as soon as the overall shape of the output has been decided upon. Then, throughout the project, they can update and refine their work as the output develops, finally delivering their work output at about the same time as the rest of the project.

The last thing you need to happen is to have the project deliverable sitting around for several weeks while the training and documentation people try to catch up with it because they were brought into the process too late in the project.

Timing of the Transfer and Implementation Process

Once someone understands you respect his time, he will be more willing to speak with you.

James Dennis
Director of Marketing Communications, Hewlett-Packard

Particularly on internal process and software projects, this is the big one. Exactly when and how are you and the project team going to implement the project output in the customer's environment? What involvement will customer personnel have in the implementation? What support will be needed from other groups? How long will the implementation take?

The majority of these discussions will be between the project leader (and possibly core-team or other project-team members) and the customer. Almost any project that involves more than a simple, "Here it is, have a nice day," type of handoff needs discussion of some or all of the following:

- When should the transfer start? Do you need to actually schedule it or can you just drop by when you're ready?

- When should transfer be completed? How long do you think you'll be hanging around? Should you order in lunch? Is there some specific time-frame that needs to be met? For example, if you're installing a new computer system over the weekend, what time Monday morning should you be out of the way so work can get started?

- Who will perform which tasks? Implementation can be an excellent opportunity to involve some of the customer's personnel in learning how to use the new process (software, machine, etc.) This can actually be an element of training. Consider this one carefully and, if necessary, build some additional tasks to prepare for involving customer personnel.

- What are the disruptions that are likely to occur during implementation? Do you need to work on this when there is no one else around or can you work around people and on-going work? If disruptions in on-going activity are likely, be very thorough in your planning of how to handle them. Consider doing the implementation in small steps rather than one big hit. Consider scheduling the work to overlap beginnings and endings of work shifts. Consider shutting down operations for a specific, short period of time and amassing excess resources to make sure you get done in the time allotted.

- What are the contingency plans needed to cover possible problems? What happens if the implementation doesn't work as planned? What's your fall-back position if you have to abort? (You should always have a fall-back position.) How do you get the customer "back in service" while you try to figure out the problem? Be very thorough in your contingency planning. It can really save your hide if something goes wrong.

- How should training be coordinated? Who's going to do what, when? If you need additional personnel to support your training requirements, get them on board early. Is training going to be on-site or offsite? During work hours or not? On-the-job or classroom? Can you overlap training and implementation? Can you have people being trained while equipment is being installed so that when they return from training, they can put what they learned to use immediately?

- How will final adjustments be performed and by whom? Most process implementations and many software and systems implementations require some period of de-bugging. How long does the project team commit to being available to adjust things? When does the responsibility for adjustment exceed the project and become either the responsibility of a support group or another project to develop enhancements? What is the cut-off point for the project team?

- How will you know when you're done? What are the indicators that the hand-off is complete? What constitutes "the end?" This one is very important. Be quite clear about what marks the end of the involvement of the project team — as a project team — and what constitutes on-going support activity. Do this even if that support will be carried out by members of the project team. Ongoing support should not be part of a project. It is an operational activity and should be treated as such. This is a common problem for some projects. Since the same people are involved in supporting the project output, it sometimes looks like the project is still going on. Don't let this happen. There is a distinct difference between a project to develop and implement something, and the activities needed to support that thing once it is implemented. Projects have to have an ending point or they will become careers. Make the end of the project clear.

Answering these questions before the actual hand-off begins generally results in a smoother process, the least disruption for the customer, and a clear ending point for the project.

PROCESS TIP
Be clear on the distinction between the project and on-going support

Few projects end with a single, total hand-off — absolutely no more involvement by project team members. Some level of on-going support is usually needed for a period of time after the project is made operational in the customer's environment. In some cases, this is simply a need to have someone available to answer questions as they arise. In other cases, it involves assigning project-team members to the customer to provide support over an extended period. This can be a major resource trap if you're not aware of it and planning for it.

This issue should be carefully considered and the transfer portion of the project plan should be updated to reflect these needs. The appropriate assignments need to be made, and if the requirements are significantly different from those originally anticipated, the affected project-team members and their managers should be involved in the negotiations.

Be very careful to draw a clear distinction between activities that are part of the project and those that are part of on-going operations. If the support activities are expected to go on for an extended period of time, they should probably not be part of the project. Developing the process by which these activities will be implemented can be part of the project — actually doing them should not be. Not drawing a clear line between project activity and on-going operations is a very good way to have your project become a career.

Completing the Transfer

Even if you're on the right track, you'll get run over if you just sit there.
Will Rogers
American Actor and Humorist

This is what is contained in the transfer plan — all the activities that must be completed in order to make the project output fully operational for the customer. The actual timing of fully meeting this milestone will vary greatly depending on the level of on-going support required from the project team by the customer. This milestone is fully met only after the project team has ceased to have any responsibilities for the implementation. The transfer is not complete until the customer no longer requires assistance from project-team members — as "project-team" members — to use the output of the project.

If long-term support is anticipated, arrangements should be made to assign project-team members to the customer as a work assignment separate from the project. This will allow the project to be closed and still provide the assistance required.

This is the period when you "tie up the loose ends" of the project in preparation for closure. If appropriate or necessary, you can execute an "acceptance of project output" when the output is fully implemented. This would provide documentation of a specific point in time when the project was finished.

Projects have a tendency to "take on a life of their own" and to just keep going long after the project plan activities have been completed. This is one of the most common problems with ending a project on time. The transfer plan (which should be agreed upon by all affected parties) should contain specific, measurable criteria for determining when each piece of the project has been transferred. Once all of the pieces have been transferred, the project is over. Gathering all of the loose ends can drag on for a very long time if these criteria are not set early, documented, agreed-upon, and used.

In a more formal environment, a final transfer document can be prepared which states the criteria for completed transfer. It should also outline those things that are the customer's responsibility. Document things like ensuring that individuals needing training are available for training, that on-going maintenance has been arranged, that on-going operational needs are understood, etc. This document need not be complex but it should be comprehensive and should clearly state the criteria for the completion of the project

PROCESS TIP
Be clear about what constitutes the end of the project
This may seem like beating a dead horse but clearly identifying the end of a project is the one thing that is most commonly overlooked. As a result, projects tend to drag on long after they should have been closed out and put away. Resources that could be doing something more productive are still stuck on the project. You can't hold your post-project evaluation because you can't get "post-project." Be clear and firm about what marks the end of a project. Resist efforts to add "just one more little thing" to the list of deliverables. Look for signs that all of the requests you're getting are actually the beginning of requirements for another project.

Closing Out the Project

What? Are you still here? It's over. Go home.

Matthew Brodrick
Actor,
Ferris Bueller's Day Off
Final line, after the credits
at the end of the movie.

Pack it in. Put it away. Put the bow on the package. Bid it goodbye. Every project comes to an end. That is one of the main characteristics that separates projects from on-going business activities. Most of the following activities occur after the project's output has been delivered to the customer. These activities are focused on closing out all aspects of the project and documenting the lessons learned. Not all of these will be necessary on every project but every project will have some of them. Don't neglect these. They may be tedious but they are part of being a good project leader.

Accounting Closeout

If there was any involvement by accounting, purchasing, or any other financial part of the company, there will likely be paperwork that requires a final close-out. Open purchase orders need to be closed. As do open work orders. Purchase agreements need to be filed. Warranties need to be filed. Everything related to accounting needs to be closed out and put away.

PROCESS TIP

Unless you're an accountant, ask for help

If you are not familiar with all the ins and outs of accounting procedures, don't worry about it. Find someone in accounting who can help you with all the details.

One aspect of being a good project leader, that we haven't really been very specific about so far, is being an effective networker. The best project leaders have extensive networks, both inside and outside their organizations. They rely on these networks for advice, resources, mentoring etc. If you don't already have a good network throughout your organization, there's no time like the present to begin developing one.

Project Documentation

The various documents and materials that make up the record of project activities need to be organized and filed so they can be retrieved as needed. There are a couple of reasons for keeping old project files.

From the practical side, other project teams may be able to use materials, formats, information, etc., developed during your project to help them with planning or implementing a project of their own. At the very least, project documentation forms a part of the on-going records of the business. For that matter, you just might find that your own past projects can be templates for future projects. In fact, for most project leaders, this is more than just possible, it's downright likely. Consider the fact that many of your projects are essentially "variations on a theme" — the same basic set of steps with differences in input and output. Why not begin to use your project plans as templates for future projects?

From the legal side, project documentation can provide legally defensible records and documentation for such things as patent and trademark applications, defense in law suits, defense of proprietary information and processes, etc. If you think your projects may butt up against one of these potential legal issues, contact someone in your company's legal department. Or find a manager who can inform you of the requirements for documentation that your company uses. Then follow those guidelines carefully.

PROCESS TIP

Consider using your project plan as a template

If your projects seem like they would lend themselves to the idea of developing templates for project planning, look for a project planning or project management software package that has this feature — projects put into the software become templates you can call up later — it could be a reason to pick one product over another.

Even if you don't use software to plan and track your projects, look for similarities among your project plans. If pieces seem to fit in multiple projects, don't reinvent the plan every time. Use what is already available.

Some organizations have a central archive of some sort where this information can be stored. Even if your organization has a central archive, keep a copy of all your project documentation for yourself.

PROCESS TIP

Use your completed projects as opportunities to learn

If you really want to become a better project leader, there is no better teacher than your own projects. Get in the habit of periodically reviewing past projects. You will probably learn more from them than from any other source. It is usually best to let a little time elapse before you go back over a project — two to three months seems about right. If you go over them too soon after completing one, you will probably tend to see what you would like to remember rather than what actually happened. If, on the other hand, you let a little time go by, you can learn a lot from reviewing your documentation.

In particular, you want to look at:

- Status reports. This is the most complete record of project activity. If you've kept complete records, the status reports will tell you what happened all the way through the project from beginning to end. Here, you're looking for trends in activity that both worked and didn't work. What seemed to go well? What problem-solving approaches worked and which ones didn't? How did the actual progress on the project match up with the original plans? Were there any issues that seemed to come up again and again? What did you do about them?

- Change control documentation. This will tell you what happened to change your original plans. This tells you how you ended up where you did. Look for things that seemed minor but turned out to be major. Were there any changes that, in retrospect, shouldn't have been made? Were there any clues that could have told you this before you made the change?

- Contingency plans that were implemented. This can be a measure of how well you anticipated the things that could go wrong. This review can help you spot long-term trends when you review contingency plan implementation on several projects. Was there a contingency plan that you had to use over and over? If so, it probably points out a planning problem — something that needs to be considered as a probable occurrence on future projects. You should also look for things that happened that you didn't anticipate. Could you have anticipated them? What would have been your contingency plans if you had?

- Post-project evaluation and the final project report. These are described in later sections of this chapter. For now, realize that they are very valuable pieces of information from any project and should be reviewed along with all the other project documentation. The post-project evaluation, if done right, is an excellent summary of the high (and low) points of a project. It provides multiple views of what occurred and is an excellent source of learning for any project leader. The final project report is a summary of the project.

Disbanding the Project Team

The extent to which personnel were devoted to the project will determine whether this becomes an issue and, if it is, how complex or time-consuming it will be. On very large projects where team members have been devoted to the project more or less full-time, the project leader has a very real responsibility to see that project-team members are successfully reintegrated into their work assignments. Some team members may be reluctant to go back to the "boring routine" after the excitement of the project. Another aspect of this is the changing nature of the interpersonal relationships that might have developed during a project. Frankly, this is rarely a serious issue, but if your project has gone

PROCESS TIP
Consider a closing event
If you think you need to bring clear closure to a project team, try holding some sort of private celebration event for the group. This should be a fun activity — something separate from other project-closure activities — and it should involve only the project team members. Make it an event where people have a chance to reminisce and remember. It's also a good time for you to offer your individual appreciation to each team member for their efforts on the project.

on for a long time and has been the primary focus for team members, be aware that "separation anxiety" is a very real condition.

For most projects, disbanding the team is not an issue. Most of the time, the project was not the main focus of their work and they didn't have a chance to form serious bonds with each other. Besides, it's not like they won't see everybody tomorrow.

There are, however, some team-member issues you should consider at the end or your projects. First and foremost, you should personally thank everyone who worked on the project. This is just common courtesy. Show your appreciation for their efforts. In addition, if the project was complex enough or involved team members being able to demonstrate exceptional skills or abilities, discussions with each team member's functional manager might be worthwhile. If you think a face-to-face discussion is inappropriate, you can always put something in writing.

Here's the issue: If a person has demonstrated better-than-average performance or unexpected skills or abilities, they deserve recognition for that. You may have seen an individual in a very different environment than their functional manager sees them in. If you can genuinely offer praise and recognition, do it. In either a discussion or written report, consider providing input on some or all of the following:

- A report on the person's participation on the project team. This can be as simple as, "Ted was a valuable addition to our project team." Or, it can be a more elaborate report on the specific contributions made and how each enhanced the project. Don't forget the "intangibles" like team participation, communication skills, problem-solving skills, leadership ability, etc.

- A discussion of the skills and knowledge the person gained from the project experience. This can be a very important issue if skill-building was a part of the overall goal of a person's participation on the project. Even if it wasn't, new or improved skills deserve recognition. Specifically, look for skills the functional manager may not be aware of or that might make the team member a more valuable employee.

- An evaluation of the person's performance on the project. You want to be somewhat careful with this one. Frankly, most people perform well on projects. The opportunity to do something new and different seems to bring out the best in them. So, for the most part, you should be able to give very positive reviews of your team members. If you feel you need to give someone a bad evaluation, be very careful about what you say, how you say it, and to whom. Most of the readers of this book will not have managerial authority or responsibility over project team members. Therefore, you may not have the "right" to evaluate their work. Positive evaluations are almost never a problem. It's the negative ones you need to watch. You may want to discuss performance problems with someone in Human Resources and let them carry the word back to the functional manager.

- A sincere "thank you" to the functional manager for his or her support of the team member's participation on the project and the contribution of the team member's time and expertise. This "thank you" note is a good place to put your praise of team members if you are uncomfortable doing it any other way.

- Finally, in most cases it's an excellent idea to copy the employee on any communication with his or her manager. You can also send a copy to the employee's personnel file. Those of you who know you have letters of commendation in your personnel files know how good it feels. For the rest of you, give it a try. The benefits are huge.

Final Project Report

Whether your organization requires final project reports or not, you should consider writing one for your own benefit. The final project report is a summary of the project. It should cover the major accomplishments of the team, describe the final deliverable, and list any key learnings or discoveries that were made as a result. The complexity of the project determines the complexity of this report. Simple projects may only require a one-page summary of what happened. More complex projects may require a significant documentation effort, including: Details of research discoveries, future lines of inquiry, significant successes and problems, etc. Even on a large project, however, this should still be a summary, not a novel. Keep it as brief as possible and still capture the important information. This report should be completed as close to the end of the project as possible.

> **PROCESS TIP**
> **Use your final report as the introduction to your archived project documents**
> This report makes a great introduction to the total package of project documents. As mentioned above, consider writing a final project report even if no one will ever see it but you. When you do your periodic review of your projects, this report makes an excellent starting point.

Post-Project Evaluation

This activity is one of the most valuable things you can do on any project. It would be difficult to over-emphasize just how important this is. In some organizations, a project is not considered finished until the post-project evaluation is completed and documented.

This should be something in which all of the project team and any others who can provide valid input (such as customers, vendors, etc.) participate. The best format for this is a meeting with flipcharts in the front of the room to capture every comment. As an alternative, you can distribute the questions you want answered (either in writing or by e-mail) and compile the responses.

The more successful the project was, the more fun this process will be, and the closer to the end of the project you can do it. For projects that were difficult or those that encountered major problems, this process is all the more important. However, you may need to let things cool down a bit before dragging it all into the light and taking it apart. Unfortunately, the window is not all that big. Two to three weeks is about all the time you can let go by between the end of the project and the post-project evaluation.

In all cases, you need to keep the evaluation focused on issues and not personalities. This process must be used to evaluate the process and outcome of the project, not the people involved (with one exception that we'll get to shortly).

The results of the post-project evaluation should be documented and included with the archived project documents. It can also become part of the final project report. This may be the most valuable single learning tool you have for improving future projects. Don't let the opportunity slip away.

PROCESS TIP
Questions for the post-project evaluation

In any post-project evaluation, you want to document several things about your project:

- *What went right and why did it go right?* By starting with the positive, you may throw people off. Most people come to one of these meetings expecting to do an autopsy to find only the diseased parts of the project. But, it's awful to have a success and not know how you did it. You need to document the things that worked well just as you need to document (and correct) those things that didn't work well. Also, starting with a focus on the positive sets a constructive tone for the process rather than a destructive "let's tear it apart" tone.

- *What went wrong and why?* Now you can get to the stuff that went wrong. Be careful in this part to keep the focus on issues and events and away from personalities. As with the previous question, you need to try to determine why something went off track. Only when you know what happened can you do something to prevent it happening the next time. You may be surprised to find that on most projects, this list is not all that long. On most projects, there are a few major problems and all the other problems are a result of, or related to, those few. This is a good place to tap into the creativity of team members. Ask for ideas about how to handle the issues that come up. Look for multiple approaches to solving a problem. Document everything.

- *What contingency plans had to be implemented? Were they implemented because of the expected problem or as a result of something else?* Not only do you want to know if your contingency plans worked, you also need to know if your anticipation of problems was on target. Another thing to look for is a trend in needing a particular contingency plan. For many of you, your projects will tend to be somewhat similar from project to project. This being the case if you have needed to implement the same contingency plan several times, it may be pointing out a planning problem. You may be building a problem into your projects. If the same thing keeps going wrong, it's more than a random occur rence. It's become something that is going to happen and you need to plan around it.

- *What totally unexpected events impacted the project?* This is where you can look for places you should have had a contingency plan and didn't. When discussing these events with the group, the first thing you should determine is whether you, realistically, could or should have anticipated the problem. It may well have been something so "off the wall" that you would never have thought of it. Or, it may actually have been something that should have been anticipated and wasn't. The latter is fodder for future plans. The former is just plain bad luck.

- *How well did the project plans work to guide the project?* In this one, you're asking whether all that up-front work was really worth the effort. There are a couple of levels to this issue. At the highest level, did the plans work for you? Were you able to track and control the project using the plans as a guide? What changes would you like to make on future projects as a result of having done this one? At a deeper level, did the plans work as a guide for the team? Were people able to self-manage better as a result of having a documented plan and schedule? What changes would team members like to see in either the content or format of future plans?

- *How good was the communication about the project?* Here's where you find out how well your information systems worked. Did team members have the information they needed to make the necessary decisions, solve their problems, and do their work? Was your sponsor adequately informed of issues and progress? Was management satisfied with the content and frequency of your status reports? Did the customer feel that they got what they were promised and that they were kept adequately informed of changes, delays, etc.? Look for tools or processes that were particularly effective and try to replicate them on future projects.

- *How well did the project team perform — as a team?* The focus here is on team behavior, not so much on work output. What you're looking for are clues about team dynamics and interpersonal behaviors that either supported or hindered project performance. Look for clues and cues that the team will provide from their perspective that you may not have seen from yours. You may be surprised at how honest and blunt teams can be in evaluating their own behavior. They saw the project from a different point of view than you did. Listen to what they can tell you about working with them as a team.

, How helpful were the project plans
What would make them better.

This is the minimum information you need from a post-project evaluation to tell you about what happened on your project. Obviously, each project will have unique aspects that may not be addressed by these rather generic questions. Give some serious thought to the information you want to get out of this process and craft questions that will get at that information.

There are two additional questions you can ask that will really help you become a better project leader. However, there is a serious caveat that goes along with these:

IF YOU DON'T WANT TO HEAR THE ANSWERS, DON'T ASK THE QUESTIONS!

If you can't stand up in front of the group and listen to what they tell you without justifying yourself, you're honestly better off not bringing the subject up. If you can stand there, write down their comments, and thank them for their input, do it. You'll learn things you never dreamed of about how you are perceived by others. If you can't stop with the question about team performance, thank everyone for their participation and close the meeting. The two questions are:

- *How well did you do as a project leader?*
- *What advice would the project team give to someone about to undertake a similar project?*

The answer you don't want to the second question is, "Give it to anybody but you." All else is fair. If you really want to get better at the people skills that make for a truly effective project leader, you need this input. And, unless you did something to really irritate the team, most of the comments will be constructive. Take them to heart and think about them.

Closing Ceremonies

To really bring closure, some sort of "event" (no matter how small) should be planned for the official end of the project. This is the other half of the brackets around the project that started with the project kickoff. Again, the size and complexity of the project dictates the extent of this event. But, even if it is only a short meeting of the project team at which you express your appreciation for the efforts of all members, a closing event adds the final touch to a project. It brings things to an end in everyone's mind and provides a final opportunity for team members to interact in the context of the project. Make this event as positive as possible. This may be your last chance to recognize the efforts of team members. Don't blow the opportunity.

Issues by Project Type

Process Projects

- Obtaining agreement from all parties about the timing and methodology for implementing the new process. Process implementations almost always result in disruptions in the customers work patterns. These disruptions should be minimized as much as possible and the customer's on-going production needs should be considered.

- Verifying training and/or documentation needs. Process implementations usually involve far more people than could practically have been included in the actual project. The means of transferring the information they need to be able to use the project results is a critical consideration.

- Defining short-term and long-term support plans. There will almost always be an overlap between the end of the project and the final activities of project-team members in the customer's environment. Sometimes this involvement can extend over several months. Clear definition of the needs, resource requirements, and customer expectations about this support is important.

- Customer takes delivery of the results of project activity. The new process is made operational in the customer's environment. Operators are trained, machinery (if needed) is installed, operational tests are conducted, adjustments in supporting processes are made, the process begins operation.

- Implementation assistance is provided. The various members of the project team with expertise in the new process provide assistance to the customer in making the process operational. The focus is on getting the customer's personnel fully acquainted with the process and how it works.

- Customer performs acceptance tests and provides feedback for adjustments (if needed). As the process is implemented, the customer evaluates the operation and provides information to the project team about acceptability. If adjustments are needed to fully meet the customer's needs, they are made, keeping in mind that trade-offs are still an issue and that significant changes will require approvals.

- Customer evaluates total project. This is the customer's input into the final review of the project that will take place upon completion of the transfer. The customer should be asked to provide feedback on the total project including such issues as the level of cooperation during development, the extent to which expectations and needs were met, the quality of the final results, the process of implementation, etc.

- On-going support (if needed) established. Short-term support to be provided by project-team members (as part of the project) should be scheduled. Long-term support (that which is not part of the project plan) should be arranged and any documentation or training needed to ensure quality should be provided.

- Project documentation carefully organized to serve as a guide for future, similar projects. The documentation of process projects should be organized in such a way that future project leaders dealing with similar projects can use the processes and experiences of your project as a guide and a source of information about what to anticipate. It should also include full explanations of any proprietary developments.

- Implementation impacts studied for possible enhancements. The issues which surfaced during the transfer and implementation of project results should be studied for clues to other improvements that could be made. Any significant discoveries should be carefully documented and brought to the attention of individuals who are in a position to make decisions about their importance.

- Critical learnings/discoveries documented for future projects. Clues about how to "work the system" within the organization should be provided for future projects.

Product/Service Projects

- Final adjustments in production/delivery systems. The "fine-tuning" of the production and delivery systems that will produce and deliver the product or deliver the service should take place at this time. Contingency plans should be developed to solve any potential problems.

- Pre-introduction samples prepared and delivered. In most product/service projects, there is a short period of time during which sample products or service demonstrations are delivered to selected representatives of the customer group. This can involve press releases, product or service demonstrations at trade shows, full-scale geographically-specific market introductions, etc. This activity also allows for further fine-tuning of production and delivery systems.

- Distribution/delivery systems verified. Few organizations maintain direct control over the entire process of delivery into the hands of the ultimate customer. The capabilities of vendors of distribution and delivery services need to be verified and any adjustments made.

- Production begins. The first actual production runs of the product or customer delivery of the service are started. The production process is monitored for a specified period of time to ensure that all is working well. Distribution begins. The delivery of the product to customers is started. The delivery system is monitored for a specified period of time to ensure that all is working well.

- Customer support system implemented. This usually involves completing training of customer support personnel. Criteria for completion should be developed.

- Initial customer feedback evaluated. The initial market reaction to the product or service provides information for the final evaluation of the project. It can also provide information for future product or service enhancements or clues to additional needs which can be met.

- Project documentation carefully organized to serve as a guide for future, similar projects. An important part of this process is the documentation of proprietary discoveries made during the project. Also, significant "short cuts" or work practices that proved useful should be documented.

- "Next generation" products/services defined. The chances are great that everything that could be included was not included in the product or service, most likely due to time constraints. Those elements which "had to be left out" should be documented for the next project dealing with the product or service.

- Critical learnings/discoveries documented for future projects. Clues about how to "work the system" within the organization, directions for future products and services, and any other significant information about possible future projects should be documented.

Software Projects
- Final integrated system tests completed. The program should be tested in every conceivable configuration in which it might be used by the customer. Any bugs detected should be addressed. This can be done through an adjustment to the program (building a "patch"). Or, it can be addressed by an addendum to the user documentation clearly detailing the limitations or conditions under which the bug is likely to surface and how the user can work around the problem.

- Production systems tested. This usually involves actually producing copies of the program using the production system and comparing the code, line for line, against the original.

- Production begins. There are two aspects to this depending on whether the software is for internal use or for external sale. For internal use, "production" means the customer begins using the software to perform work. For external sale, "production" means software duplication.

- Initial customer feedback evaluated. From internal customers, this feedback includes comments on ease of use, accuracy, speed, etc. From external customers, it includes market survey responses. The purpose of this feedback is to define refinements, improvements, and the direction of future development projects.

- Project documentation carefully organized to serve as a guide for future, similar projects. An important part of this process is the documentation of proprietary discoveries made during the project. Also, significant "short cuts" or work practices that proved useful should be documented. Bits and pieces of code not used should be stored for possible use in enhancements.

- "Next generation" or enhanced products defined. Most software goes through several revisions and enhancements during its functional life. Many of the elements of these enhancements are a direct result of work done on the original project which couldn't be included in the first release due to time constraints. This work should be documented.

- Critical learnings/discoveries documented for future projects. Clues about how to "work the system" within the organization, directions for future products, work methods developed, short cuts in the programming or testing process, etc., should be documented for future projects.

Process Tips for Distributed Projects

Introduction

There is a relatively new phenomenon that is emerging in some organizations. Distributed teams (virtual teams, multiple-location teams, whatever you want to call them) are becoming much more common. These working groups (they rarely become real teams) are geographically diverse. They share some specific characteristics that impact how projects are done by them. They need to communicate over long distances. They infrequently (if ever) meet in person. They frequently are in different time zones and may even be in different countries. This is not an ideal project environment. But, more and more companies are putting projects together with this type of dislocated group. If you find yourself with one of these projects, you will need to take special care with the communication systems and the general project-management processes for your group. Think of this chapter as one big Process Tip for working in this dislocated environment.

First of all, many of the processes described in this book won't work as well for you — at least not exactly as they've been described. For example, the whole Post-It® Note planning process becomes a bit difficult to use when everyone is in a different city. Likewise, a team meeting by conference call is not going to work the same way as a meeting where everyone is in the same room. The following are some very general tips for dealing with some of the more obvious problems of working on a project with a distributed team.

- Some, if not most, aspects of the project are probably going to take more time than they would with everyone in the same place. Recognize this and figure it into your planning.

- A distributed project team usually means distributed stakeholders. This can complicate the stakeholder analysis process. Develop a documented process for gathering, evaluating, and making decisions about stakeholder issues. Involve the team members at the location in gathering and documenting their stakeholders' issues. Create a distribution list of identified stakeholders and circulate information in a timely manner.

- Like stakeholder analysis, the Needs and Wants identification process will need to be done in a distributed fashion. Actually, this one works fairly well in an e-mail format once the original list and ranking is established. Creating the original list may require a few rounds of the team going through a develop-circulate-for-comment-return-compile-re-circulate cycle. Circulating the list once it's developed should only require one or two editing loops.

- Basic project planning may need to be done by one or a few individuals and distributed to team members for their review and comment. This can require more than one round of distribution and you need to take this added time into account. On the issue of planning, there are some other things to consider as well:

- You will need to create your plans in a format that can be distributed easily by whatever means is available. If you use the Post-It® Note process, consider capturing the developing (or completed) plan in a program like Visio®. This is a business graphics program that has all the capabilities you need to build a duplicate of your project flowchart. There are other programs available such as ABC Flowcharter 4.0®. The major criteria for picking one needs to be its availability to the entire team. Everyone needs to be able to open, read, print, and possibly edit the files. Therefore, everyone needs to have the same software. It is possible to create a version of your project flowchart in most of the current word processing programs but, since this is not their main function, it's more difficult. Both Microsoft® Word® and Corel® WordPerfect® have graphic capabilities that are sufficient for building a flowchart, what they lack is the automated functions and drag-and-drop capabilities of the graphics programs.

- Project planning issues will need to be documented somehow. Probably the easiest way to do this is to have team members edit the copy they are given (highlighting their changes in some way) and return it to you (and the planning group) for consideration and consolidation. This whole develop-distribute-review-comment-return-consolidate-redistribute cycle can get pretty involved. It can also take longer than you might think. Plan for it.

- Updating the project plan and schedule will need to be faithfully done. Virtually every change will need to be documented and distributed to every team member. One of the first things you should probably do is set up a project-team distribution list in your e-mail program. You can set up distribution lists for all the other information related to the project as well, but the team list is a must.

- Dealing with the everyday issues of the project will probably require a bit more discipline than you might need if you're wandering around talking to the players. You'll need to read and respond to e-mails. You'll need to route information to the appropriate people as soon as possible. You'll simply have to stay on top of the communications about the project. This is a discipline that is critical in a distributed-team setting. Even short delays in turning information around can have major impacts on the pace of work.

- One of the things that actually works pretty well via e-mail is the written status report. The trick is to set and adhere to a firm schedule for when these essential pieces of project communication need to be received and then to follow-up on anything that needs attention. As a slight complication on this issue, you should probably ask for a bit more in the way of detailed information from a distributed team. The recommended bullet-point format may not be enough when you can't easily contact someone for additional information (or go look at what they're actually doing).

- The whole monitoring and measuring process of daily project management is complicated by distance. You'll need to establish many more controls and check points than you might require on a project that is all in one location. Try to develop these processes early in the project and monitor them for effectiveness as they're being used. Make adjustments as needed along the way. Distributed projects have a greater-than-average tendency to get off track. Watch for the clues and take action immediately if something seems to be slipping.

- Problem-solving almost always takes longer. The normal process of a group gathering around the problem and working it through to solution gets spread out over a series of back-and-forth e-mails, an occasional phone call, or a couple of faxes. This does not lend itself to the best problem-solving techniques. Documentation of problems and solutions is also somewhat more important in the distributed world. You'll need more documentation about problems and their proposed (or implemented) solutions when you can't actually see the solution in place.

- Closing out a distributed project can also be a bit more complicated. There are usually many more players involved and making sure everything is finished can require some time. Documentation is critical in a distributed project. Keep careful records and build yourself some checklists to make sure that everything that needs to be done is done. If you end up opening work orders or accounting paperwork in a number of locations, you'll need to be sure that it all gets closed out properly.

- The post-project evaluation usually needs to be done the same way everything else has been done — by e-mail. Timing becomes a little more important when you have to do it this way. You want to get feedback while it's still fresh in people's minds. Ask detailed questions and set a deadline for responses. When all the comments have been received, compile and distribute them to the team and anyone else who should see this evaluation.

- Working in a distributed-team environment just takes more attention to detail than the same work in a single location. You'll need to build and maintain processes to ensure that information flows smoothly and continuously through and around the project. Be aware of the limitations of this type of approach. Take the time to plan carefully. Plan not only for the work of the project but also for the maintenance of the information and communication systems that will support it.

8

Process Tips for Multiple Projects

Introduction

If you have the responsibility for managing multiple projects, you face some challenges that your single-project peers do not. If managing a single project is a juggling act, keeping track of several projects is juggling fifteen or twenty balls instead of just three or four. This chapter is by no means a definitive exploration of the issues surrounding managing multiple projects. It it intended as an overview of the major challenges.

One way to get control of multiple projects is to create a project to manage them. By treating each individual project as a part of the whole, and by treating the resources as part of the larger project and not the smaller pieces, you will be able to keep better track of where resources are being utilized and where they might be getting dangerously overbooked.

Resource Issues

In the more comprehensive project management software packages, there are tools for linking projects and tasks to a common resource pool. The difficulty with most of these programs is that they treat people as components in a computer program. Most of the people you will deal with don't behave in anything approaching that level of consistency.

The trick with multiple projects is keeping everything straight. Who's working on which activity, right now? Who were you supposed to meet with today, and what was the topic? Which activities are behind schedule on which projects? Where is the latest crisis?

A slight variation on this concept is the idea of a Project Portfolio. Under this concept, all projects (defined as deadline driven activities larger than a single task) are viewed as part of a total package, or portfolio. This list of known commitments is the first step in getting control of them. Carried to its logical conclusion, organizations should be looking at all the projects currently underway (the Organizational Project Portfolio) in the same way.

Unfortunately, this is fairly rare. Guiding multiple projects requires a high level of attention to detail. And, as is the case with individual projects, the better you plan, the better the outcome. There are two specific issues you should look at very carefully when doing your planning:

1. Individuals who will provide work on multiple projects, and,

2. Work activities or work outputs that might serve double (or even triple) duty on more than one project.

In the first case, the obvious danger is overbooking someone — scheduling them to work more time than they can realistically put in. Here's and example of a cross-project resource matrix.

List Projects across the top, either by name or using some other identifier.

List the resources down the left.

Indicate the total number of hours per month each resource can devote to project work (excluding other work commitments. The maximum hours should be based on the company's standard work month.

Indicate the hours committed to each project by individual.

Calculate hours available for project work but not currently scheduled.

Indicate the hours over-committed.

Resources	Total Hours Available (Max. 176/Mo.)	Hours Committed Current Month Project #1	Hours Committed Current Month Project #2	Hours Committed Current Month Project #3	Hours Committed Current Month Project #4	Hours Potentially Available for Scheduling	Hours Over-Committed

This example is based on a standard 22-day work-month, eight hours per day.

Resources	Total Hours Available (Max. 176/Mo.)	Hours Committed Current Month Project #1	Hours Committed Current Month Project #2	Hours Committed Current Month Project #3	Hours Committed Current Month Project #4	Hours Potentially Available for Scheduling	Hours Over-Committed
Karl Wilson	176	32	48	96	40	0	40
Joan Borden	176	20	96	20	16	24	0
Bill Murphy	120	0	40	80	16	0	16
Carol Hinley	176	120	20	0	16	20	0
John Chen	120	20	0	0	108	0	8
Maria Gonzales	80	48	24	16	0	0	8
Bashir al Hasad	108	24	0	12	60	12	0
Jean-Marie Lucard	64	0	12	32	0	20	0

- From this it's easy to see that Karl, Bill, John, and Maria are over-booked. In the case of John and Maria, the over-scheduling isn't terribly serious. Neither of them was scheduled for a full month's worth of work on project-related activities and the over-booking is not extreme, particularly in Maria's case.

- Maria has 12 days that are not scheduled for project work. It is likely that she will be able to complete the 8 hours of required tasks within the 96 hours she has available. Most people have some level of flexibility in their schedules.

- John may have a bit more trouble. Based on the 22-day month, John only has seven days (56 hours) of unscheduled time. He is over-booked by 8 hours. This amount of additional work may be more difficult to work into an already full schedule.

- Bill's situation is still more difficult. He was scheduled for three full weeks of work on three of the projects. The remaining seven days are, presumably, dedicated to on-going job activities. Picking up the additional two full days of work could present a fairly serious scheduling problem.

- Karl is in serious trouble. His entire month is scheduled on project-related activity. And, as it currently stands, he's scheduled to put in at least forty hours of overtime. If this scheduling problem can't be resolved, someone will need to authorize the overtime and John will need to agree to work it.

- One way the over-scheduling issues might be addressed is by utilizing some of the time available from Joan, Carol, Bashir, or Jean-Marie. This will only work if their skills match the work to be done and if they are not fully scheduled for non-project work.

Most of these people have "real jobs" that they will need to keep doing at the same time that they're working on the projects. In this example, only Karl, Joan, and Carol appear to be assigned to project work full time. The rest are splitting time between the projects and other activities. As most anyone who has worked on projects as an in-house player will tell you, when there is a conflict between the needs of a project and the needs of the on-going business, the business will trump the project in almost every case.

As has been stated repeatedly in this book, the project leader in most in-house situations rarely has scheduling authority over the people working on their projects. The first step in resolving an over-scheduling problem is to recognize that it has happened. The second step is to begin the dialogue with whomever you need to in order to get it dealt with. There is no simple solution to the problem of over-scheduling. But, it needs to be addressed.

The second situation, looking for work that can do double-duty on more than one project, is a bit easier to do and can pay huge dividends. This works best when the projects are similar and have common activities spread among them. Try to avoid the tendency to take something that is "almost right" and put it into a situation it wasn't designed to fit. You may lose the benefits of having the work do double-duty in the course of "making it fit."

When there is a real opportunity to have work done on one project transfer directly to another project, take advantage of it. As an additional benefit, it is frequently possible, when you have identified potential double-duty work ahead of time, to assign it to the most capable people even if they are not "officially" on the project where the work is needed first. This is one of the advantages of working from a "resource pool" when you're dealing with multiple projects. It allows you to shift your best people to where they will be able to have the greatest impact.

Obviously, all of this requires you to have a very clear picture of your projects and of the commitments and capabilities of the people working with you on them. Consider creating a Cross-Project Resource Matrix and keep it continuously updated. Talk to the people you have available to you to get a picture of their actual availability, their commitments outside the projects, and potential scheduling conflicts. When in doubt, try to under-book people rather than over-booking from the beginning. On most projects, the unanticipated problems that will arise will take up any slack time that might be available, and then some.

Multitasking

The whole idea of multitasking (working on two or more activities at the same time) is more jargon than reality. Walking and chewing gum at the same time is about all most people can really manage as true multitasking. In reality, what this means is the ability to keep multiple activities moving ahead at the same time. That's not the same as actually working on them simultaneously. It requires the ability to efficiently switch between activities to keep them moving. Have you ever seen the circus act where someone keeps several plates spinning on the top of long sticks? The only way to do it is to keep moving from stick to stick to renew the momentum as they begin to slow down. This is what most people actually mean by multitasking. And, contrary to conventional wisdom, success in multitasking lies in having an established, systematic method for jumping from one thing to another — not in randomly running around spinning plates.

There is no simple, transferable process for this. What works for one is overly cumbersome for another. The key is planning — careful, detailed planning that acknowledges that there are more work activities than there are people to do them. This type of planning requires that you have a clear picture of the demands of the projects and the demands on all contributors' time.

This is a place where collaborative planning is almost essential. You really need the input from the resources who will be doing the work in order to fully understand what their constraints are. Some things are more important than other things. This is so obvious it may seem pointless to state it. However, this is a critical concept that far too many organizations routinely ignore. One of the most maddening problems in-house project leaders face is the seemingly constant shifting of priorities within the business that cause resources to be pulled from the project to "deal with something that is more important, right now." The last two words in that statement are the key — "right now." This is an insidious problem that can't be solved by employees. This is a management problem and that's the only place it can be addressed.

Prioritization

Now having made that depressing statement, there are some things that you can do within your projects to help avoid creating your own prioritization problems. The first is to recognize and deal with this issue of some things being more important than others. One tool that can help with this is the Priority Matrix.

Requirement	Priority #1	Priority #2	Priority #3	Priority #4	Priority #5	Priority #6

In its simplest form, a Priority Matrix lists requirements down the left and assigns a priority to each. The key is: There can only be ONE activity at each priority level — just one number one, one number two, one number three, etc. Using this tool forces you to make judgments about the relative importance of each activity.

An example of a completed matrix is shown below. This example shows the six major features, characteristics, or constraints of a particular project. One might surmise that each of these is considered critical to the overall success of the project. Unfortunately, some of them are in conflict. The problem is to determine the relative ranking of each item so that the project leader and the project team can make informed decisions when the inherent conflicts begin to cause problems as the project proceeds. This is not a decision that can be made by most project leaders without input from management and other stakeholders. However, the decision still needs to be made. The Priority Matrix can be a tool to help guide the discussion and force a decision.

Requirement	Priority #1	Priority #2	Priority #3	Priority #4	Priority #5	Priority #6
Hit Marketing's price point +/- 5%				X		
Do not exceed the resources allocated					X	
Meet the deadline	X					
Complete the prototype in time for the trade show		X				
Keep all work in house — no outside resources						X
Meet every functional specification in the first iteration			X			

Here is one way to interpret this information:

- Meeting the deadline is the most important thing. Everything else takes second place to that.
- Directly related to meeting the overall project deadline is meeting the interim deadline of having a prototype ready for presentation at a trade

show. If these were the only things that the team needed to worry about, this project would probably move ahead rather smoothly. Everything would be geared to meeting these two deadlines.

- The third most important requirement is "meeting every functional specification." Nice to say; may be hard to do. If every specification must be met by the prototype, the need to mobilize and focus resources to meet that deadline could be a real problem.

- Now, let's complicate things by adding the requirement of meeting a projected cost/price point that has been established by another department (possibly without input from the people who will be doing the actual development).

- Fortunately, the resource constraints are far enough down this list to provide the possibility of either getting more in-house resources to help with the work or, as a last resort, sending some of it outside.

The real key to using this tool effectively is getting the buy-off of the people who make the ultimate decisions about your project. This is a tool that should be developed and discussed as early in the planning process as possible. Unfortunately, if you simple ask the question: "Which of these requirements is most important?" you are likely to get a response like: "They're all equally important." This is not much help. One way around this is to develop a series of questions that might go something like this:

- If we have a situation where we can't meet the deadline without additional resources, which would you prefer: That we miss the deadline but keep the resources in check, or that we get whatever resources necessary to meet the deadline?

- If we can meet most of the functional requirements within the deadline and resource constraints to meet the trade show date, but there is one that will require significant extra effort, which do you prefer: That we get the resources necessary to complete it or that we let the prototype go without that feature and work toward getting it done for the final product?

- If we are getting close to one of our deadlines and simply can't hit it with the resources available in house, should we miss the deadline or bring in the outside resources necessary to hit it?

Phrasing things in this either/or format can force a decision and result in the establishment of fairly realistic priorities.

Watch Out for Overload: Yours and Others

Most people like to be engaged in what they're doing. When there isn't enough to do, many people become bored and listless. To combat this, some people continuously take on more than they can effectively handle. This certainly keeps them from getting bored but it also puts them is a state of continuous overload. In today's highly competitive business environments, the push is on to "do more with less." Up to a point, this is not a bad thing. But, when that point is reached, and the over-commitment and the attendant stress becomes chronic, several things happen.

Since most organizations do not have a clear picture of their commitment load — the volume of work they are trying to get done balanced against the resources available to do it — there is a tendency to continue to take on more and more as new opportunities present themselves. In many organizations this overload is on the order of a 200% to 300% over-commitment.

Not only does this make for a stressful environment, when something unexpected happens, the resources to deal with it, already stretched to the breaking point, may not be able to respond effectively.

Even when an organization tries to deal with this situation by lowering expectations and demands, things don't recover immediately. It takes time to clear the backlog. It takes time to re-prioritize the work. It takes time for people to recover.

On an individual level, the physical and emotional impact of over-commitment can be severe. First off, most people tend to blame themselves for the problem. This may or may not be appropriate. They may look at themselves as failing personally when, in fact, they're in a no-win situation. So, the first thing to do is acknowledge that you may not be to blame. Get past the guilt and get on to the solution.

In most cases, there is no one person responsible for an over-commitment situation. These things don't usually come about suddenly. It's the cumulative effect of numerous small commitments that, taken together, add up to a substantial problem. Therefore, don't look for someone to blame. Look at the situation and determine which things actually NEED to get done and which do not. Eliminate the unnecessary and get to work on the important things. This may mean you need to make some phone calls or have a few meetings with the people to whom you've made your commitments. It's better to get this out in the open and dealt with than to wait until it's time to deliver and you aren't ready. Give them a chance to find some other way to get things done.

Here are some strategies for dealing with the over-commitment problem:

- Shuffle your resources. This may involve moving people from one project to another, temporarily, to get things back on track. Or, it may involve bringing in additional people for the short term to take up the slack. Note that this is usually short-term solution. Unless you're in a position where you control the labor budget for the project, making permanent additions to the work force is not likely to be an option. Be sure to look at the possibility of outsourcing some of the work. Most organizations are reluctant to do this, but it's fairly easy to build a convincing cost-benefit case if the project is important enough.

- Overtime is never a pleasant option especially if it becomes a way of life. There is also the problem of diminishing returns on the excess hours worked. Numerous studies show that both efficiency and effectiveness both begin to drop dramatically after about the 50-hour mark. Short-term overtime can be an effective way to catch up, but as a way of life, it doesn't work. The myth that the 60-to-80-hour-work-week is effective is just that, a myth.

- Look for ways to increase efficiency. A pressure situation is not the best time to try to truly re-work a process, but there are likely to be ways to make some incremental gains if you take the time to look for them.

If none of the above strategies work, you will probably need to go to someone and renegotiate one or more of the projects. There is no particular order to the following list. In other words, the first item is not necessarily the first thing you should try, but all of these a potentially negotiable.

- The deadline. Is there any way more time can be made available to complete the work? Can overtime be authorized?

- The resources. What options are available for additional resources? Is outsourcing an option?

- The deliverable. Might it be possible to deliver most of the final output by the deadline and the remainder later? Is there some portion of the deliverable that is less important than the rest? Can it be delivered in stages?

Monitoring and Measuring

This activity, while important on any project, is critical to maintaining control of multiple projects. Without a reliable method for gathering status and other information, analyzing that information, and basing decisions on it, chaos will ensue.

Whether you are treating the management of multiple projects as a project or as a portfolio of individual projects, the tracking system that you use for a single project simply needs to be scaled up to meet the demands of more input. The major differences will be in the time this activity requires and the need to track resources across multiple projects. This is by no means an insignificant difference.

Once you move into the arena of multiple projects, the monitoring and measuring activities usually take on a somewhat more formal tone. Scheduling updates and meetings on each project on a regular, recurring basis is a good start. If the projects are closely interrelated, joint meetings and reviews might be appropriate.

Project Status Reporting also takes on added importance. You still need to keep the status-reporting process regular and as simple as possible but you may have specific information requirements for individual projects (or all projects). Examples of this might include early warnings of potential schedule slips, any activity that is experiencing even minor problems, conflicts between projects for resources or output, etc. If you determine that information on these or any other issues is necessary, modify your status report procedure to ensure that the information is provided.

All in all, managing multiple projects requires a much greater attention to detail than does a single project. The communication systems that support the projects are extremely important and need serious attention from the beginning.

Appendix A
Project Planning and Management Checklists

The following checklists cover a wide range of project planning and management activities. Not every checklist is appropriate for every project. Select and use (or modify to fit your needs) those that are appropriate for your projects.

These checklists are also available for download on the Project Management Tools web site:

www.ProjectManagementTools.com

Needs Analysis Activities

☐ A project leader has been selected.

☐ The project's Customer has been identified.

☐ The problem to be addressed by the project has been defined.

    ☐ Needs have been identified and verified.

    ☐ Wants have been identified and weighted.

    ☐ Alternative solutions have been developed.

    ☐ Alternatives have been compared to Needs and those not meeting all identified needs have been eliminated.

    ☐ Alternatives have been screened through the Wants.

    ☐ Risks have been evaluated.

    ☐ The best alternative has been selected.

☐ The constraints have been identified:

    ☐ Time (starting date, due date, any significant milestone dates).

    ☐ Resources (people, materials, money).

    ☐ Output (performance or quality characteristics).

☐ A project Sponsor has been identified and has agreed to support the project.

☐ Stakeholders in the project have been identified.

☐ The core members of the project team have been identified.

☐ The first draft of the project goal has been completed.

    ☐ Connection of project goal to organizational goals has been established.

☐ Preliminary planning has been completed.

☐ Planning resources have been requested.

☐ Project goal has been approved.

☐ Priority of the project has been established.

Goal Development

The project goal should be tested and verified through a series of dialogues with both the management that is responsible for the project and the customers of the project. The project goal should be:

☐ Specific enough that there can be no doubt about the desired final outcome of the project.

☐ Measurable in terms that are appropriate for determining when the goal has been achieved and whether the project has answered the need which caused its creation.

☐ Agreed-upon by everyone who will be affected by the project. This will include management, customers, support, and maintenance functions.

☐ Realistic in the sense that the project falls within the expertise of those who will work on it, that it is appropriate for the business, and in terms of the resources available for its completion.

☐ Time-framed as realistically as possible to meet the real needs of the customer and the business.

Assumptions

Plan assumptions should be developed and shared with everyone who is affected by the project. Assumptions should cover those things over which project personnel have little or no direct control but which could seriously impact the project. Each assumption should be tested and verified if possible. You can include your assumptions on the Needs and Wants Comment Form. At a minimum, verify assumptions about the following:

☐ We have identified factors inside the company we assume will support project activities.

☐ We have identified factors inside the company we assume will restrict project activities.

☐ We have identified factors outside the company we assume will support project activities.

☐ We have identified factors outside the company we assume will restrict project activities.

☐ We have ranked these factors in their order of importance to the project.

☐ We have determined how we can test each assumption.

☐ We have tested each assumption.

Planning Activities

☐ Planning has been done with the key players involved.

    ☐ The project has been flow-charted including:

        ☐ Phases of work.

        ☐ Major tasks in each phase.

        ☐ Major deliverables in each phase.

        ☐ Key decisions/approvals.

        ☐ Sub-tasks and detail tasks.

        ☐ Responsibilities and involvement.

        ☐ Schedule estimates.

☐ A Responsibility Matrix has been completed.

    ☐ Commitment has been gained from all managers contributing resources to the project.

    ☐ Commitment has been gained from all team members for the work they must complete.

☐ Relationships and interdependencies between tasks have been identified and confirmed.

☐ Task assignments have been negotiated with each team member and agreement gained about:

    ☐ The deliverable to be provided.

    ☐ The estimated task time required.

    ☐ The estimated duration of the task.

    ☐ The assistance or other resources required to complete the task.

    ☐ The responsibility and authority to complete the task.

☐ The project schedule is complete:

    ☐ Conflicts have been resolved and known "trade-offs" have been negotiated.

    ☐ The critical path has been established.

☐ Contingency plans have been developed for:

    ☐ Each major or critical milestone (specifically those along the critical path).

    ☐ All "high impact" risk conditions throughout the project.

☐ Costs have been developed for all external resources (non-staff personnel, materials, etc.) and a budget has been prepared.

☐ The project goal has been completed and includes time and resource measures.

☐ The customer's priority and the project priority within the organization have been reconciled.

☐ Additional plan details (project leader's monitoring and other plans) have been completed.

☐ The project plan has been approved by the appropriate management.

If the scope or any other significant project parameter changes, negotiate the changes and repeat the Project Planning Activities and the Needs Analysis Activities if necessary.

Objectives

Objectives should be developed for every major activity of the project. Objectives should be function-specific and developed under the same criteria as the project goal. Objectives should be:

☐ Specific. They should define the exact nature of the deliverables expected and tie them to the accomplishment of the project goal.

☐ Measurable in terms that are appropriate for the function and the tasks to be performed. This should also tie into the measures that will be applied to the total project.

☐ Agreed-upon by the functional manager and the project participants from that function.

☐ Realistic in terms of the abilities and expertise of the function and the resources available.

☐ Time-framed to meet the overall needs of the project schedule and the needs of other functions with which the group or individual must interact.

Flowchart

The flowchart developed as part of the planning activity is the basis for all subsequent project planning. It is a graphic representation of the series of activities and deliverables that will lead to the accomplishment of the project goal. Remember to identify the Critical Path through the project:

> The **Critical Path** of the project is the longest single string of events and activities through the project (the end-to-end finish-start relationships). If a delay occurs in an activity along the critical path, the whole project is delayed.

It is sometimes helpful (depending on the complexity or duration of the project) to construct several flow charts based on manageable pieces of the project and to then combine these into a single flow chart for the total project. Verify that all of the following have been done:

☐ We have identified the significant deliverables throughout the project.

☐ We have determined what activities must be completed in order to accomplish each deliverable.

☐ We know the peripheral activities that support major activities.

☐ We know the order in which activities must be completed.

☐ We know which activities result in critical deliverables (those which must be completed before succeeding activities can begin).

☐ We know who is responsible for each activity.

☐ We know the time estimate (task time and duration) for each activity.

Work Breakdown Structure

Developing the work breakdown structure (WBS) for the project should begin at the highest level of activity and proceed, step by step, to the lowest appropriate level of detail. This process begins at the level of group or individual objectives. For each objective, ask "how will this be accomplished" between two or three times or until the appropriate level of detail has been reached.

☐ We have determined the objectives for each individual or group involved with the project.

☐ We have determined how the highest level of activity for each objective will be accomplished

☐ We have determined how each successive level of activity for each objective will be accomplished (as far as you believe it is necessary for you to understand, track, and assist with the activity).

☐ We have determined the level of involvement of all resources needed to accomplish either the entire objective or some activity leading to its accomplishment.

☐ We have verified the work breakdown with the people who will be responsible for accomplishing the objectives.

Integration Planning

The integration plan is a tool for ensuring that critical interdependencies and interconnections between activities are considered and carried out. Your integration plan should allow you to determine:

☐ Which activities result in deliverables which must be integrated with deliverables from other activities and how they must integrate.

☐ Which points in the project are appropriate for testing the results of interconnected activities

☐ What criteria should be used to determine the success of the integration.

☐ What specific elements of the performance or quality criteria can be tested at each integration point.

☐ Who needs to be involved in the integration, testing, and the evaluation of results.

Responsibility Matrix

There should be no event or activity on either the project flow chart or the project schedule that does not have a specific individual responsible for its accomplishment. Events and activities are listed down the vertical axis and individuals are listed across the horizontal axis. The intersection of an event or activity and an individual should show that person's level of involvement in the accomplishment of the task.

The PARIS code is useful for indicating levels of involvement:

P = Participant. This person participates in the work of the task.

A = Accountable. This person is accountable for seeing to it that the work gets completed.

R = Review required. This person needs to see and review either the work or the output.

I = Input required. This person has information that is necessary for the task.

S = Sign-off required. This person must approve the work.

The responsibility matrix should be discussed with each individual shown on the matrix and their agreement to accept the various responsibilities assigned to them should be obtained. You should:

☐ Specify one, and only one, individual accountable (responsible) for every task.

☐ Discuss their involvement with every person listed on the chart and gain their commitment.

☐ Verify that all activities have been included.

Scheduling

The project schedule is best displayed as a Gantt chart, which lists tasks or activities down the vertical axis and time along the horizontal axis. The project schedule should show:

☐ The critical activities of the project.
☐ The order in which they must be accomplished.
☐ Task-time estimates for each activity.
☐ Duration-time estimates for each activity.
☐ Activities that connect at critical deliverables.

An alternative to the "task/ duration" method of collecting time estimates requires that you ask for three estimates for the duration of a task:

The Optimistic time (if all goes well, how long will it take to deliver?).

The Pessimistic time (if everything goes wrong, how long will it take to deliver?).

The Most Likely time (in your best judgement, what is a realistic estimate of how long it will take to deliver?).

The following formula can be used to calculate time estimates when there is a significant discrepancy between any of the estimates for optimistic, most likely, and pessimistic time required to complete a task:

$$te = \frac{ot + (4mlt) + pt}{6}$$

te   =   time estimate
ot   =   optimistic time (the time required to complete the activity under ideal conditions)
mlt   =   most likely (the most realistic time estimate under normal conditions)
pt   =   pessimistic time (the time required to complete the activity under the worst conditions)

To develop the time estimate, add the optimistic time to four times the most likely time and the pessimistic time. Divide the result by 6.

Your method of updating the project schedule should allow you to show progress on an activity in terms of:

☐ Activities that are on schedule.
☐ Activities that are ahead of schedule.
☐ Activities that are behind schedule.
☐ Activities that have been completed.

Budgeting

Budgets should be developed in cooperation with the functional areas involved in the project and with the assistance of accounting personnel if possible. The budget should include:

☐ Estimated direct labor costs.

☐ Estimated indirect (support) labor costs.

☐ Overhead and fringe benefits. (Most companies have a formula for this computation; check with accounting.)

☐ Estimated materials costs.

☐ All other anticipated expenses related to the project.

The budgeting process can also be applied to non-monetary things such as time available, equipment usage and availability, etc. Just remember to "budget" in the appropriate "currency", i.e., hours, machine through-put capacity, etc.

Transfer Planning

The initial transfer plan, developed as part of the project plan package, will likely be updated several times as the project progresses. The basic concerns of the transfer should, however, be outlined and whatever detail is available should be included. Your transfer plan should include:

☐ The specific deliverables to be handed over at the end of the project and to whom they are to be delivered.

☐ The documentation and training that will accompany the transfer of deliverables.

☐ The timing of the transfer.

☐ The process of the transfer.

☐ The customer's involvement (if any) in the transfer.

☐ How disruptions to the customer's work will be overcome (if appropriate).

☐ The test and measurement criteria by which the customer will judge the acceptability of the deliverables and the implementation.

☐ The anticipated level of on-going support that will be needed, how long it will be needed, and who will provide it.

Contingency Planning Activities

At a minimum, contingency plans should be developed for each activity along the critical path of the project where the Probability and Impact have been rated at Medium-Medium or higher. In addition, plans should be developed for other activities where significant risk has been identified. Each contingency plan should include:

☐ The event or events which will signal the need to implement the plan (the "trigger" events).

☐ A rating of the Probability of the identified problem occurring.

☐ A rating of the Impact on the project if the problem occurs.

☐ An analysis of the project plan for ways to mitigate either the Probability or Impact or both.

☐ The specific actions to be taken to implement the plan.

☐ The specific changes implementation of the contingency plan will cause in the total project plan.

☐ A means of analyzing the total project plan for unexpected impacts.

☐ A list of individuals who should be notified that the contingency plan has been implemented.

Project Implementation Activities

☐ Hold an appropriate project "Kickoff" event.

On a regular basis, remember to:

☐ Manage project priorities, considering time, resources, and performance parameters.

☐ Hold regularly scheduled project-team meetings and collect written status reports from all team members.

☐ Re-plan based on progress-to-date, changes in priorities, or changes in any of the "triple constraint" parameters.

    ☐ Always evaluate changes in resources, time, and performance parameters for impact on the project before committing to them.

☐ Track and document all changes to the project.

☐ Keep everyone associated with the project updated with frequent status reports.

☐ Manage customer expectations. Be sure your customer is expecting what you will deliver.

☐ Implement contingency plans if needed:

    ☐ Inform the customer and/or the sponsor of the change.

    ☐ Involve the team in the decision.

    ☐ Inform everyone associated with the project of the change.

☐ Talk to team members daily.

☐ Facilitate team members' work.

☐ Remove obstacles.

☐ Refine and update the plan to transfer project results:

    ☐ Work closely with the customer.

    ☐ Involve anyone who may be impacted by implementation of the project.

    ☐ Define who will do what, when.

    ☐ Define how disruptions in the customer's work patterns will be managed.

    ☐ Refine the completion criteria.

Monitoring Activities

The monitoring plan is your tool for anticipating and dealing with the problems which will occur during the project. The monitoring plan should allow you to track:

☐ Differences between planned start dates and actual start dates for each activity.

☐ Differences between planned finish dates and actual finish dates for each activity.

☐ The percentage of completion for each activity and for the project as a whole.

☐ Activities performed out of sequence.

☐ Milestones achieved or missed.

☐ Differences between estimated costs and actual costs for activities and the project as a whole.

☐ Differences between estimated resource requirements and actual resource requirements for activities and the project as a whole.

☐ Activities, issues, or individuals of particular importance or concern.

Management Reporting

The management reporting plan is your plan for keeping various managers and other interested parties informed about project activity. Your management reporting plan should include:

☐ Identification of who needs to be kept up-to-date on the project.

☐ Their level of "need-to-know".

☐ How they can best be informed based on their level of "need-to-know".

☐ An appropriate schedule of updates.

☐ The points during the project it is likely (or certain) that formal management presentations will be needed.

☐ A general format for management presentations.

Team Meetings

The team meeting schedule should specify the basic information team members will need in order to prepare for, and schedule participation in, meetings. The team meeting schedule and plan should include:

☐ The frequency, duration, and location of regular project-team meetings.

☐ The general agenda format for meetings.

☐ The format for minutes that will be taken and distributed.

☐ A distribution list for meeting minutes.

Status Reports

Status Reports should be collected from all team members on a weekly basis. At a minimum, Status Reports should include:

- ☐ The tasks accomplished or started since the last status report.
- ☐ The problems or discoveries encountered while working on the project.
- ☐ The actions taken, or the people informed, about the problems or discoveries.
- ☐ The plans for future activity.

Transfer Activities

☐ Transfer plans have been reviewed and finalized with the project's customer.

☐ Project results meet the completion criteria in the transfer plan.

☐ All training and documentation has been prepared and is ready to present to the customer.

☐ The customer has accepted project results.

☐ Follow-up, enhancement, or extension projects have been identified.

Project Closure

☐ Organizational documentation related to the project (accounting, work orders, etc.) has been completed and submitted.

☐ The Post-project evaluation has been completed.

    ☐ It included all of the project team, the customer, and others who had valid input.

    ☐ Results of the Post-project evaluation have been documented.

☐ On-going support for the customer (if appropriate) has been established.

☐ Final project report has been written and submitted.

☐ Project documentation has been archived.

Post-Project Evaluation

Everyone who can provide you with valid input (team members and others) should participate in this post-project review. Ask the following questions:

- ☐ What went right? Why?
- ☐ What went wrong? Why?
- ☐ What contingency plans had to be implemented? Why?
- ☐ What totally unexpected events impacted the project? Why were they unexpected? Could they have been anticipated? How could they be anticipated on future projects?
- ☐ How well did the project plan package guide the project? How could it have been better?
- ☐ How well did the information systems which supported the project (internally and outside the project itself) work? What could have made them better?
- ☐ How well did the project team, as a whole, perform? What could have made it better?
- ☐ How did you do as a project leader?
- ☐ What advice would the project team give to someone about to undertake a similar project?

Appendix B
Project Planning and Management Forms

The following forms and templates (most referenced in the text) cover a wide range of project planning, management, and tracking activities. Select and use (or modify to fit your needs) those that are appropriate for your projects.

These forms and templates are also available for download on the Project Management Tools web site:

www.ProjectManagementTools.com

Stakeholder Analysis Worksheet

Project:	Date:
Project Leader:	
Project Sponsor:	

Stakeholder: ☐ Supports ☐ Opposes ☐ Unsure/Undecided

Features	Benefits	Value

Strategy:

Stakeholder: ☐ Supports ☐ Opposes ☐ Unsure/Undecided

Features	Benefits	Value

Strategy:

Instructions

Identify Stakeholders and determine their current position in relation to the project: Support, Oppose, or Undecided. List the "Features" of the project output that you believe hold "Benefit" and "Value" for the stakeholder. Develop a strategy for increasing support, overcoming or circumventing opposition, and converting the undecided.

Commitment Form

Project:	Date:
Project Leader:	
Project Sponsor:	

Individual	Commitment Needed	For	Against	Unsure

Instructions

List the individuals from whom a commitment is needed for the project. Describe the commitment needed from each (resources, assistance, budget, etc.). Check your understanding of the individual's current attitude toward the project: For, Against, or Unsure. Use this list to develop strategies to strengthen existing commitment, swing the "unsure" to committed, and convert or circumvent those "Against" or in opposition to the project.

Skills and Influence Matrix

Project:	Date:
Project Leader:	
Project Sponsor:	

	Potential Team Members																							
Skills																								

Individuals to be Influenced

Instructions

List "Potential Team Members" across the top. List the "Skills" needed for the project down the left. Connect individuals to skills to determine missing or unnecessarily duplicated skills. This form can also be used to connect potential team members to individuals who need to be "influenced" about the project in some way.

Needs and Wants Comment Form

Project:	Date:
Project Leader:	Date Comments Required:
Project Sponsor:	Comments by:

The following is a list of the Needs and Wants identified for this project. A Need is defined as: "a feature or characteristic that MUST be part of the final deliverable in order for the project to be seen as minimally successful." A Want is defined as: "a feature or characteristic that should, if possible, be included in the final deliverable, but is not essential for project success." Wants are ranked according to their importance using a scale of 1 = low importance to 10 = high importance. Needs, being absolute requirements, are not ranked.

This list is being circulated for comment and input. The Needs and Wants and the ranking given to each Want are a "first cut." Your input and comments are being solicited. Please review, comment, and return this form by the date indicated above.

Project Assumptions:
1.
2.
3.

Needs (Absolute Requirements)	Shift (Need to Want -> <- Want to Need)	Wants (Desirable, but optional features. Importance ranked 1=low to 10=high)	Rank	Alternate Rank

Additional Comments:

Instructions

List the "Assumptions" about the project. List "Needs" in the first column. List "Wants" in the third column and the "Rank" (importance rating) that has been assigned to each in the fourth column. Circulate this list among stakeholders for their input. Discuss and resolve any discrepencies.

Options Rating Form

Project:	Date:
Project Leader:	
Project Sponsor:	

		Options					
Wants	**Rank**	**Score**	**Total**	**Score**	**Total**	**Score**	**Total**
Total Points							

Instructions

List "Options" across the top. Remember, in order to make this list, an Option must meet all identified Needs. List "Wants" in the first column and the "Rank" (importance rating) for each in the second column. Discuss and determine how well each option meets or satisfies each Want. Use a scale of 10 = fully satisfies the Want to 1 = does not satisfy the Want for scoring. Multiply the "Score" by the "Rank" to achieve the total. Add totals for each Option. The highest scoring Option should satisfy the majority of high-level Wants.

Probability/Impact Calculator

Probability Rating

Probability of Occurrance	Very Low 1	Low 3	Moderate 5	High 7	Very High 9
	Very unlikely to occur (less than 10% chance)	Possible but still unlikely to occur (10%-25% chance)	25%-50% chance of occurance	50%-75% chance of occurance	Greater than 75% chance of occurance

Impact Rating

Impact on Constraint	Very Low .5	Low 1	Moderate 2	High 4	Very High 8
Cost or Resources	Insignificant cost increase or impact on resource utilization	Less than a 5% cost increase or 5% change in resource utilization	5%-10% cost increase or 5%-10% change in resource utilization	10%-20% cost increase or 10%-20% change in resource utilization	Greater than 20% cost increase or 20% increase in resource utilization
Schedule	Insignificant schedule impact	Less than 5% slipage in schedule	Overall project schedule slipage of 5%-10%	10%-20% cost increase or 10%-20% change in resource utilization	Overall project schedule slipage greater than 20%
Output Quality or Performance	Impact on quality or performance barely noticeable	Only very demanding applications are affected	The change in quality or performance requires customer approval	10%-20% cost increase or 10%-20% change in resource utilization	Project deliverable is effectively unusable

Probability/Impact Matrix

Probability	Risk Score = Probability X Impact				
9	4.5	9	18	36	72
7	3.5	7	14	28	56
5	2.5	5	10	20	40
3	1.5	3	6	12	24
1	.5	1	2	4	8
	.5	1	2	4	8
	Impact				

Project Risk

☐ Low overall project risk   ☐ Medium overall project risk   ☐ High overall project risk

Contingency Plan Risk

☐ Contingency plan probably not required   ☐ Contingency plan should be considered   ☐ Contingency plan required

Contingency Planning Form

Project:	Date:
Project Leader:	
Project Sponsor:	

Description of the "Trigger Event"

_____

_____

_____

_____

Probability   Impact   Planning Actions

☐ High   ☐ High
☐ Medium   ☐ Medium   _____
☐ Low   ☐ Low
                          _____

                          _____

                          _____

                          _____

                          _____

                          _____

Contingency Plan

_____

_____

_____

_____

_____

_____

_____

_____

Notification List   **Notified Date**

_____ ☐ _____

_____ ☐ _____

_____ ☐ _____

_____ ☐ _____

_____ ☐ _____

_____ ☐ _____

Instructions

Describe the "trigger event" that will indicate the need to implement the contingency plan. Rate the "Probability" that the problem will occur and the "Impact" it will have on the project if it does occur. Describe any actions that can be taken in planning to mitigate the probability, the impact, or both. Describe the specific action that will be taken if the problem occurs. List all who will need to be notified of the change in activity. Check off and date when each person has been notified.

Responsibility Matrix

Project:				Date:																			
Project Leader:																							
Project Sponsor:																							

Team Members and Stakeholders

The PARIS Code:
P = Participant
A = Accountable
R = Review Required
I = Input Required
S = Sign-off Required

ID	Tasks	Task Start	Task End																				

Instructions

List "Task Identification Numbers" (if used) in the first column. List "Tasks" in the second column. "Task Start" and "Task End" dates can be included in the third and fourth columns. List "Team Members and Stakeholders" across the top. Connect team members and stakeholders to tasks using the "PARIS" code designations.

Project Budget Worksheet - Labor

Project:	Date:
Project Leader:	
Project Sponsor:	

Team Member	Rate	Hours per Project Phase or Task Group								Total
Totals										

Instructions

List team members in the first column. Indicate the labor-charge rate for each team member in the column headed "Rate". List project phases or major task groupings across the top. Estimate the number of hours each team member is expected to contribute to each project phase or major task grouping. Multiply the total hours estimated for each team member by their charge rate and enter the total in the last column. Totaling each project phase column will yield the total hours anticipated for that phase. Totaling the last column will yield the estimated labor cost for the project.

Project Budget Worksheet - Non-Labor

Project:	Date:
Project Leader:	
Project Sponsor:	

Item	Cost/ Unit	Units per Project Phase or Task Group								Total
Totals										

Instructions

List non-labor items in the first column. Indicate the cost-per-unit-rate for each item in the column headed "Cost/Unit". List project phases or major task groupings across the top. Estimate the number of items expected to be consumed in each project phase or major task grouping. Multiply the total units estimated for each item by the charge rate per unit and enter the total in the last column. Totaling each project phase column will yield the total units anticipated to be consumed in that phase. Totaling the last column will yield the estimated non-labor cost for the project.

Priority Matrix

Feature, Characteristic, or Constraint	Priority (Importance)				
	1	2	3	4	5

Instructions

The Priority Matrix is used to identify and order important features, characteristics, or constraints related to a project or activity. List the features down the left. Assign each feature a priority from 1 = most important to 5 = least important.

IMPORTANT: Each priority can only be used once. You may only have one number 1 priority, one number 2 priority, etc. The purpose of the tool is to help determine which feature or constraint is actually the most important. Circulate the form for input from stakeholders.

Project Proposal

Project:	Date of Proposal:
Proposed Project Leader:	Proposed Due Date:
Proposed Project Sponsor:	

Related Projects

Preceding Projects	Completion Date(s)	Responsible Person(s)
Succeeding Projects	Start Date(s)	Responsible Person(s)
Parallel Projects	Completion Date(s)	Responsible Person(s)

Project Description

	Detail
Problem or Opportunity to be addressed by this project	Detail
Business Purpose of this project	Detail
Expected Impacts/Effects of this project	Detail
Project Deliverables	Detail
Key Milestones (based on deliverables)	Detail
Major Constraints and Key Assumptions	Detail
Items/Issues specifically excluded from this project	Detail
Resources Expected for this project	Detail

Estimated Total Person Hours	Detail	Estimated Cost	Detail

Instructions

Not every project will require all of this information. Complete the appropriate sections. Include or reference any additional detail needed for a complete understanding of the proposed project.

Meeting Agenda

Meeting Time: _____ **Duration:** _____ **Location:** _____

Meeting Purpose: _____

_____

_____

Expected Outcome: _____

_____

_____

Participants:

_____   _____

_____   _____

_____   _____

_____   _____

Topic:	**Person Responsible:**	**Time:**
_____	_____	_____
_____	_____	_____
_____	_____	_____
_____	_____	_____
_____	_____	_____
_____	_____	_____
_____	_____	_____

Review Action Items and Assignments
Develop Agenda for Next Meeting
Critique This Meeting

Meeting Minutes

Meeting Time: —————— Duration: —————— Location: ————————————————

Meeting Purpose: ——

_____

_____

Expected Outcome: ——————————————————————————————————————

_____

_____

Participants:

_____   _____

_____   _____

_____   _____

_____   _____

_____   _____

Summary of Meeting:

_____

_____

_____

Action Items:	Person Responsible:	Due:

Agenda for Next Meeting: Critique of This Meeting:

_____   _____

_____   _____

_____   _____

Status Report

Project:	Date:
Project Leader:	Reported by:
Project Sponsor:	Interval Since Last Report:

Activities/Accomplishments	Since your last Status Report, what have you accomplished on your project work?
Challenges/Discoveries	In working on the project, what problems did you encounter and what discoveries did you make?
Actions Taken on Challenges/Discoveries	What did you do about these problems or discoveries - actions taken, results achieved, people informed, etc.?
Planned Activities	What are you planning to accomplish prior to your next scheduled Status Report?

Project Change Control Document

Project:	Date:
Project Leader:	Change Requested by:
Project Sponsor:	Request Received by:

Description of the Requested Change

_____

_____

_____

_____

_____

Priority   **Impact**   **Description of the Impact**

☐ High   ☐ High   _____

☐ Medium   ☐ Medium   _____

☐ Low   ☐ Low   _____

_____

_____

_____

_____

Decision: ☐ **Proceed**   ☐ **Put on Hold**   ☐ **Modify**   ☐ **Do Not Change**

If Put on Hold or Modified, explain:

_____

_____

_____

_____

_____

Change Authorized by: _____ **Date of Decision:** _____ **Date of Action:** _____

Notification List   **Notified   Date**

_____ ☐ _____

_____ ☐ _____

_____ ☐ _____

_____ ☐ _____

_____ ☐ _____

_____ ☐ _____

Instructions

Describe the requested change. Include as much detail as necessary to thoroughly understand the change. Based on the requestor's input, rate the "Priority" (importance) of making the change. Rate the "Impact" of making the change on the project constraints of time, resource, and output. Describe the impact. When a decision is made, check the appropriate box. Explain "on hold" and "modified" decisions. Sign this form, or have it signed by the appropriate individual, to authorize making the change in light of the impact it will have on the constraints of the project. Record the date of the decision and the date the change was made. List all who need to be notified. Check off and date when each is notified. Keep this form as part of the permanent project record.

Multiple-Project Resource Worksheet

Resources	Total Hours Available for Project Work	Hours Committed Current Month Project _____	Hours Committed Current Month Project _____	Hours Committed Current Month Project _____	Hours Committed Current Month Project _____	Hours Potentially Available for Scheduling	Hours Over-Committed

Directions

List Projects across the top, either by name or using some other identifier. List the resources down the left. Indicate the total number of hours per month each resource can devote to project work (excluding other work commitments). The maximum hours should be based on the company's standard work month. Indicate the hours committed to each project by individual. Calculate hours available for project work but not currently scheduled. Indicate the hours over-committed.

Appendix C
A Problem-Solving Process

Introduction

It seems to be part of the nature of projects that they are riddled with problems. Much of a project leader's time will be spent working with team members to solve the problems that come up throughout the life of the project. In doing this, it is helpful to have some tools that will make the job easier.

Prior to getting into the model and the tools that support it, a discussion of problem-solving in general is appropriate.

The Approach

For some reason western societies are, on the surface, much more action-driven than most other cultures. In the West, we like to "get things going." While this is an admirable quality under some circumstances, it is not always the best approach to solving problems. There is a tendency to "shoot from the hip" when confronted with a problem. The "Ready! Fire! Aim!" mentality was discussed briefly in an earlier chapter and bears repeating here.

The phrase "just do it," that became an advertising slogan for the fitness craze, is also part of the thinking of most organizations. Other manifestations of this thought pattern are phrases like:

- "Don't just sit there. Do something!"
- "Anyone who can remain calm in the midst of all this chaos simply doesn't understand the situation."
- "Idle hands are the devil's playthings."

Our folklore is loaded with heroes who have triumphed over overwhelming odds. Most of these stories are about individuals who just "jumped in and did it." The stories don't tell anything about thinking through what needed to be done, planning how to best accomplish it, and then methodically carrying out the plans.

The tendency to start acting without planning is not only less likely to actually solve the problem, it is also likely to be very expensive. False starts, having to backtrack and redo work, finding out after the designs are complete that the manufacturing process can't make the product, etc., are just some of the ways the "just do it" approach can cost in both time and money.

Using a structured problem-solving process serves two main functions:

1. It provides a framework for thinking about the problem, potential solutions, and effective implementation.

2. It provides a process by which ideas and alternatives can be examined and evaluated before much time or money is spent finding out which ones will work.

Having said that, it should be noted that the complete process, in all of its detail, is not necessarily appropriate for every problem encountered during a project. The process is not overly complex but it can be time-consuming, and time is something in short supply on most projects. There are, however, situations that demand a comprehensive approach to problem-solving. In these cases, the process should be followed carefully. One example of a good place to use the whole process is the Needs Analysis which should be conducted at the beginning of a project. In fact, the process itself is a model of how to plan and implement a project.

"As Is" and "To Be"   At the foundation of any problem-solving process is the problem statement and some idea of what a desirable solution would look like. According to this process, a good problem statement contains two specific parts:

The "As Is" portion of the statement contains a description of the situation exactly as it is — with no implication of why it is the way it is and with no indication of what should be done about it. This portion of the statement should be based on facts as much as possible. For example:

- Employees rate the food selection, quality, and service in the company cafeteria at 2.3 on a scale of 1 to 5 (with 1 being lowest and 5 being highest), according to a survey conducted on March 1st of this year.

This statement simply states the facts according to the survey. There is no indication of why the employees don't think much of their cafeteria. There is no indication that, for instance, hiring more servers or offering a wider variety of food would solve the problem. In fact, from this statement, the solution (or solutions) are not at all clear.

The "To Be" portion of a good problem statement contains the desired outcome of solving the problem. It does not contain any indication of how the problem will be solved — only how we will know that it has been solved. For example:

- Employees will rate the overall food selection, quality, and service in the company cafeteria at 4 or above when the March 1st survey is re-administered in July of this year.

There is no indication of how this improvement will be accomplished. This statement simply provides a statement of how to determine whether the problem was solved.

Working on a problem stated in this manner requires that the problem be analyzed to determine exactly why the "As Is" situation exists and how the "To

Be" condition can be achieved.

Defining problems using this method will go a long way toward preventing jumping into solutions without really looking at the problem.

The Process

This problem-solving process is a structured approach to the identification, analysis, and solution of problems.

In Appendix B of this section are instructions for using a number of tools. Most of the tools are presented as worksheets that can be copied or used as models for working on various aspects of the problem-solving process. Others are described as processes that can be used in specific situations. Review them and test the tools that seem interesting or appropriate.

The process consists of six specific steps:

1. Stating the problem.

2. Analyzing the problem.

3. Generating potential solutions.

4. Selecting and planning the solution.

5. Implementing the solution.

6. Evaluating the solution.

Even though these steps are illustrated as sequential, problems rarely lend themselves to a single trip around the wheel. In many cases, it is necessary to back up and repeat one or more of the steps as new information becomes available.

Overall, the process is a logical progression of questions. The answers to the questions lead to the next step in the process. In steps one through four, there are brainstorming activities followed by evaluation and selection activities. In the brainstorming pieces, creativity and innovation are encouraged — the search for wide-ranging alternatives. In the evaluation and selection activities, the alternatives are examined and measured against criteria to determine which to pursue and which to discard.

Define the Problem

Every good problem-solving process begins with a clear definition of the problem to be addressed. This is the basis for all the work that follows. There are two pieces to a good problem statement:

- The "As Is" portion of the statement describes the problem in objective, measurable terms. It should contain only those aspects of the problem that can be observed. It should not contain implications of either causes or solutions. In other words, it is a statement of "what," not "why" or "how.

Developing this objective statement can be more difficult than it appears on the surface. It is sometimes hard to keep the implication of cause and solution out of it.

- The second part of the statement is the "To Be" portion in which the desired outcome of the problem-solving effort is stated. This also needs to be an objective statement of observable, measurable results. As with the "As Is" portion, this part of the problem statement should not contain implications of either cause or solution.

Since what you are really doing in developing the problem statement is developing a goal for the problem-solving activity, consider using the goal development process described in Chapter 2: *Project Pre-Work*. Build the problem statement in pieces, using the Post-It® Note process. You can rearrange the parts in several ways and remove anything that implies cause and solution. The object is to achieve a statement that will guide the work of solving the problem.

Process   The process of developing the problem statement should encourage exploration of the situation in detail. Some of the questions you could use include:

- What do we see that tells us that something is wrong?
- How can we measure the difference between what we're seeing and what we think we should be seeing?
- What are the apparent parts of this problem?
- Is there a pattern to what we're seeing?

Various techniques can help with this initial evaluation. Flowcharting is a good one to use to get a good picture of how the problem situation works.

- Map the situation from beginning to end.
- Place a decision diamond after each identifiable step. The decision is a "Yes" or "No" answer to the question: "Is this correct?" or "Is this what we should expect?" When the answer is "No," examine that step further to determine what is wrong. The descriptions of what is wrong become part of the "As Is" portion of the problem statement. The information about what should be becomes part of the "To Be" portion.
- Develop a draft problem statement from the resulting information.
- Discuss the statement and refine it.

Another way to approach writing the problem statement is to have a group brainstorm about the situation.

- Let the brainstorming run freely until a number of possibilities have been advanced.
- Discuss each idea, clarifying the details and probing for additional information.
- Eliminate those pieces that are obviously not part of the problem and combine those that have distinct similarities.
- Develop one or more problem statements for the remaining items.
- Discuss the resulting problem statements and further refine them into a single "As Is" and "To Be" description of the problem.

Before moving on to the next step, be sure you can answer "Yes" to the following:

- Is the problem statement objective, stated in terms that only describe the observable facts and that do not imply either cause or solution?
- Is the "To Be" portion of the statement also objective, stated in terms that

describe what will be observable when completed and that do not imply either cause or solution?

- Is the problem sufficiently limited in scope or does the problem statement describe a series or group of problems that should be dealt with separately?

Tools   Tools that can help with this step include:

- Brainstorming
- The Post-It® Goal Development Process
- Problem Selection Worksheet
- Weighted Voting

Analyze the Problem

With a clear, measurable problem statement, the scope and direction of analysis should be fairly obvious. One thing to remember in doing problem analysis is that, particularly when working with a group of people, graphic visual tools are very helpful. Use the tools that will allow you to display data visually. Cause and Effect Analysis, Why-Why Analysis, and Force Field Analysis are all examples of tools that lend themselves to this.

In analyzing the problem, the goal is to determine the root cause or causes of the problem. The symptoms of the problem are a clue to the root causes out they are not usually the actual root cause. Discovering the symptoms can lead to discovering the root cause. In a very simple example, the route to the root cause might look some thing like this:

- Problem: There is oil on the floor around the base of machine #3. This presents a safety hazard.
- Symptom: Oil is observed on the floor at the base of machine #3.
- Question: Why is there oil on the floor?
- Answer: Because there is a leak in the lubrication system of the machine.

It would be easy to stop at this point, fix the leak, and get on with other things. However, the real question is: "Why did the leak develop?"

So, we follow the process a little further:

- Question: Why is there a leak in the lubrication system?
- Answer: Because a worn part was not replaced as scheduled.
- Question: Why wasn't the part replaced?
- Answer: Because, due to work load, scheduled preventative maintenance was not done.

We now find that the problem was preventable. In addition, we now know that preventative maintenance was not done as scheduled which, in turn, could lead us to look for other potential problems that could result from this lack of maintenance. Also, if we simply fix the existing leak and do nothing to ensure that preventative maintenance occurs as scheduled, we could see this same problem develop in other machines in the area.

Notice how each of the questions in the above example starts with the word "Why." This is the question that you need to answer in this step of the problem-solving process. Asking the "Why" question several times can often lead to the root cause. (See: Why-Why Analysis in the *Problem Solving Tools* section.)

Another way to approach problem analysis is to use the Cause and Effect Analysis technique developed by Professor Kaoru Ishikawa. (See: Cause and Effect Analysis in the *Problem Solving Tools* section.)

Before moving on to the next step, be sure you can answer "Yes" to the following questions:

- Does the data we have collected confirm that the problem exists?

- Does the data we have collected support our description of the problem?

- Are the root causes of the problem, as we've defined them, supported by our analysis?

Tools Tools that can help with this step include:

- Cause and Effect Analysis

- Checksheets

- Force Field Analysis

- Point-Scoring Evaluation Form

- Paired Comparison Evaluation Form

- Why-Why Analysis

Generate Possible Solutions

Distrust the obvious. Don't jump to the conclusion that the first solution you come up with is the best solution.

With the data from the previous step in hand, turn your mind loose to see how many ways you can solve the problem. This is another excellent application for Brainstorming. At this point, however, limit the brainstorming activity to the generation of ideas. Save the analysis and evaluation for the next step.

The goal here is quantity — not necessarily quality. You are looking for as many ways as possible to solve the problem, including some that are pretty "off the wall." Even the most ridiculous idea may lead to the development of an idea that will actually work. Encourage people to "think outside the box" of their expertise and experience. This also means that you must maintain careful control over the brainstorming process to ensure that there is no evaluation or criticism of ideas as they are generated.

Process Set up a classic brainstorming session. Have a flipchart, a white board, or other visible place to record ideas.

- Start the process by reviewing both the problem statement and the data from the analysis.

- Ask one or more of the following questions to get the process moving:

- How can the causes of this problem, either individually or in groups, be eliminated?
- How can we overcome this problem?
- What can we do to ensure that this problem doesn't occur again?
- What is the simplest and the most creative way you can think of to solve this problem?

- Record the resulting ideas as presented. Try to record the exact words used to state the idea. Discourage explanations and justifications. Encourage the free flow of ideas. If you can't write that fast, ask for a chance to catch up and then let the free flow pick up again.

- If the group gets stuck, refer to the Thought Provokers in Appendix D: *Problem Solving Tools*. This list can help break the blockage and stimulate some fresh thinking.

When the list seems as complete as it is likely to get, ask for clarification. This activity is for clarification only — it should not be used to defend or promote specific ideas. Encourage people to state what they meant in clearer terms and to provide some specific information if that will help others understand the idea.

With few exceptions, this step and the first part of the next step, Select and Plan the Solution, are completed in the same working session. Just keep in mind that they are two distinct steps.

Before moving on the next step, be sure you can answer "Yes" to the following questions:

- Is this as complete a list of possible solutions as we can develop within a reasonable time?
- Have we been as creative as possible?
- Are the ideas clear?

Tools   Tools that can help with this step include:
- Brainstorming
- Mind Mapping
- Thought Provokers

Select and Plan the Solution

The first part of this step, the selection of the solution to be implemented, can follow the previous step immediately. The planning portion of this step may take longer than one working session depending on the complexity of the solution.

Process   For the first part of this step, the selection process, try the following process:
- Have the group suggest, and list on a flipchart, white board, or other medium, criteria that could be used to evaluate alternative solutions.
- Discuss and select the criteria to be used.
- Apply the criteria to each proposed solution. Use both opinion-based

methods such as Weighted Voting and more data-driven methods such as Alternative Rating Forms or Point Scoring Evaluation Forms as appropriate. The key is to apply the same process to every alternative.

- Remember that new solutions are likely to arise during this process. Do not discount them. Record them and run them through the same analysis process. These new alternatives frequently incorporate the best aspects of several other alternatives and may yield the best overall alternative.

- When agreement about which alternatives might best solve the problem seems close, consider using Force Field Analysis as a final test for a viable solution.

- Decide on the actual solution to be implemented.

The second part of this step, the planning of the implementation and measurement of the results, should follow the same basic process as project planning in general. The Post-It® Note process can be used for this planning if desired.

- Determine the major tasks to be accomplished and order them in sequence and in parallel.

- Add detail in the form of sub-tasks.

- Assign responsibilities and other levels of involvement for the individuals who will work on the implementation.

- Assign schedule estimates.

- Review the total plan for logical order and utilization of resources.

- Identify points where problems could occur and develop contingency plans.

- Determine how the effectiveness of the solution will be measured and develop whatever plans are necessary to carry out this evaluation.

- Document the plan.

Before moving on the next step, be sure that you can answer "Yes" to the following questions:

- Have we worked through all the options and decided on the one most likely to actually solve the problem?

- Have we taken into account all the steps needed to implement the solution?

- Have we included the measurement criteria we will use to determine the effectiveness of the solution?

- Have we documented our plan?

Tools   Tools that can help with this step include:
- Alternative Rating Form
- Brainstorming
- How-How Analysis
- Paired Comparison Evaluation Form

- Point-Scoring Evaluation Form
- Post-It® Note Planning Process
- Solution Selection Worksheet

Implement the Solution

Here, also, the processes of project management in general apply. In this case, it is the Monitor, Measure, Problem-Solve, Report cycle of on-going project management.

Implementation of the solution should be treated as a separate project. It should be monitored and measured against its own criteria.

Process Some things to keep in mind include:

- Monitor activities frequently. Keep yourself and the people working on the implementation informed about activities as often as necessary to ensure smooth implementation.
- Measure the work being done against the criteria developed for this purpose. When deviations occur, find out why and fix them if necessary.
- Be flexible. If reality says the plan is wrong, you have two choices: you can try to change reality or you can change the plan to reflect the real situation. Changing the plan is usually a lot easier than changing reality.
- Implement contingency plans as needed. Don't hope the problem will go away by itself. They rarely do.
- Communicate frequently and thoroughly with everyone impacted by the implementation.

Before moving on the next step, be sure you can answer "Yes" to the following questions:

- Have we followed our plan?
- Did we make the adjustments necessary along the way?
- Have we documented what we did?
- Are we ready to measure the effectiveness of our solution?

Tool The tool that can help with this step is:

- The implementation plan

Evaluate the Solution

Evaluation is the piece that is missing from many problem-solving processes. Many of them stop at the implementation phase. What this fails to take into consideration is whether the problem has actually been solved, whether it will stay solved, and whether something else got broken in the process.

This evaluation "closes the loop" on the problem-solving process. Here is where you find out whether you have achieved your "To Be" state as defined in the original problem statement. Without this evaluation, your problem-solving work is not done.

Process Evaluation of the effectiveness of the solution should follow much the same process as a Post-Project Evaluation (See the Post-Project Evaluation Checklist in the *Forms and Checklists* section).

To gather the information to evaluate:

- Collect data according to the evaluation process developed as part of the plan.
- Compare this information against the "To Be" state as defined in the problem statement.
- Compare it against the analysis of the problem from the second step of the process to verify that all the causes have been addressed.
- Verify that no new problems have resulted from the implementation.

Before leaving the problem-solving process, be sure you can answer "Yes" to the following questions:

- Have we solved the problem we set out to solve?
- Do we believe it will stay solved?
- Are we sure we haven't created any new problems in the process?

Tools Tools that can help with this step include:

- The implementation plan
- The evaluation criteria developed as part of the implementation plan
- Post-Project Evaluation checklist

Conclusion

This structured problem-solving process is useful when there is enough time to actually complete the work involved in using it. Obviously, this process is time-consuming and data-intensive. It is not intended to be used on every little problem that comes up.

However, the concepts and the steps of the process — a step-by-step examination of the problem and its potential solutions — are valuable in virtually every problem situation.

The tools included in Appendix D can be used with or without the process, as the situation warrants.

Appendix D
Problem-Solving Tools

This Appendix contains a set of problem-analysis and problem-solving tools to assist with the identification, analysis, and solution of problems encountered in defining, planning, or working on projects.

Many of these tools are available for download on the following web site:

www.ProjectManagementTools.com

The tools in this Appendix include:

Brainstorming

The purpose of brainstorming is to generate a large quantity of ideas from a group in a relatively short period of time. Brainstorming is best done in a small group.

Description

Brainstorming is an idea-generating technique pioneered by Alex Osborn, an advertising executive. A group of people throw out their ideas as they think of them, so that each has the opportunity to build on the ideas of others.

Brainstorming is not a free-for-all. There is a discipline to the process that helps maintain both a sense of order and a reasonable level of freedom. There are two phases to the brainstorming process: Idea-generation and idea-sorting and evaluation.

Directions, Phase 1

The rules for the idea-generation phase of brainstorming are:
- No evaluation. Ideas must not be criticized or praised during the idea-generating phase.
- Encourage wild ideas. Some of the most off-the-wall ideas lead to practical solutions.
- Hitchhike. Build on the ideas of others.
- Strive for quantity. Quality comes later.

There are three basic methods of brainstorming. Each has its advantages and disadvantages. Each is described below.

Free-Wheeling Brainstorming

- Group members call out their ideas as they think of them.
- Ideas are recorded, usually on a flip chart or white board, as fast as they are generated.
- An attempt is made to record the idea exactly as stated, using the contributor's exact words.

The advantages of the Free-Wheeling process are:
- It is very spontaneous — ideas come from all over, all at once.
- It tends to be very creative — if the "no criticism" rule is strictly observed, the ideas tend to be more creative as the process unfolds.
- It is easy to build on the ideas of others — because there is no need to wait, if an idea sparks a thought, it can be added to the list immediately.

The disadvantages of the Free-Wheeling process are:
- Strong individuals may dominate the session — everyone must be encouraged to participate.
- It can be confusing, particularly for the person recording the ideas, when too many people talk at once. Ideas can get missed.

Round-Robin Brainstorming

- The group leader or the person recording the ideas asks each person, in turn, for an idea — people need to wait for their turn to speak.
- Group members can pass on any round — if you don't have an idea, you pass.
- The session continues until everyone has passed during the round.
- Ideas are recorded in the same manner as in Free-Wheeling Brainstorming.

The advantages of the Round-Robin process are:
- It is difficult for one person to dominate the session since everyone gets a turn.
- The generation of ideas tends to be somewhat more focused.

- Everyone is encouraged to take part in the process.

The disadvantages of the Round-Robin process are:
- It can be difficult to wait for one's turn to speak.
- Due to the structured nature of the process, some loss of energy usually occurs.
- Some people will show a reluctance to pass. This can hold up the process while they try to think of something to contribute, further draining energy.
- Because of the one-at-a-time approach, it is more difficult to build on the ideas of others.

Slip Method Brainstorming
- This method is quite different from the previous two.
- The leader asks participants to write down ideas on small slips of paper, Post-It® Notes, or index cards.
- The cards are then collected and organized.
- Review of the submitted ideas can be by the group that generated them or by another group.

The advantages of the Slip Method are:
- The anonymous nature of the input can be used to deal with sensitive subjects.
- This method can be very useful with large groups.
- The fact that no one need speak can be a relief for some people who are reluctant to speak in groups.

The disadvantages of the Slip Method are:
- Due to the anonymous nature of the input, it is impossible to build on the ideas of others.
- The process is slow.
- Some ideas may be illegible or incomplete and hard to understand.
- It is difficult to get clarification.

Directions, Phase 2 The second phase of brainstorming is the idea-sorting and evaluation phase. This needs to be a separate activity from the first phase. Do not get the two mixed up. Evaluation during the idea-generating process can be fatal to the creation of new ideas. Ideas are fragile things when they are fresh. They don't survive criticism very well. Let the generation phase run until the ideas begin to dry up, then move on to the sorting and evaluation phase.

Idea Sorting This activity is intended to reduce the size of the list of ideas generated by grouping them logically together. After a group has stopped presenting new ideas, ask them to help with the sorting by identifying those ideas that seem to belong together. The groupings should be fairly obvious. Ideas that are similar in intent, content, wording, etc., should be grouped together. The can generate a whole new (but shorter) list. Try for agreement about how to word the explanation of the newly grouped ideas. This should result in more fully described ideas.

Idea Evaluation In this part of the exercise, the ideas are open for debate, criticism, and evaluation. They can be examined for merit and debated for viability. The results of this proces should be a list of ideas to be pursued and developed. The decision about which ideas to pursue should be a group decision.

Cause and Effect Diagrams

Description
Cause and Effect Analysis is used to help structure the examination of a problem in order to determine the root cause of the problem rather than the symptoms. The process is useful on a wide range of problem types.

General Directions
Begin by drawing the basic Cause and Effect Diagram. This consists of the Effect box at the right, the center line, and branches to Categories of Causes. Determine the Categories. (As a starting point, the standard categories are Machines, Materials, Methods, Manpower, and sometimes Money.) Any categories that are appropriate to the problem can be used.

Standard Cause and Effect Directions
Begin to brainstorm causes within each category. As causes are identified, it may become apparent that there are secondary causes driving the primary causes. These are branched from the primary cause. If a cause seems significant enough, it can become the Effect in another analysis. Once causes have been identifed, data can be collected to determine the extent and impact of the each cause.

Process-Analysis Using the Cause and Effect Diagram
To look at a complete process using this technique, create a series of diagrams corresponding to the steps in the process. The Effect of each diagram is the output of that process step. The Causes or each Effect are the process activities that create the output. Processes can be examined for efficiency, effectiveness, and problems created along the process.

Reverse Cause and Effect Analysis
This technique can be used to determine the Causes needed to create or drive a desired Effect. For this analysis, place the desited Effect in the Effect box, create the appropriate Categories, and brainstorm the Causes that will create the desired Effect.

Checksheet

Description of the Event or Item to be Tracked	**Time Periods** during which data is to be collected (hours, days, weeks, etc.)										Totals
Totals											

Description

There are two questions to be answered in order to set up a Checksheet:

1. What do we want to know?
2. What is the most reliable way to collect the data?

Information on Checksheets is usually collected in categories: by product, by production operation, by date, by work shift, etc. In constructing the Checksheet, try to form categories that will be easy for the person recording the data to use. The data recorder should not have to make difficult judgements about when to put information on the form.

Directions

Prepare the blank Checksheet. List the time periods during which data will be collected across the top. List the data being collected down the left. (The occurance of defects is the most common data tracked.) The number of times a particular defect is discovered during each time period is indicated by a simple "hash mark" (/) in the appropriate box. Totals are developed both vertically and horizontally.

Cost-Benefit Analysis

Description
Cost-Benefit Analysis is a tool for comparing the known cost and potential benefits of a proposed action. Some things are relatively easy to evaluate using Cost-Benefit Analysis, even if they involve making some assumptions, (e.g., that the proposed solution will result in a 25% improvement in productivity) that will have to be verfied after the implementation. If you can get agreement that the assumptions are valid, you should have little trouble getting your analysis accepted.

Some situations do not lend themselves to "hard numbers" analysis. In other words, the evaluation should be based on something other than the cost and the dollar value of benefits. For these "softer" issues, it may be helpful to simple answer two questions: "What do I give?" and "What do I get?" In all cases the approach is to find some measure, usually dollars, and estimate the coste and benefits associated with a given choice.

Directions
Develop a list of the costs associated with the proposed action. This should include "out-of-pocket" expenses such as purchase price and installation costs, etc. It should also include "hidden" costs such as production down-time during installation, operator retraining, etc.

Develop a list of the benefits associated with the proposed action. This should include such things as increased productivity, reductions in waste, faster turnaround, money saved, etc. This may involve making some assumptions about what those benefits will be. If so, be sure to gain agreement about your assumptions before proceeding.

Develop the analysis using a format similar to the example below.

Costs

Machine	$1,000
Rewiring and installation expense	500
Cost of operator training	250
Cost of lost production during installation	500
Total Cost	**$2,250**

Benefits

Reduce rejects by 10% (assumption)	$750
Reduce personnel hours for the job (assumption)	500
Reduce set-up time (assumption)	250
Total Benefits	**$1,500**

Conclusion:

Comparing the cost and the benefits over two years shows:

	Costs	Benefits	Profit
Year #1	$2,250	$1,500	($750)
Year #2	0	$1,500	$750
Totals	**$2,250**	**$3,000**	**$750**

In two years the new equipment will pay back the original cost and generate $750 in additional income.

Force-Field Analysis — Example

Force Field Analysis helps groups identify those forces within the organization that will help drive a desired change and those that will hinder the change. The "To Be" statement (the desired result of the change) is represented by the center line of the diagram. Forces are usually represented by arrows of various lengths. The Driving forces are pushing from the left toward the center while the Hindering forces are pushing from the right against the center.

Some groups use a scale (e.g.: 1 = very weak to 5 = very strong) to evaluate the relative impact of the forces. For graphic representation, arrows of a length that represents their relative strength are used.

"As Is" Statement: Morale, as identifed in the latest Employee Opinion Survey, is low. Department
(current situation)   employees rated morale at an average of 2 on a scale where 1 = low and 5 = high.

"To Be" Statement: Department employees will rate morale at or above 4 on the same scale when the
(desired situation)   same survey is retaken in three months.

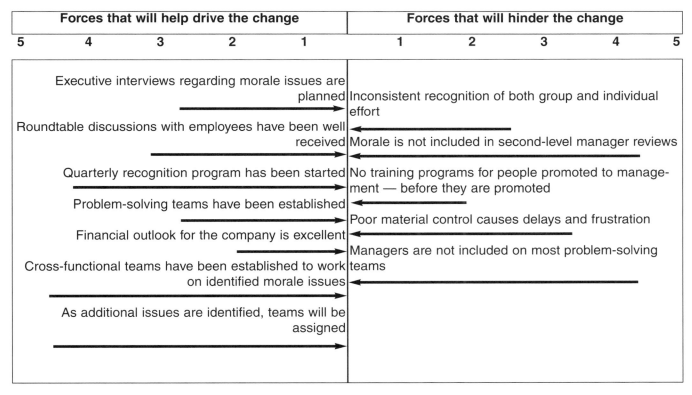

Forces that will help drive the change	Forces that will hinder the change
5 4 3 2 1	1 2 3 4 5

Executive interviews regarding morale issues are planned | Inconsistent recognition of both group and individual effort

Roundtable discussions with employees have been well received | Morale is not included in second-level manager reviews

Quarterly recognition program has been started | No training programs for people promoted to management — before they are promoted

Problem-solving teams have been established | Poor material control causes delays and frustration

Financial outlook for the company is excellent | Managers are not included on most problem-solving teams

Cross-functional teams have been established to work on identified morale issues

As additional issues are identified, teams will be assigned

Draw a line down the center of a sheet of paper. This represents the "To Be" statement — what you want the situation to be when the change is complete. The group then identifies and lists the Driving forces to the left of the center line and the Hindering forces to the right of the center line.

Arrows are drawn which represent the perceived strength of each force. Once the diagram is complete, the group can use the information to generate potential ways of strengthening Driving forces and weakening Hindering forces.

Note: In most situations, the data developed in Force-Field Analysis is primarily subjective (based on opinion rather than verifiable facts). It should therefore be tested for accuracy.

Force-Field Analysis

Force Field Analysis helps groups identify those forces within the organization that will help drive a desired change and those that will hinder the change. The "To Be" statement (the desired result of the change) is represented by the center line of the diagram. Forces are usually represented by arrows of various lengths. The Driving forces are pushing from the left toward the center while the Hindering forces are pushing from the right against the center.

Some groups use a scale (e.g.: 1 = very weak to 5 = very strong) to evaluate the relative impact of the forces. For graphic representation, arrows of a length that represents their relative strength are used.

"As Is" Statement:
(current situation)

"To Be" Statement:
(desired situation)

Forces that will help drive the change					Forces that will hinder the change				
5	4	3	2	1	1	2	3	4	5

Draw a line down the center of a sheet of paper. This represents the "To Be" statement — what you want the situation to be when the change is complete. The group then identifies and lists the Driving forces to the left of the center line and the Hindering forces to the right of the center line.

Arrows are drawn which represent the perceived strength of each force. Once the diagram is complete, the group can use the information to generate potential ways of strengthening Driving forces and weakening Hindering forces.

Note: In most situations, the data developed in Force-Field Analysis is primarily subjective (based on opinion rather than verifiable facts). It should therefore be tested for accuracy.

How-How Analysis

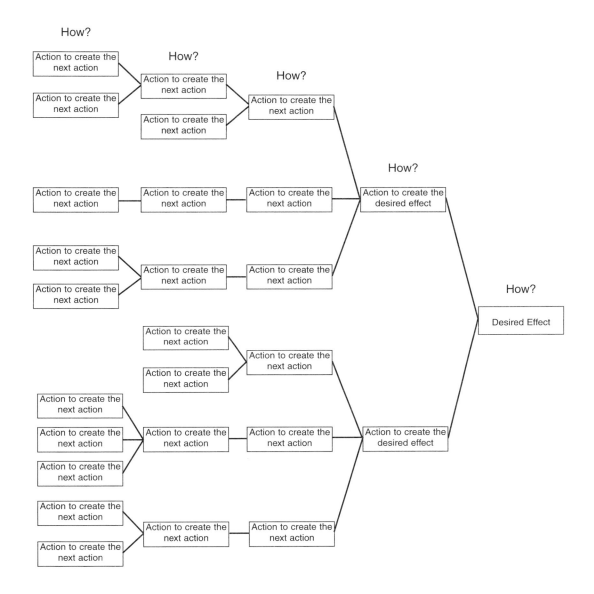

Description

How-How Analysis is similar to the Cause and Effect Diagram in that both processes can be used to uncover the root causes of a problem. They both begin with a specific situation that needs to be broken down into causative elements. Unlike Cause and Effect Analysis (and its variation, Why-Why Analysis), this process asks how you can intentionally bring about the result in the future, not focus on understanding a past effect. It can be used to test the implementability of a proposed solution. In structure, it looks like a Why-Why Analysis diagram reversed and is frequently used to test solutions developed using the Why-Why technique.

Directions

Begin by creating the first box of the diagram at the right side of the page. Place the "effect" (the desired result) in this box. Ask the question, "How?" This is the question at every stage of this process. "How can this be achieved? How can this be done?" Branch the most obvious answers into the next column to the left. Ask the same questions for each of the elements in this column and continue to branch the answers to the left. As a general rule, if you take this to about the fifth level, you will most likely be at the lowest practical level of detail.

Paired Comparison Evaluation Form

Options	Comparisons						
	A vs B	A vs C	A vs D	B vs C	B vs D	C vs D	Totals
A							
B							
C							
D							

Description

Like Weighted Voting, Paired Comparisons will help a group to quantify the preferences of its members. Each option (e.g.: potential solution) is compared against every other option. Votes are recorded. They are totaled only when all possible comparisons have been made.

The power of Paired Comparisons comes from the choices it forces group members to make. Even when two options seem equal, members must choose one over the other. Having to make these choices often leads to seeing advantages and disadvantages that might otherwise have been overlooked. This process can be helpful when comparing options to Wants in project pre-work.

Directions

See the chart below to determine the number of comparisons required for a given number of options. Set up the necessary grid. In each comparison, each member has one, and only one, vote. He or she must decide which of the two alternatives in the pair is better. (The total number of votes cast should equal the number of members in the group.) Everyone must cast a vote in each comparison, even if neither choice is particularly appealing.

Number of Options	Number of Comparisons
2	1
3	3
4	6
5	10
6	15
7	21
8	28

Point-Scoring Evaluation Form

Criteria	Max. Points	Items or Options to be Evaluated				
	Totals					

Description

A Point-Scoring system is a variation on Options Rating. One thousand (1,000) points are divided among criteria in accordance with their relative importance. The group then reviews and discusses the options, assigning a number of points up to the maximun for that criteria. The totals help clarify the group's preferences.

Directions

Determine and define the criteria to be used in the evaluation. Distribute 1,000 points among the criteria in proportion to their importance. Review all options with respect to the first criteria and decide, as a group, how many points to allocate to each option — from 0 to the maximum for that criteria. Continue with the second cirteria, then the third, etc.

Problem Selection Worksheet

Problem Statements ->				
Control Low 1 2 3 4 5 High				
Importance Low 1 2 3 4 5 High				
Difficulty High 1 2 3 4 5 Low				
Time High 1 2 3 4 5 Low				
Return on Investment Low 1 2 3 4 5 High				
Resource Requirements High 1 2 3 4 5 Low				
Total Points				

Control: The extent to which the group can control the problem and can control the solution.

Importance : The seriousness or urgency of the problem.

Difficulty: A judgement about the relative difficulty of working through the problem to a solution.

Time: A judgement about the relative length of time it will take to resolve the problem.

Return on Investment: The expected payoff from implementing the solution.

Resource Requirements: The amount of resources required to solve the problem (people, time, money, equipment, etc.).

Directions

In the boxes across the top, write statements describing the various problems the group is considering. Rate each problem against the listed criteria by working across each row. The objective is to have the group reach agreement about the rating to give to each problem in turn, based on each of the criteria. The higher the score, the greater the likelihood that the problem is appropriate for the group to undertake.

Special Note

The scales for three criteria: "Difficulty," "Time," and "Resource Requirements" run from High to Low. In these cases, the lower the score, the better. This is the opposite of the scales for "Control" and "Return on Investment", where a higher score is desirable.

Solution Selection Worksheet

Solution Statements ->				
Control Low 1 2 3 4 5 High				
Appropriateness Low 1 2 3 4 5 High				
Resource Availability Low 1 2 3 4 5 High				
Time High 1 2 3 4 5 Low				
Return on Investment Low 1 2 3 4 5 High				
Acceptability Low 1 2 3 4 5 High				
Total Points				

Control: The extent to which implementation of the solution is within the control of the group.

Appropriateness : The degree to which the solution satisfies the requirements of solving the problem.

Resource Availability: The extent to which the resources are available to the group.

Time: A judgement about the relative length of time it will take to resolve the problem.

Return on Investment: The expected payoff from implementing the solution.

Acceptability: The degree to which the people (and organization) involved will accept the changes.

Directions

In the boxes across the top, write statements describing the various solutions the group is considering. Rate each solution against the listed criteria by working across each row. The objective is to have the group reach agreement about the rating to give to each solution in turn, based on each criteria. The higher the score, the greater the likelihood that the solution can be effectively implemented.

Special Note

The scale for the "Time" criteria runs from High to Low. In this case, the lower the score, the better. This is the opposite of the scales for the other criteria where a higher score is desirable.

"T" Chart

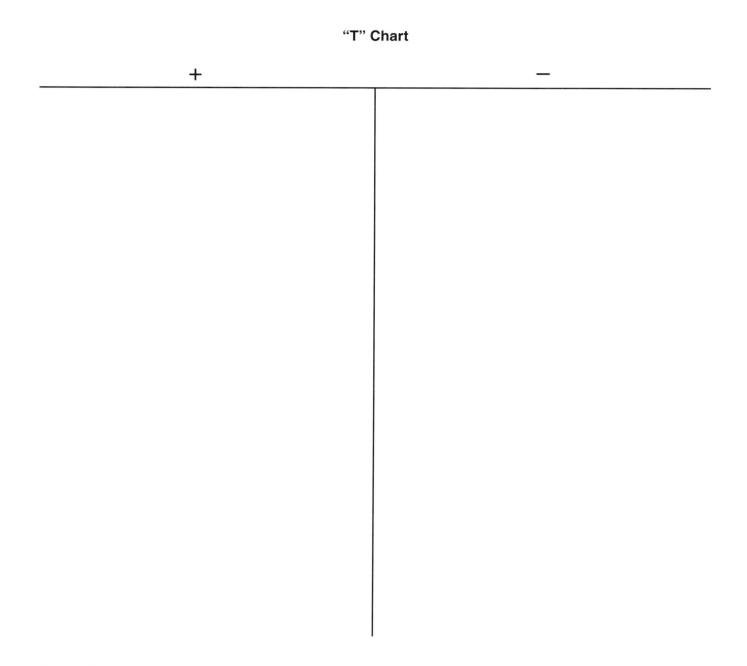

Description

T-Charts, also known as Balance Sheets or Balance Charts, allow a group to identify and review the pros and cons of a variety of options. Like other tools for reaching consensus, T-Charts won't make the decision. They will, however, help organize information and facilitate discussion among group members. T-Charts can be particularly useful during meeting critique as a quick way to capture positive and negative comments about the meeting process. T-Charts look much like Force-Field Analysis, but they are quite different in purpose. Force-Field is used to contrast the "As Is" situation and the "To Be" state to determine what is helping and what is hindering movement toward the "To Be" state. A T-Chart is a quick way to document the pros and cons of one or more choices.

Directions

Simply mark a large "T" on a flipchart or white board. Label the left side "+" (pros) and the right side "-" (cons). List the positives in the left-hand column and the negatives in the right-hand column. The group can then discuss the relative merits (or disadvantages) of the items in each column.

Thought-Provokers

When faced with a problem, consider the questions on this list to help stimulate your thinking along alternative lines. Creativity is more a matter of looking at a problem from a slightly different angle than looking at it from a completely different direction.

Put to other uses?
- A new way to use it as is?
- Other uses for it if modified?

Adapt it?
- What else is like this?
- What else does this suggest?
- Does the past offer a parallel?
- What could I copy?
- Whom could I emulate?

Modify it?
- Is there a new twist I could put on this?
- Could I change the meaning, color, motion, sound, odor, form, shape, etc.?
- Are there other changes I could make?

Magnify it?
- What could I add to this?
- Would more time make a difference?
- Would greater frequency make a difference?
- Could it be stronger?
- Could it be larger?
- Could it be higher?
- Could it be longer?
- Could it be thicker?
- Could I add extra value?
- What ingredient(s) could I add?
- Could I duplicate it?
- Could I multiply it?
- Could I exaggerate it?

Minimize it?
- What could I subtract from this?
- Could I make it smaller?
- Could it be condensed?
- How about a miniature version?
- Could it be lower?
- Could it be shorter?
- Could it be lighter?
- Could I omit something?
- Can it be streamlined?
- Can it be split up?

Substitute something?
- Who else could do it?
- What else could be used instead?
- Can I use some other ingredient?
- Can I use some other material?
- Can I use some other process?
- Can it be some other place?
- Can it be some other time?
- Can it use some other form of power?
- Is there some other approach?
- Can I use some other tone of voice?

Rearrange it?
- Can I interchange components?
- Can I use another pattern?
- Can I use another layout?
- Would it work in some other sequence?
- Can I transpose the cause and effect?
- Can I change the pace?
- Can I change the schedule?

Reverse it?
- Can I transpose the positive and negative?
- How about opposites?
- Can I turn it backwards?
- Can I turn it upside-down?
- Can I turn it inside-out?
- Can I reverse the roles?
- Change shoes?
- Turn the tables?
- Turn the other cheek?

Combine it?
- How about a blend, an alloy, an assortment, an ensemble?
- Can I combine units?
- Can I combine the purpose with another?
- Can I combine the appeal with another?
- Can I combine the ideas with others?

Weighted Voting Form

Individuals	Options				

Description

Weighted Voting is a way to quantify the positions of group members. It differs from Criteria Rating in two ways. First, no decision criteria are used. Second, individual member votes are recorded; there is no discussion or attempt to reach agreement on a single number. Once the voting is completed, the group can discuss the relative positions of various members and attempt to reach consensus.

Directions

List the options being considered across the top. List individual group members down the left. Assign the number of votes each member will have to distribute among the options. (As a general rule, the number of votes should be approximately 1-1/2 times the number of options.) Ask members, in turn, to distribute their votes among the options. Members may assign their votes to one option or distribute them among several.

Why-Why Analysis

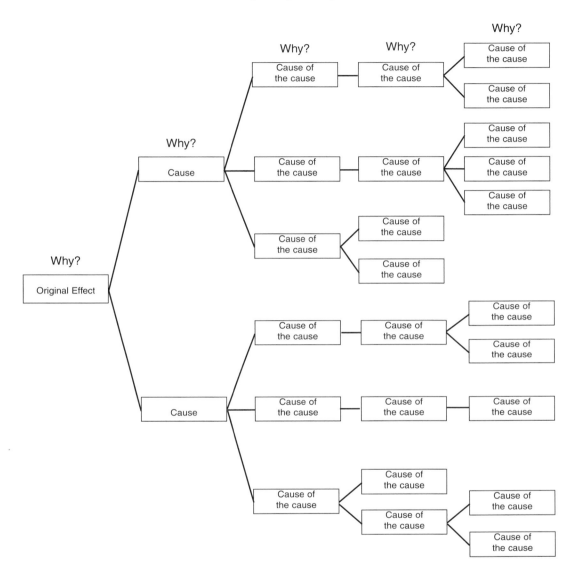

Description

Why-Why Analysis is a variation of the Cause and Effect Diagram. Like Cause and Effect Analysis, it can be used to uncover the root causes of a problem. Also, like Cause and Effect Analysis, the process can be reversed (See: How-How Analysis) to develop the steps needed to achieve a desired effect.

Directions

Begin by creating the first box of the diagram at the left of the page (roughly in the middle vertically). Place the "effect" (the observable condition) in this box. Ask the question: "Why?" This is the question asked at every stage of this process. "Why is this happening?" "Why is this the case?" Branch the most ovious answers into the next column to the right. Then, taking each answer in turn, ask the "Why?" question again and branch those answers into the next column. This process can be extended as far as necessary to uncover the root cause of the problem. As a general rule, if you ask "Why?" five times, you will most likely reach the root cause of the situation.